Better Parenting with the

"Ann Gadd has written a concise and accessibl[e] [introduction to] the Enneagram. It can be enjoyed by beginning Enneagram enthusiast[s] [and] still provides depth for experienced practitioners. *Better Parenting with the Enneagram* focuses on the positive characteristics of each type and gently challenges us to recognize the places we go to under the specific stresses of parenting. As a child of a Type Four mother, I was blown away by the book's accuracy. Ann was able to capture my experience growing up and articulate what I needed as a little child. As a psychotherapist and a parent of two small children this book has become my go-to guide to help the little people and parents in my life!"

—LYNDSEY FRASER, MA, LMFT, CST, marriage and family therapist and certified sex therapist

"*Better Parenting with the Enneagram* is yet another incredibly valuable contribution by Ann Gadd to the rapidly expanding list of Enneagram literature. Ann is proving again that the Enneagram is not just an abstract spiritual tool but that our passions show up in every aspect of our daily life. Parenting can be extremely challenging, and Ann explains in her enviably eloquent and humorous style how we tend to make things needlessly worse for ourselves and our kids. This book will help any parent to worry less and actually enjoy some of the weird behaviour of our kids."

—FREDERIK COENE, Ph.D., Enneagram researcher and member of the International Enneagram Association

"Ann's book *Better Parenting with the Enneagram* is a clear, accessible read for those of us who want to parent with awareness, understanding, and acceptance. Her simple yet detailed presentation of the information makes it enjoyable and easy to digest (coming from a Type Seven parent with two small children!)."

—CHARLOTTE HAGGIE, health and well-being coach

"A gem of a read! As a soon-to-be parent, this book helped me acknowledge the natural strengths that I am already bringing to the table and also provided insight on where to be mindful of how my own stress/fixation can impact the parent–child relationship."

—VALERIE WANAMAKER, LCSW, sex and relationship psychotherapist

"Ann Gadd has made an engaging introduction to the Enneagram, focusing on the most important relationship we might ever have—the parent–child relationship. We are all someone's child, which makes the book relevant to everyone. Gadd allows us to reflect both on ourselves as parents and as children. You don't need to know about the Enneagram to benefit from this book; you are handed the Enneagram's view on the important aspects of the parent–child relationship and can immediately start using it. With this tool, you can be closer to having a conscious relationship, not only to your children, but also to your parents.

Using the lost childhood messages (in the back of the book) is like adding magic dust to your relationships; try it, and you will most probably find that your child sinks into a peaceful, loving state immediately!"

—PATRICK HOUGAARD SIMONSEN, Enneagram coach and NLP trainer
& ANNABELLA AL-NAFUSI, stress release therapist and Enneagram
speaker and coach

"This book is pure magic. An essential and practical resource for any parent interested in their own self-development journey of growth alongside their child. Ann uses clear, easy to digest language with examples and descriptions that accurately reflect the uniqueness of each style of parent and child."

—MARY J. FOURIE, millennial mother and Enneagram coach

Better Parenting
with the Enneagram

9 Types of Children &
9 Types of Parents

ANN GADD

 FINDHORN PRESS

Findhorn Press
One Park Street
Rochester, Vermont 05767
www.findhornpress.com

Text stock is SFI certified

Findhorn Press is a division of Inner Traditions International

Disclaimer
The information in this book is given in good faith and is neither intended
to diagnose any physical or mental condition nor to serve as a substitute for
informed medical advice or care. The author of this book does not dispense
medical advice nor prescribe the use of any technique as a form of treatment for
medical problems. Please contact your health professional for medical advice and
treatment. Neither author nor publisher can be held liable by any person for any
loss or damage whatsoever which may arise directly or indirectly from the use of
this book or any of the information therein.

Cataloging-in-Publication Data for this title is available from the Library of Congress

ISBN 978-1-64411-422-3 (print)
ISBN 978-1-64411-423-0 (ebook)

Printed and bound in the United States by Lake Book Manufacturing, Inc.
The text stock is SFI certified. The Sustainable Forestry Initiative® program promotes
sustainable forest management.

10 9 8 7 6 5 4 3 2 1

Edited by Nicola Rijsdijk
Artwork by Dorothy Ann Gadd
Text design and layout by Damian Keenan
This book was typeset in Adobe Garamond Pro and Calluna Sans
with ITC Century Std used as a display typeface.

To send correspondence to the author of this book, mail a first-class letter to the
author c/o Inner Traditions • Bear & Company, One Park Street, Rochester,
VT 05767, and we will forward the communication, or contact the author directly at
https://anngadd.co.za or **https://enneagrams9paths.com**.

To Luke, Tess, and Taun,
for all you've taught me

Contents

.... **PART 3** ....

Parent–Child Combinations

Introduction

I wish I'd had the information I'm about to share with you when I became a parent—it would have saved much heartache. I'd have understood that my three-year-old daughter's desire to organize my sewing box (and me) wasn't a passing fad, but part of her Three makeup. I'd have known that setting strict studying rules for my 15-year-old son would only lead to resistance and rebellion, and that I'd be more successful if I helped him to see the consequences of *not* studying and worked *with* him on creating a study routine.

If I'd known back then about the Enneagram types, I'd have been a happier parent, and they would have been happier kids.

I can say (with no bias whatsoever, of course!) that my children—now adults themselves—have turned out rather well but, like many of us, I walked into parenting with loads of idealism and a considerable lack of practical skill. My kids were *never* going to eat sweets, were going to be naturally brilliant and impeccably behaved, were going to radically uplift the world ... Their father had, of course, had a different upbringing to me, and brought his own expectations to the mix.

How much energy and effort we could have saved if we'd been more aware of our distinct but innate parenting styles, and if we'd understood our children's own particular strengths and challenges.

Understanding how and why we parent the way we do, and understanding the emotional core of our kids, helps us to be better parents—and better people. Working with an insight into your own and your child's healthy and less healthy aspects provides you with your best chance of achieving your parenting potential.

The information in this book is like a personal manual for each child. It takes into account the core of who they are—what drives them, what their fears are, what inspires them, and most importantly how you relate to them.

My own parenting experience would have been so much easier to navigate if I could have:

1. Understood myself on a deeper level. I thought I did. Years of doing every alternative workshop available, from Sacred Breath to numerology, was hugely valuable—but nothing has been as profound, growth-inspiring, and revealing as the Enneagram was, and continues to be.

2. Understood what made my children tick. I often wondered how two kids from the same parents could turn out to be so very different.

As parents, we tend to believe there is one way to correctly parent a child—our way. If your way of parenting differs radically from your partner's, you may be led to wonder whose method is right. Which style will make for a happier, emotionally healthier child? It may come as a surprise to discover through the Enneagram that there are nine different parenting styles, each with its own positive and less productive characteristic, that can be experienced differently by each child in the family.

As an adult, your personality affects the way you understand all aspects of life—your personality acts as a filter. In parenting, you are inclined to emphasize the aspects of parenting that resonate most with you, and deemphasize those aspects that do not. If your child is not the same personality type as you are, you might struggle to understand the motivations for their behaviour. For instance, a Seven parent (The Enthusiast) prioritizes living adventurously and seeking new stimulation—and they don't shy away from being the center of attention. But they may have a quiet Five child who prefers to fly under the radar and avoid "superficial" social gatherings. Understanding the personality type of the child will help this parent act with greater wisdom and insight.

It needs to be said that in my understanding, **parents do not create a child's personality type.** Parents can, however, affect the development of healthy or unhealthy aspects of a child's Enneagram type. A traumatic childhood is more likely to create a stressed-out child who has more trouble accessing the integrated (conscious) aspects of their type. A child who has always felt loved, nurtured, and heard will enjoy a smoother path. It's also important to understand that different children in a single family may experience different types of parenting, depending on environmental stress during their formative years.

There is way more to the Enneagram than just the personality-profiling aspect. The Enneagram is a spiritual and psychological guide to help you shine a light on those parts of yourself of which you're unaware, enabling you to become your own change agent. I have experienced the extraordinary benefits of understanding my children on a deeper level, and through knowing my own type, I have also seen the potentials and pitfalls I bring to my parenting. My kids and husband would agree that for us as a family, the Enneagram has been a deeply enriching experience—despite some self-mistyping along the way.

With knowledge of the Enneagram, you can be the best parent you can be—and that's a truly great start for your child.

PART 1
Parenting and the Enneagram

1

The Enneagram—
Your Parenting How-To

I magine you were given a manual that explained everything about you: what motivates you, your hidden fixations, aspects of your behavior you're unaware of, even how you behave under stress. When you have a framework for understanding why you act, think, and feel as you do, and you're aware of your own path to increased health, you're better equipped to deal with life. Having a better relationship with yourself means having better relationships with others—including your child. Even if you don't know your child's type, knowing *your* Enneagram type will help you on your journey through parenthood.

What Exactly *Is* the Enneagram?

The Enneagram of Personality consists of nine main personality types with many potential nuances. To describe this very complex system in a nutshell: the Enneagram describes nine different types of neurosis that manifest according to our stress levels. For instance, a cerebral Type Five's neurosis is the need to be competent and confident in all they do. However, the very fear of not being like this can make them feel incompetent and incapable. The deep desire of the Five is avarice. It's a fear of lack—so they are inclined to hold on to their resources, feeling that there will never be sufficient for their needs. Although Fives may be miserly with others, in terms of resources or time, they tend to hoard information and possessions, fearing that others will take these from them. An integrated (healthy) Five may seldom act on this tendency, but it becomes more apparent as stress increases. Each different Enneagram type reflects a specific inbuilt neurosis.

In the Enneagram workshops I run, I often hear people saying, "But I don't want to be put in a box." I agree completely. The Enneagram is not about boxing you, but rather about showing you the box you're already in. Part of the work of the Enneagram is to understand the neurosis associated with our type so that we notice when it arises. We can then work consciously to reduce our stress and thus the need for the behavior. The Enneagram is a sacred energetic path to liberation from our wounds and resulting personalities—it's about showing you how to free yourself from the confines of the "box" to reach your fullest potential.

So How Do I Find My Type?

Start by reading up on all the Enneagram types and then exploring the type that resonates most with you. If you're not sure, choose the type you'd rather *not* be, because a strong reaction *against* a particular type can also be a clue. (I never wanted to be a Nine—I misunderstood what the type was about—so it was a shock to find out, after trying out being a Three, a Seven, and a Six, that I was in fact a Nine!)

There are loads of online resources and tests for you to do, both free and at a cost. Tests are helpful, but not always accurate. My advice is to do several tests and to ask friends, family, and colleagues—they often see what you don't. Over time you'll develop a feel for your type.

It's very important to realize that we are not limited to our types—our type simply reflects the personality style we have adopted in response to our core fear. As we develop (becoming healthier or more integrated), we start to access aspects of *all* the types. (It's a little like being the corner-back in American Football and then realizing that you are, in fact able to access the qualities of all the other players in the team. There's much to be learned on the journey!)

How Long Will It Take Me to Discover My Type?

For some people, identifying your type is almost instantaneous and there's a sense of "coming home." Others gain from taking a slower journey to themselves. There's no right or wrong. Often the other types you resonate with are indeed aspects of your personality. In that case, spending time exploring other types helps you to gain a richer understanding of yourself when you do discover your actual type.

What If I See Myself in Several of the Types?

You'll often see yourself in several types. That's because, although we are born a particular type and stay that same type throughout our lives, we can reflect aspects of some or all of the other types because of our wings and the Points of Stretch and Release. (See page 37 for more information on these terms.) In time, one type will resonate more strongly with you.

Can My Type Change?

Nope. If you're a Seven, you'll be a Seven for this lifetime. Your wings can alter and your Instinctual Drives (see page 40) can shift in emphasis (although we usually maintain the most developed one), but unless you've incorrectly typed yourself, your Sevenish self will remain.

At What Age Will My Child's Type Be Evident?

Although some Enneagram teachers say that a child can be typed from the age of seven, Enneagram-type behavior may be clear in some children from an even younger age. In other children, it can be hard to gauge their types until their personalities are clearly formed, largely because kids often mimic the people around them while they are trying to find who they really are.

Importantly, before you look to discover your child's potential type, become aware of your own. Just as you may be confused about your type, it is easy to mistake a child's type, so it's wise to keep an open mind (and heart).

What's the *Best* Type for a Parent to Be?

The type you already are. Really. You and your child are together for a reason, which makes you the perfect parent for them. Each type brings with it unique gifts, strengths, and virtues, and has an associated set of challenges. No type is better than any other—they're just different. It's up to you what you make of yourself.

Irrespective of your type, the information in this book can help you become a more integrated parent—and the healthier and more integrated your thinking, feeling, and behaving, the better parent you'll be. As we evolve into healthier states of being, we access more of our own type's gifts, as well as the gifts of other types. So the issue is not what type you are—it's how healthy you choose to be.

What's the *Best* Type for a Child to Be?

The type your child already is. You can learn much from your child no matter what type they are. Relish and encourage the special gifts each child brings to the world, and use your role as caretaker to help them grow into the healthiest adults they can be.

Does Gender, Culture, Religion, or Upbringing Make a Difference to My Type?

No—whatever you are and however you identify, you share the commonalities of your type. It's part of what I love about the Enneagram.

A Warning about Typing Your Child

"We were convinced our five-year-old was a Type Two. She was kind and caring and seemed to imbue the qualities we admired. As she got older, though, traits started appearing that looked more Three-ish—and that's what she is. She has a Two-wing, so it's easy to see where the traits came from, but because she's a counterphobic Three, we misunderstood them." (For a definition of the wings, see page 35 and for counterphobic types, see page 45.)

Here's why I found it hard to make the decision to write this book. As much as the Enneagram can be a tool to help you become more integrated or conscious, and as such an even better parent, it carries with it the potential to label your child, and in so doing, limit their potential by becoming judgmental and prescriptive about their behavior—as the parent above might have done. The idea of "boxing" a young child via the Enneagram does not sit well with me, and is not what the Enneagram of Personality was ever intended for.

There may also be the temptation, even subconsciously, to *want* your child to be a certain type and to nudge them in that direction—much as parents have always said things like, "My James is going to be a doctor," when young James really wants to be a poet. Certain types of behavior may be encouraged or discouraged according to a parent's conscious (or unconscious) desires. Instead of accepting a child for who they are, parents may try to influence a child to act in certain ways—"I want Christie to be sporty like me, so I've signed her up for basketball, baseball, tennis ..." Christie may actually be a bit of a bookworm who loves baking with Grandma.

No parenting strategy can prevent a child from or encourage them into a particular Enneagram type. For a child, trying to conform to a parent's belief of who they should be can be very harmful. The pressure will only add to the neurosis of the child, pushing them in the direction of disintegration. The reality is you can't change your child's Enneagram type. Your child is the type they were born to be—relish them for being who they are, rather than who you want them to be. That's the way to help them on a healthy path.

It helps to acknowledge that we have parts of *all* types within us, but one type is dominant. Rather than label a child, use the potential of all the types to help them grow into healthy adulthood. Keep an open mind, and always remember that you may have got it wrong.

For your child, discovering who they are for themselves carries way more powerful self-development potential than being told who they are. Use the Enneagram as a gradual opening to your child's being and allow them to explore and unfold.

How to Use This Book

The next chapter explains the Enneagram terminology that is used throughout the book. Part 2 then describes parents and children of the nine different Enneagram types—you're invited to explore these descriptions in the hope that you will "see" yourself and your child in the descriptions. In this section, I give the integrated relationship pointers, as well as what to be aware of when you are becoming less integrated (see page 36 for an explanation of these terms). This is so you can begin to recognize when you're becoming stressed and displaying the behavior most associated with your type. This awareness is the Enneagram's gift, as once you have "seen" where you are, you can consciously take measures to reduce your stress levels and get back to healthier living.

I introduce names to describe parents and children of each type—for example, I call the Type One parent "The Parenting Perfectionist" and the Type One child "The Good Boy/Girl." Please note that different schools and authors use different titles to describe each type. For the purposes of this book, I have chosen names that focus specifically on parenting styles and the childhood experience of each type.

Once you have a sense of the parent and children of each type, Part 3 introduces the relationship markers of specific combinations of parents and their children—for example, a Seven parent with a One child, a Two child, a Three child, et cetera. These parent–child combinations are, of course, an overview. Many other factors will affect your relationship with your child, including your Instinctual Drive stacking and your wings. As you will see in the descriptions in this part of the book, your level of integration is the most relevant in determining the health of your relationship. It's a given that the less integrated or conscious you or your child are, the greater potential for conflict and unhappiness in your relationship.

The descriptions in this book generally explore your relationship with a slightly older child, as typing younger children may not be possible and is not always in their best interests. If your child is young or you are still unsure about their type, it might be useful to check back from time to time to see if your relationship dynamics are starting to become clearer.

How to Explain the Enneagram to Children

It is my hope that this book will give you greater insight into the nature of your relationship with your child and the areas of your parenting that might need work. But the question remains, how do you explain the Enneagram types to children so they too can discover more about themselves and others?

I believe there is value in helping children explore the differences in the Enneagram types. When this information is presented at their level of comprehension, children are able to develop an appreciation not only for their own gifts, but also for the contributions of the people in their lives. To help parents introduce these ideas to their children, I created a series of fun illustrated Enneagram books that help children understand that being different doesn't mean being wrong, and that there is room for all types in the world. The books present simple but insightful examinations of each of the Enneagram types and their unique path to emotional and mental health—I hope they will be a useful accompaniment on your Enneagram parenting journey.

PERCY PERFECT—The Enneagram Type One for Kids
Percy Perfect wants his house to stay perfectly neat and tidy, but his messy friends have other ideas. Is it worth being perfect if you miss all the fun?

HAZEL HELPER—The Enneagram Type Two for Kids
Hazel Helper is always busy helping everyone else—but one day she realizes that she needs help too! Hazel learns not just to nurture and be kind to others, but to be kind to herself.

SALLY STAR—The Enneagram Type Three for Kids
Sally Star loves to be the best at everything. But what happens when the other kids also start excelling? Sally learns that sometimes being kind makes you the real winner.

ARTHUR ARTSY—The Enneagram Type Four for Kids
Arthur Artsy is original and creative, but he often feels sad and misunderstood. Arthur discovers that he doesn't need to try to be special and unique—like all of us, he already is!

SEBASTIAN STUDY—The Enneagram Type Five for Kids
Sebastian Study just loves learning new things, but his friends sometimes get in the way. If he stays in his room, he can do his own thing . . . but is he missing some fun in the park?

KATY CAUTIOUS—The Enneagram Type Six for Kids
Katy Cautious is a loyal, responsible friend, but sometimes her fear stops her from having a good time. Katy learns to find the courage to act despite her fear.

FELIX FUN—The Enneagram Type Seven for Kids
Felix Fun loves having adventures and is always busy planning the next one. One day Felix gets sick and has to stay in bed—boring! It's a visit from his friends that makes him feel better.

BEN BOSS—The Enneagram Type Eight for Kids
Ben Boss is always in charge in the playground, but when he can't catch the ball, he starts to cry! His friends already know how brave Ben is—but it takes true strength to also be gentle.

POSIE PEACE—The Enneagram Type Nine for Kids
Posie Peace doesn't like to speak out or make a fuss. But when all her friends start fighting, it's up to her to find her voice and create peace and harmony between the others.

And Finally, the Tough Stuff . . .

Like aging, working with the Enneagram is not for sissies. We all love to hear about how great we are—and we *are* pretty amazing. But (and this is a rather huge "but") awareness is what creates change (and back-patting just bolsters the ego and keeps us trapped in our "box"). The Enneagram of Personality allows us to *become aware* of what's stopping us from being all we could be, and what's holding us back in life. Our Enneagram type gives us unique insights into parts of ourselves of which we may not have noticed.

The thing is, if we're too big a fan of the great aspects of our type and ignore the less pleasant ones—"Who, *me*?"—then there's no desire to grow beyond ourselves. We get stuck. Writing only about the positive aspects of each type would definitely improve my book ratings (and it's tempting, I'll admit), but shying away from the tough stuff would be to fail you—the reader who wants to grow and learn to be an even better parent.

Showing both healthy and less healthy aspects of each type is the nature of the Enneagram. Not doing so is like sitting alone on a seesaw. To truly shift, we need to hold and accept our type's behavior and its (often less attractive) opposite in a non-judgmental way. When we understand both sides (for example, a Type One's need to be excellent in all they do versus their overly critical judgment of others), we can transcend the fixations that don't serve our best interests.

The Enneagram is a beautiful ray of insight to help lead you home to yourself. As a springboard to self-awareness and personal growth, working with the Enneagram involves honest reflection and acknowledgment of all aspects of our unique selves. You're going to need some loving acceptance when it comes to seeing both the positive and the less positive aspects of yourself. (Side note: Having a sense of humor helps!)

When it comes to the people around you and exploring their types, the Enneagram is a wonderful tool, not a weapon. Never use it to judge or condemn. Eyeing your partner or child and saying, "That's so typical of a damn Four!" is not going to help your cause—it will only alienate and infuriate your loved one. If you use the Enneagram to encourage, uplift, and inspire, then this book will have served its purpose.

A Fun Enneagram Test

Take this test to start your journey.

- Quickly read through the list of words.
- Circle the 12 words or phrases that resonate *most* with how you see yourself now and in the past (rather than how you'd like to be in the future).
- Starting from page 27, find the type where each of those words are listed and tick the relevant box.
- Add up the number of ticks to see which type rates highest for you.

accepting	confronting
accommodating	conscientious
adaptable	considerate
adventurous	creative
aesthetic	cultured
affectionate	curious
ambitious	decisive
anxious	deep
big-hearted	demonstrative
caring	doubting
cautious	down-to-earth
cerebral	dutiful
charming	dynamic
comfortable	easy-going
compassionate	emotional
competitive	energetic

expressive	motivational
extroverted	neat
exuberant	observant
fair	optimistic
faithful	orderly
feeling	organized
focused	other-orientated
fun-loving	overly protective
future-orientated	patient
goal-orientated	peaceful
good listener	perceptive
helping	perfectionistic
honest	persevering
image-conscious	planning
imaginative	popular
impatient	power-focused
independent	prepared
informed	private
innovative	protective
intelligent	punctual
intense	receptive
logical	reflective
loyal	relationship-orientated
moral	resourceful

responsible	successful
restless	supportive
romantic	takes charge
sacrificing	talkative
seductive	thorough
self-disciplined	trustworthy
self-sufficient	unassuming/humble
sensible	uncomplicated
sensitive	uninhibited
sensual	unique
skeptical	unselfconscious
spontaneous	unsentimental
straight-talking	uses "should" a lot
strong	
strong-willed	

Type One Characteristics	
conscientious	perfectionistic
fair	punctual
honest	self-disciplined
moral	sensible
neat	thorough
orderly	uses "should" a lot

Type Two Characteristics	
affectionate	other-orientated
caring	overly protective
considerate	relationship-orientated
demonstrative	sacrificing
good listener	seductive
helping	supportive

Type Three Characteristics	
adaptable	image-conscious
ambitious	impatient
charming	motivational
dynamic	organized
focused	popular
goal-orientated	successful

Type Four Characteristics	
aesthetic	feeling
creative	imaginative
cultured	intense
deep	romantic
emotional	sensitive
expressive	unique

Type Five Characteristics	
cerebral	observant
curious	perceptive
informed	private
innovative	reflective
intelligent	self-sufficient
logical	unsentimental

Type Six Characteristics	
anxious	loyal
cautious	persevering
compassionate	prepared
doubting	responsible
dutiful	skeptical
faithful	trustworthy

Type Seven Characteristics	
adventurous	optimistic
energetic	planning
extroverted	restless
exuberant	spontaneous
fun-loving	talkative
future-orientated	uninhibited

Type Eight Characteristics	
big-hearted	protective
competitive	resourceful
confronting	straight-talking
decisive	strong
independent	strong-willed
power-focused	takes charge

Type Nine Characteristics	
accepting	peaceful
accommodating	receptive
comfortable	sensual
down-to-earth	unassuming/humble
easy-going	uncomplicated
patient	unselfconscious

Easy-Peasy Enneagram Terminology Explained

The Enneagram has so many terms, it can feel as if it's too much to take in. Here's your cheat sheet of terms used in this book and other Enneagram writing—you can refer back here if you're unsure.

The Enneagram Symbol

First, let's look at the actual symbol. There are three parts to the Enneagram symbol itself:

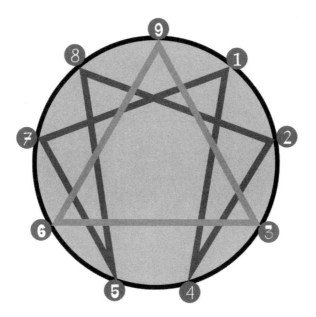

The Circle: The circle represents wholeness, all-is-one, completeness, the beginning and end.

The Triangle: The triangle's three points represent an active (Type Three), a passive (Type Nine), and a reconciling (Type Six) force.

To explain this concept, let's head to the tennis court. The player hitting the ball could be said to be the active force. The ball, being reliant on the tennis player, would be the passive force. The tennis racket could be seen to be the reconciling or neutralizing force between the activity of the player and the passivity of the ball. This concept of three points or stations on the circumference of the circle plays itself out in the Enneagram.

Passive force

Neutralizing force

Active force

The Hexagram: The hexagram is the six-pointed aspect of the Enneagram symbol that, together with the triangle's three points, makes up the Enneagram's nine points.

It also relates to what is known as "The Law of Seven," which has its origins in the Sufi tradition. This complex study is beyond the scope of this book—Google if interested!

The Triads

The Enneagram symbol can also be divided into triads—the Body, Thinking, and Feeling centers.[i] The three centers represent the areas of each type's primary wounding. Body or gut-centered types are action-orientated, Head-centered types are about thinking, and Heart-centered types are about feeling. As you become more integrated, you engage with healthier aspects of all three centers.

---

i   These terms are from the Riso/Hudson description of the Triadic self in Riso and Hudson's *The Wisdom of the Enneagram*.

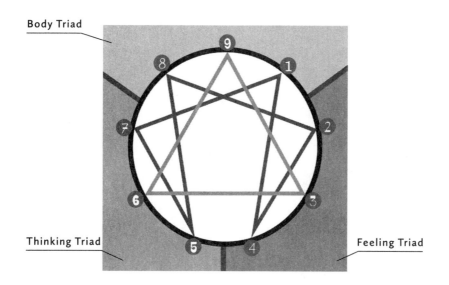

Body Triad

Thinking Triad

Feeling Triad

Body/Action Triad: Types Eight, Nine, and One. These are action-orientated types, where the issue is expression or repression of anger that stems from the gut. Autonomy is desired as these types resist reality in different ways.

Head/Thinking Triad: Types Five, Six, and Seven. These types are focused on thinking, and place less emphasis on the other two centers. The focus is anxiety stemming from deep-rooted fear. As a result, they seek security and safety.

Heart/Feeling Triad: Types Two, Three, and Four. These types are focused on feelings, self-image and idealized personalities. Shame occurs when they feel they don't match their desired identity.

Knowing which center your type falls in helps you to understand the dynamics at play. This focus doesn't mean that if you're a Thinking type, you don't *feel* anything. It's just that you'll be more inclined to *think* your feelings, while Heart-centered types will be more aware of their feelings and will act from the heart rather than the head. Body or anger types will either overly express rage or attempt to repress it, acting first and possibly thinking or feeling later.

The work of the Enneagram leads us to engage with the world through all three centers, rather than limit ourselves to one, as in: "I'm a thinker."

Are you more inclined to think, feel, or act?

In which triad (Body, Thinking, and Feeling) does your type lie? Here's a hint: Which sentence rings truest for you?

- When under pressure, I take immediate action to solve the problem or deliberately avoid doing so and use the words, "I'll do . . .".
- When under pressure, I think about what to do, plan my next move, and use the words, "I think . . .".
- When under pressure, I spend more time feeling the pain and uncomfortableness of the situation and use the words, "I feel . . .".

Observe yourself over the next few days to see how you approach various situations. The "doing" types tend to be Types One, Eight, and Nine. The "thinking" types are Types Five, Six, and Seven. The "feeling" types are Types Two, Three, and Four.

Tritypes

In 1994 Katherine Fauvre began researching her theory of Tritypes, which adds a further dimension to the Enneagram. The Tritypes suggest that we have a dominant type in all three of the centers: Head/Thinking, Heart/Feeling, and Body/Action.

The model examines the behaviors or motivations that result from 27 possible stackings, with each Tritype forming a new type. For example, you could be an Enneagram Type Six (dominant Head type), with a dominant Nine in the Body center, and a dominant Four in the Heart center—a (6, 9, 4) Tritype. Being the least dominant in the stack, the Type Four coping mechanisms would be utilised less often, but would still affect the other two aspects, while the Type Six aspects would be the most noticeable. The three types in the Tritype enhance their shared qualities, and reduce those they don't share.

From a parenting perspective, say you're a Type Five and your child is a Type Two. Although you and your child don't share a type, if your Tritype is (5, 2, 9), then you share a Type Two commonality with your child. The Tritypes form an entire study of its own, but is something to bear in mind when you look into your parenting style. You can take the Tritype test at **www.katherinefauvre.com/enneagramtritypetest**.

The Wings

No need to flap—wings are just the numbers on either side of your type, which influence your behavior.

For example, as a Type One, your wings could be either a Nine, a Two, or both—and some people don't have any wings. If you're a One with a Nine-wing, you'll have some of the traits of a Nine, but not the core wounding of a Nine.

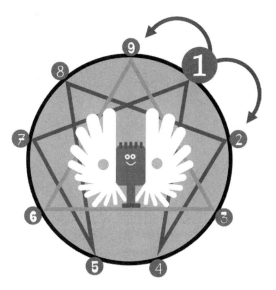

In this illustration, Type One has a Nine- and a Two-wing.

This illustration shows how a person can have two balanced wings, a stronger and weaker wing, or no wings at all.

While your Enneagram type remains constant throughout your life, your wings can strengthen, weaken, or alter. You can also show more of a certain wing in different situations. For example, you may be a Type Eight who reveals a more nurturing Nine-wing at home, but a more charismatic Seven-wing at work.

Integration and Disintegration

These terms explain how emotionally and mentally healthy we are—or how conscious or unconscious. As we shift between integrated and less integrated states of being, our behavior shifts accordingly. When we act from the lower levels of consciousness of our type, our neuroses or fixations become more dominant and have greater control over us and how we behave. When we live from a healthier or more integrated space, our fears and resultant fixations have less control over us and we are more able to share the gifts of our type. A person's level of integration and disintegration can explain some of the differences between people of the same type. An integrated (healthy/conscious) Type Eight, for instance, will behave very differently to a disintegrated (unhealthy/unconscious) Type Eight.

Russ Hudson and the late Don Riso described nine levels of integration. We can move up and down the levels depending on what's happening in our world, although it usually takes a traumatic event to move from the average levels to the disintegrated levels.

Most of us tend to hang out in the three "average" levels, with less than 10 percent of people being in the "integrated" levels. Interestingly, we tend to exhibit the opposite of a certain behavior when we compare the disintegrated version with the integrated version of a type. For example, a disintegrated person who preys on the weak will, when integrated, redeem or assist those who have been victims. Or we may be prideful (disintegrated), becoming humble (integrated) as we evolve. Being able to hold both our pride and humility without judgment is where we transcend duality.

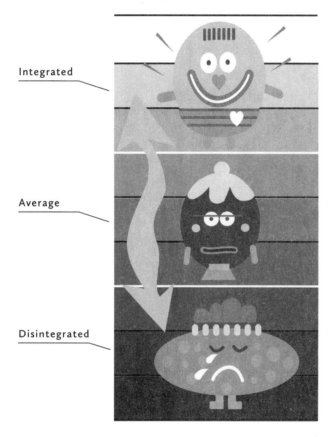

Lines of Stretch and Release

Sounds like some kind of exercise program, right? [ii] It is—just not physical exercise. There's so much more to the Enneagram than just your type, and in this case the lines that connect your type to other types indicate the potential to gain extra resources and balance your type.

---

ii   The terms "Lines of Stretch and Release" and "Stretch and Release Points" were first used by the iEQ9 Integrative Enneagram school.

We more easily access aspects of the types connected by the lines from our own type. We tend to move to them at the same level of integration or consciousness that we are currently at, unless we consciously challenge ourselves to move to the higher aspects represented by those types. Let's say, for example, you're a Type Four. Under stress or pressure, you could move to aspects of a less conscious Type Two or One (see the direction of the lines on the Enneagram symbol). Likewise, when integrated, you could embody healthier aspects of either of these types.

Lines of Stretch

Lines of Stretch: The lines that move towards a type (indicated by the direction of the arrows) are known as Stretch Lines. Why? Because they indicate the challenges you can work with/stretch towards. The type they connect with is known as the **Stretch Point**—where you go when under pressure or stress. For example, a Nine moving to their Stretch Point of Six will challenge themselves to stand up for themselves and access the courage to change, like an integrated Six.

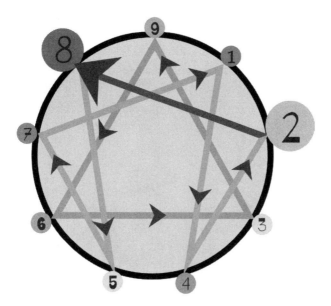

Eight is the Stretch Point of Type Two

Lines of Release

Lines of Release: The lines that move away from a type are known as Release Lines. Why? These represent the place where you can choose to release what is not serving you. The type they connect with is known as the **Release Point:** This is where you go when you're more relaxed. For example, a Seven moving to their Release Point of Five will slow down and focus more deeply on an issue or on their inner self, becoming less scattered as a result.

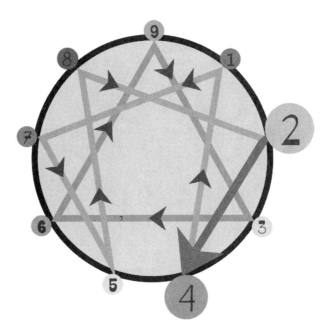

Four is the Release Point of Type Two

The Instinctual Drives

The study of the Instinctual Drives [iii], also known as "Subtypes," is remarkably interesting and can be incorporated into the Enneagram or understood as a stand-alone tool. It's another way in which people of the same type can appear and act differently. I don't address the Instinctual Drives much in this book, but it's something to bear in mind when you study the Enneagram further.

---

iii   My use of this term comes from John Luckovich of the *New York Enneagram*.

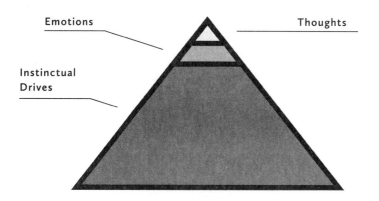

The Power of our Instinctual Drives

The Instinctual Drives are much stronger than your thoughts or emotions in controlling the way you act in life, even though their impact is mostly unconscious.

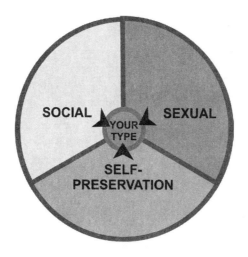

Our Enneagram Type and the effect of the Instinctual Drives

NOTE: In this example all three drives are equal, which is seldom the case. In earlier times, our Instinctual Drives are what would have ensured the safety and survival of our tribe. They are also clearly seen in animals.

The Instinctual Drives are:

Self-preservation drive: Concern with our physical selves. For protection we need a home, finances, comfort, and caring for our bodies. (This drive can also be seen in the opposite—for example, self-neglect.) We find security and safety in having physical stuff. When disintegrated, we may feel the need to hoard our resources.

Social drive: How we navigate groups of people. Safety in our "tribe"/ group. When a horse is thrown out of the herd, its chance of survival is drastically reduced. This drive is about our social standing in society, power, fame, and connections with individuals and groups. With this instinct foremost, we put a greater focus on society, social awareness, and working together with others.

One-on-one or Sexual drive: The buzz of engaging with another person, mostly (but not always) with sex in mind. Tribal safety is ensured through procreation. It's about the intensity of connection. It involves how we dress to attract others, our looks and the emphasis we place on them, and how we attract others generally, sustain relationships or fear that we can't. It's the chemistry that happens when two people meet—whether to discuss a new scientific breakthrough or whose bed we're heading to.

SELF-PRESERVATION	SOCIAL	SEXUAL
Survival through taking care of physical needs	*Survival through being part of a group*	*Survival through procreation and sexual drive*
Material security	Navigating groups	The buzz of connection between two people
Physical safety	Power	
Structure	Fame	
Physical needs, e.g. home, food.	Personal value	Intensity
Body: Health and fitness (or ignoring these)	Accomplishments	Excitement
	Standing in society	Appearance
	Ability to adapt	Passion for life
Comfort	Groups/community	Boundary issues
Issues with risk-taking	Social awareness	Intimacy focused
Hoarding	Shared purpose	Over-identifying with attraction
	Friendships	

YOUR ENNEAGRAM TYPE

As depicted below, we seldom have an equal balance between all three instincts. Rather, we tend to have a dominant instinct and one we use less although, as these illustrations show, circumstances and time can alter levels of dominance. The Instinctual Drives create our Subtypes, which explains why people of the same core type may behave differently.

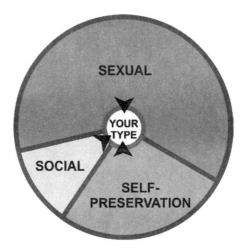

SX or Sexually dominant, followed by Self-preservation and the area needing work: Social. This person's "stack" would be SX/SP/SO.

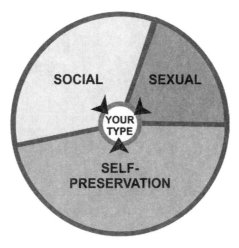

SP or Self-preservation dominant, followed by Social and the area needing work: Sexual. This person's "stack," would be SP/SO/SX.

Counterphobic Types

Counterphobic types, or countertypes, behave in the opposite way to the type's "Passion." For example, Type Six seeks safety and security. But Type Six's countertype may involve looking for dangerous activities that go against their cautious nature.

PART 2

The Enneagram Types–
Parents and Children

Type One

The Type One Parent
The Parenting Perfectionist

General Description

Integrated One parents are responsible and dedicated to their roles as caretakers. You're the reliable, responsible, wise, dedicated, and fair parent every child can benefit from being raised by. You encourage your child's development and have a sensible, balanced approach to life. You provide good boundaries and instil a strong sense of morality and impeccable action.

If you're a One parent, you work hard to improve yourself and your child. You're likely to be neat, tending towards pastels or navy over shocking pink or neon orange, and suits or classic designs rather than jeans and a grubby T-shirt. Chances are that you walk with a sense of purpose, as if embarking on an important mission (which you probably are). You're a dutiful parent and aim to raise your kids to be solid, upstanding citizens.

Many Ones report having had childhoods where parents were demanding and punitive; alternatively, you may have had no discipline as a child, and so created your own rules. You may insist on certain things for your child, such as not eating any sweets or cake at a party, following a strict diet, or not playing with specific children.

One parents will expect their child to keep their clothes clean and their rooms tidy, and to be polite and well-behaved. Neatness is important to Ones, so even when your kid is very young, you'll insist that they pack away their toys after every play. (Right now you'll probably be thinking, "Doesn't every parent do that?")

You may find yourself becoming somewhat preachy to kids on subjects such as morality, being truthful, the right way to behave, manners, and knowing right from wrong. You have high moral standards and berate yourself emotionally for any slight deviation from your own high expectation of yourself. When I was at school, there was a very One hall monitor who would always call me out over the length of my skirt or my untidy hair. After I left school, we lost contact for 40 years until I received a message from her on my cell phone telling me there was a spelling error in one of my books! Now, that's a very One thing to do!

What you may want in your child: You'd like your child to be self-controlled, reasonable, regular, and have the ability to delay rewards—a "little adult" or the "good boy/girl."

Advantages of Being a One Parent

When we are healthy and integrated, we are able to share the gifts of our type. These are the advantages of the Type One parent.

You have firm boundaries: The great part about being a One parent is that your kids know where they stand—things are either right or wrong. There's no grey area. At your more integrated levels, you know the need for empathetic limits, and the difference between control and rigidity. You also understand that having a few age-appropriate rules (such as around safety and treating other people with respect) and adding to them over time is way better than having a long list of rules that are impossible to enforce. You know this makes for secure, better-adjusted children. When rules are obeyed, life is good.

You are punctual: It's highly unlikely that you'll ever be late to collect your child, because Ones pride themselves on being punctual. You do the same for your kids: you'll make sure they show up at the party on time, or even a few minutes early, despite any protests that this is uncool.

You are detail orientated: For you, the devil is not in the detail—rather, the detail is divine. You easily focus on your tasks, including your role as a parent, which means you will actually read report cards, attend school functions, check school emails, and sign homework books.

You are hardworking: You expect your kids to work as hard as you do— and you work hard! You have no time for slackers, although you may sometimes procrastinate finishing a job (because you're afraid it is not perfect). You definitely believe in "homework before fun." Even if you aren't gifted with extreme talent, you have diligently worked your way to being who you are—and you expect nothing less than the same level of perseverance from your offspring.

You are fair: You are serious about parenting and have a need to be fair. If there are two enchiladas remaining and three kids who want a second helping, you'll take great pains to divide the food fairly.

You are responsible, sensible, and reliable: Your kids can bank on you. You are a solid and dedicated parent who gets things done effectively, be it baking for the school bazaar or signing off homework. You react logically to a crisis as opposed to being overly reactive. You're a guiding light through the travails of life.

You are honest: You put much effort into teaching your kids the value of being truthful. If asked an awkward question, you'll try to answer as honestly as possible, although may occasionally resort to "white lies" where you deem the honest answer would not be suitable for the child.

You have wisdom: Ones can be wise and serene parents who are able to give their children impartial advice. As they become healthier, they become more accepting.

You have self-discipline: You use this to help improve yourself and to work hard—you want to be a better person and you expect the same self-discipline from your child.

You strive for excellence: You are simply not prepared to accept anything less. You want the world to be a better place, and whether it's saving the rainforests, fighting poverty, or reducing plastic waste in your own home, you are fully committed to the cause.

You are thoughtful: As a One, you approach life practically and with a desire to be helpful. You want to improve your child and show them better ways of doing things. My own One mother was always helping me to be better—whether it was improving my manners or showing me how to fold my laundry—because she didn't want me to be humiliated by not knowing these things. (I fear that in matters of folding laundry, I've failed her!)

Ways to Be a Better One Parent

You may recognize yourself in the description above. What's not to like, right? Well, when you are less self-aware, stressed, and disintegrated, those ideal attributes can be taken to the other extreme. These represent the opposite of integrated behavior, which in turn prompts us to become healthier. Not all of the following aspects may be relevant to you.

Try to loosen up: Sometimes your need to follow the rules can mean you're a tad inflexible or strict. If supper is at 6pm sharp, it will take a lot of persuasion for you to alter the rules—even on a special occasion. The problem is that if there are too many "shoulds", more rebellious kids will react against the authoritarian rule, and more compliant kids will bow resentfully to it. Also bear in mind that while being rigid may control bad behavior, it won't necessarily help a child learn self-discipline, or take responsibility for themselves. The trick is getting children to *want* to behave well, rather than enforcing them to do so.

Be less critical: You have high standards. I was at a cooking class once when the women next to me let out a big sigh, leaned over, and started making my dim sum for me—without asking! Apparently mine wasn't being made correctly, but I was happy with my less-than-perfect creations, and resented the intrusion. Sometimes, Ones set the bar a bit too high—and when your child doesn't meet these standards, you become critical. You may also find it hard to accept some physical attributes of your child, such as being a bit overweight, having pimples, or not being athletic. You can also be a tad critical of people whose parenting style is different from yours. Be aware of this tendency and move towards the healthier, more accepting aspect of your type. Understand that different parenting styles bring different advantages.

Don't repress your anger: Unlike Eights who express their anger, Ones attempt to repress it (because getting angry is not "perfect" behavior). This can mean, however, that it festers as resentment. Rather, have your say and move on.

Don't try to "fix" your child: Deep down, Ones see themselves as being intrinsically flawed, and try to overcome this by placing extra emphasis on being "perfect." This can extend to the child—One parents can, if stressed, view a child as a project that requires being shaped into their idea of perfection. You may look for whatever you view as a "flaw"—perhaps a manner of speech, a way of dressing, nail-biting, or a weight issue—and want to perfect it.

Don't be overly directive: "Be quiet!" "Sit up straight!" "Walk properly!" "Use your table napkin!" Commands like this make it difficult for your child to make their own choices. Allowing kids to make their own small decisions shows that you trust their abilities—and this gets their buy-in. Having to do everything your way (or the "right" way) doesn't allow a child to explore and try things out—both vital for growing their creativity and sense of self. Find the balance between direction and flexibility.

Stop sweating the small stuff: You're a perfectionist and you expect the same perfectionism from your kids. You get stressed when things aren't done perfectly (in your eyes). Kids will be reprimanded and judged too harshly for common kid habits like being messy. It's hard for you to understand that your high standards can't always be applied to your child and that your standards, while being correct for you, are not the same for everyone. Remember "different strokes for different folks."

Encourage exploration and be open to failure: One of the mottos of a Type One parent is "waste not, want not." While this is great for protecting the environment and avoiding wretched excess, it can be taken to extremes. For example, your child makes cookies but uses a cup rather than a teaspoon of salt, so the cookie dough is wasted. In the eyes of a One parent, this legitimate mistake can take on the proportion of a major disaster. Similarly, children making mud pies in the garden, or doing any messy art activity can be problematic for neat Ones. Your child needs to explore—failure along the way is just part of the process. Be open about your own failures and successes. Let your child see that human side of yourself.

Have more fun: It can be hard for One parents to let go—there are so many dos and don'ts that pleasure is lost in the pursuit of perfection. As a result, you may become resentful if your partner is having fun with the kids, because you feel like the "bad cop." This can feel hard for you because Seven is your Line of Release (see page 40)—you really *want* to have some spontaneous Sevenish fun. So, do that. Find the playful space inside you and enjoy expressing it to your child.

Don't push your beliefs too hard: This may be contentious as many Ones are educators or religious leaders wanting to uplift and reform. You might have found that meditating with a Mongolian monk and living off barley-grass juice, or joining the religious cult next door does wonders for your own sense of self, and that's great, but insisting that your child shares your enthusiasm could be seen as dictatorial. It's all about respecting your child's rights to exercise their own choices in who or what to believe, especially as they get older.

Be patient: As a One parent, you believe you know how things should be done and can become impatient with a child who is slow or simply not of an age to be able to color inside the lines. If a child is struggling with a task, you may find yourself wanting to take over—which tells the child that their efforts are not good enough. Appreciate your child's efforts, breathe deeply, and adopt a hands-off approach to simple tasks.

Drop the role of hard taskmaster: You work hard and expect the same from your offspring. "You should be able to play the piano better—you just need to practice more." "This homework is careless. You really should put in more effort." Sound familiar?

Some Other Ones . . .

In the *Harry Potter* series by J. K. Rowling:
- *Albus Dumbledore* is a wise mentor and teacher and epitomizes goodness.

In the *Fellowship of the Ring* by J. R. R. Tolkien:
- *Gandalf* takes the role of wise teacher.

In the *Mr. Men* and *Little Miss* books by Roger Hargreaves:
- *Mr. Fussy*, because he wants everything neat and tidy.
- *Mr. Good*, because he always makes his bed, brushes his teeth, and wipes his feet.

- *Mr. Perfect,* because he seeks perfection in everything.
- *Little Miss Neat,* because ... you guessed it!
- *Little Miss Busy,* because she's always cleaning the house, shopping, and cooking.
- *Little Miss Wise,* because she is wise and sensible.

The Type One Child

The Good Boy/Girl

General Description

Margery Meanwell was a fictitious character from the 1765 children's book *The History of Little Goody Two-Shoes.* The tale focused on a poor orphaned child, nicknamed Goody Two-Shoes, who only had one shoe until a rich man gave her a pair. Margery goes on to become a teacher and marries into wealth. The name "Meanwell" is true of young Ones.

They want to be good, and they *do* mean well in their attempt to improve their classmates, siblings, and parents. They are the North Star, shining their light for others to follow—and this gives meaning to their existence. Life would be better for everyone, they believe, if they just conformed to the rules, and all became like Goody Two-Shoes.

One kids quickly learn that being good and responsible is the way to garner strokes and praise from their parents. They're self-disciplining and they discipline others—even their parents. Little Ones can be frustrated by their playmates, who they see as being lazy, untidy, noisy, and unreliable. Remember the kid on the playground who had you all playing by the rules? Who'd get furious if you dared move up the snakes and down the ladders, just because it was fun? The bossy child who'd tear up with frustration at non-conforming children's irreverence?

One kids can assume the role of parenting their siblings, instilling in them the rules and values they believe their parents lack, as this person discovered:

> "My One brother was forever trying to discipline me, and he was merciless. If I dared have my elbows on the table, he'd hit them out from under me; if I didn't wash up immediately, he'd leave the dirty plates on my bed. Deep down, I know he felt he was doing it for my own good—to save me from being an uneducated, lazy

slob—but as a child, it was extremely taxing and would invariably end up in a fight. He was more of a parent than my parents were."

As One kids don't take kindly to criticism, pointing out inappropriate behavior can spark outrage, particularly if it's in front of other children.

Ones often experience their parent(s) as being inadequate or not available when it comes to discipline. As a result, a young One starts to create their own rules—their own guiding star. By contrast, some Ones may feel their parent(s) are too strict or punitive. When a parent is overly strict, Ones may internalize rather than externalize this code of conduct—feeling flawed, they try to become perfect.

Ones work really hard to please teachers and parents, and do what is right and expected of them. At school and home, their uniforms or clothes will be neat and clean, and Ones will look down their noses at kids whose rough-and-tumble play has created dirty marks or tears.

These kids love being the hall monitors in school—legitimately keeping other kids in line. As it resonates with being good, this kind of role also gives them a sense of purpose. Similarly, they love being given tasks like making sure everyone is quiet when the teacher leaves the room or handing out the juice. Life can be hard for these little perfectionists, who are always trying to take what they believe to be the right course of action. As such, they can sometimes appear overly serious or older than they really are. It's important to understand that as critical as they are of others, they can be equally critical or even harder on themselves.

Positive Traits of a One Child

As with adults, the more integrated your child is, the more they can express the unique gifts of their type. A child who is relaxed and happy will be more able to express these traits in a positive way than a child who is stressed and unhappy.

They are responsible: Even from a young age, One kids take life seriously and approach whatever tasks they are given responsibly and conscientiously. Whether it's feeding the cat or doing their homework, little Ones will be reliably up for the task.

They want to be the best they can be: One kids want to be the best. Not in the way of a Three or an Eight child, who *needs* to win, but rather to strive to be their *personal* best. They'll study longer and harder, train with dedication, work long hours—whatever it takes to be conscientious and thorough in their chosen field. It's not unusual for a One child to choose to do their homework before going outside to play—the reward only comes after the effort.

They are punctual: One kids like to be on time. It's important to be timeous in getting them to where they need to be, as being late makes them stressed.

They are fair: Ones get very annoyed with parents, teachers, and other children if they feel that they or others are not being treated fairly. If they are dividing a bag of sweets, a One child will be adamant that everyone receives an equal share. (And they'll likely be the ones sharing out the treasure.)

They are honest: One kids like to tell the truth. You can most often rely on their word—which doesn't always make them popular with other kids, as you can imagine.

They persevere: Long after their classmates have given up, little Ones will still be trying to master the task.

They like order: One children generally like a neat bedroom where everything has its place. Some may even be obsessive about lining up their teddies or dolls in a certain order. Rooms shared with a messy sibling can prove tricky.

They stick to the rules: If they have a deadline for playtime or watching TV, or if they are playing with others, One kids will generally stick to the rules of the home or the game. One children intent on doing the right thing tend to be well-mannered and do what they feel is expected of them.

Challenging Traits of a One Child

As with adults, positive traits can degenerate into their opposite extreme. By understanding these potential pitfalls, you can consciously work with your child to reverse them. Not all of these traits will necessarily apply to your child.

They might snitch on other children: Because truth is important to them, One children are inclined to be tattletales—seldom a popular playground trait. Even from a young age, they can be quite prim and stoic, getting furious with other kids who don't share the same ideals.

They act superior: Because they believe that they are better behaved than other kids, they can assume the high moral ground and take on the role of teaching other kids the correct way (according to their standards) to do things. They may do the same with a parent who they believe is not acting correctly.

They dislike criticism: Calling out a One child in front of siblings or classmates won't go down well. Because they put so much emphasis on doing the right thing, being told they are wrong can be mortifying.

They won't accept blame or responsibility: One children may refuse to accept blame when things go wrong. Perfectionistic little Ones just can't see that they may be at fault. Their desperate need to be right inevitably makes other kids wrong, so you'll hear things like: "Yes, I did smack him, but he wasn't playing by the rules of the game!" "She cheated so I told on her." "He took my train, so I broke his to teach him a lesson."

They need to feel in control: One children like to assert themselves with what comes across as self-righteous behavior to other kids. The trouble is that other kids, especially certain types, like Type Eights, don't want to be told what to do. So, with the very best of intentions, Type One kids can create enemies with the very people they believed they were trying to help.

They can be intolerant: One kids feel that they alone know the right way to approach a task, whether it's building a sandcastle or hitting a ball. They believe they need to help "improve" other children or projects, and don't easily accept other approaches or methods.

They are fussy eaters: The same intolerance they exhibit in life can translate to food choices, and One children may quickly develop certain likes or dislikes: "I don't like it when the sauce is too mushy." "I don't like ice cream if it has bits in it." As a parent of a fussy eater, you'll need to find a balance between respecting a child's preferences and becoming a slave to their desires.

One Preteens and Teenagers

The teenage years are usually tough for everyone, as your child's desire for greater independence meets their need to revert to the comforts of childhood. With unexpected erections, pimples, growth spurts, menstrual leaks, and urges that arise seemingly out of the blue, developing bodies can lead to embarrassing situations. For One teenagers, trying to suppress their natural urges and control their bodies can feel like a hopeless task. As a result, the body can easily become something to feel ashamed about—something that lets them down. Some Ones may try to correct what they see as faults in their bodies, in extreme cases through eating disorders.

The One teenager who tries to do the moral and correct thing can become the target of more rebellious types—a classic "good" child versus "bad" child dynamic. Like most teens, Ones desire to feel part of their social group, but doing the right and expected thing can be a veritable minefield as they try to both abide by and create rules for themselves and their peers. Fearing rejection, they may try to conform stoically to desired norms (being thin, having certain facial features, or dressing in certain ways) while at the same time finding these at odds with their beliefs in what is right or wrong. For example, sex before marriage may be frowned upon by their family, but upholding this rule can make them feel excluded in their peer group. Needless to say, social media can amplify these confusions.

Ones may resent siblings or classmates who seem carefree and uninhibited, and they may feel angry with parents who don't seem to be conforming to the very rules they established: as when parents tell them, "You shouldn't drink underage," yet think nothing of having a few drinks with supper every night. Resentment and hormones build and churn and are expressed as sarcastic retorts followed by penance and self-recrimination. This self-criticism can swing into sharp criticism of a parent: "You didn't raise me the way I should have been raised!"

Bringing Out the Best in Your One Child

No matter *your* type, here are some ways you can help your One child to be the healthiest they can be.

Teach your child to be accepting: Gently help your child to understand that the world and other people are not there to be fixed or corrected. One children need to understand that people are different, that being different isn't wrong, and that they don't always have all the answers for everyone.

Show them it's okay to have fun: Taking it easy, relaxing into the flow of an experience and not forcing a particular outcome reduces stress. Let your child see that letting go, enjoying moments of humor, and having fun are good for them.

Don't give them undue responsibility: Let your child know that they don't always have to assume the role of a rule enforcer—and they are not the parent.

Teach them about nuance and flexibility: Allow your child to grasp the idea that between black and white there are many shades of grey.

Help them keep a positive perspective: Teach your child to focus on what is good or right in the world, rather than fixating on what is bad or wrong.

Avoid perfectionistic behavior: Help your child to understand that failure is the road to success and not a disaster. Allow your child the opportunity to do a task only half-well, and free them from the belief that perfection is the only option. One children need to know that you're happy for them to try new things, even if they don't succeed. To try itself is to win.

Model compassion: Show compassion to yourself and others, so your child learns to have compassion for themselves. Teach them to accept themselves and to be less self-critical—they are good and worthy of love just as they are.

4

Type Two

The Type Two Parent
The Pleasing and Praising Parent

General Description

What a great parent! Integrated Two parents are nurturing, loving, and giving. You willingly sacrifice your time, energy, and resources to help your child. As such, you are supportive and affirming, and you empathetically tune in to your child's needs. You imbue a love of self and others.

When it comes to your child's efforts, you'll happily and unselfishly find the time to help with homework or a school project—because family comes first. Twos are the most people-orientated of all the Enneagram types, which bodes well for your child's playdate schedule.

If the school needs a volunteer to take kids on an outing, your hand will be quickly raised. When integrated, you truly accept and listen to your child, lovingly getting them to see all the positive traits they have and encouraging those they have yet to develop. When your child has failed or made a mistake, you are quick to forgive and move on.

Two mothers are the archetype of the earth mother, enveloping their offspring into their kind and loving embrace. You provide a warm home that other children love to visit—and no one is going to leave hungry. You are genuinely concerned about the children with whom your child interacts. If you feel these children are not getting enough care in their own homes, loving Twos will do their best to help and be kind towards them. As such, other children may long to have a parent like you. You will patiently teach elementary physics or join in a board game, understanding when to praise and when to allow a child to find their own way.

Other mothers may resent as you genuinely get involved with the game, rather than feigning interest while sending texts. Love, you believe, is earned through helpful deeds—so you may try to fix pain in others that you are unable to acknowledge in yourself.

You may crave deep connection with others, including your child, yet be unable to create this connection. As you become less integrated, your shadow aspects appear: you may become overly possessive and self-deceptive regarding your motives, giving time, attention or gifts only because you expect to get the same in return.

What you may want in your child: You'd like your child to be generous, thoughtful, helpful, and attentive to others—a "little helper."

Advantages of Being a Two Parent

When we are healthy and integrated, we are able to share the gifts of our type. These are the advantages of the Type Two parent.

You like to praise: Two parents shower praise on their children—in your eyes, no child is quite as wonderful as yours is. This is very affirming for your child, particularly if they are shy or less confident.

You're a good listener: Integrated Two parents make it seem as if they have all the time in the world to listen attentively, offering sympathetic input when required. The empathy you show towards your child will benefit you later in life when they still turn to you for advice or with their problems.

You emphasize relationships: Relationships are very important to Twos, and you highly value the parent–child relationship. In wanting to be loved yourself, you shower love on your child.

You put your child first: Twos will sacrifice much for the sake of their child. You will seldom miss a prize-giving or school concert, and will be the parent applauding loudly when your child stars as a bulrush in the nativity play. (Yes, mine actually was a bulrush!)

You're considerate: Twos consider the needs of those they love: "What is his favorite dish?" "He'll be exhausted after the exam, so I'll run him a lovely bath when he gets home." You are often the parent who ends up doing more than your fair share of the lifting, hosting, and catering. Through their own desire to help others, Two parents teach their children to be thoughtful and caring.

You're sociable: Twos generally enjoy having people around them, so they're happy to organize playdates and entertain another parent at the same time. You like your home to be the neighborhood play hub.

You teach independence: When integrated, Twos are able to move beyond their own need to be needed and are good at teaching their children how to be independent, capable individuals.

Ways to Be a Better Two Parent

You may recognize yourself in the description above. What's not to like, right? Well, when you are less self-aware, stressed, and disintegrated, those ideal attributes can be taken to the other extreme. These represent the opposite of integrated behavior, which in turn prompts us to become healthier. Not all of the following aspects may be relevant to you.

Avoid overpraising: Sometimes praise becomes more like flattery and feels insincere. Kids can see through this and may start to distrust your praise as a result: "If *everything* I do is amazing, am I really that great?" Praise can also degenerate into a form of manipulation, with the Two parent thinking: "If I praise her enough, maybe she'll carry on with ballet classes, even though I know she doesn't really enjoy them." Be careful that you don't pressurize your child to do things just so you can bask in their achievement.

Become aware when you are giving to get: As they become less integrated, Twos start wanting reciprocation, and love becomes conditional: "After all I do for my child, they treat me like this?" Twos can also use their child to "social climb" with desirable contacts: "If little Noah needs company, my Oliver would be *happy* to join you for your weekend in the Hamptons . . ." Giving can also become a way of winning the approval of teachers and other parents—a Two parent might donate three cakes to the bake sale instead of the requested one.

Don't fall into the prideful belief that no one in the family can exist without you: This may be somewhat true when your child is young, but as they get older, they don't want to be made to feel that in giving them life, you have constrained yours.

Realise that love isn't earned: An integrated Two's natural need to nurture and love unconditionally can slide into a belief that love has to be earned through doing things for other people. Being a good parent seems to demand some sort of physical or emotional reward or payback. The message to your child is: "We are loved for what we do, rather than who we are."

Give up being a rescuer: It's always painful when your child experiences difficulties—but when you are overprotective of your child, they never learn to stand up for themselves and find their own ways of dealing with life's hardships. This can result in them always being dependent on you. Instead, encourage them to face challenges and congratulate them when they do.

Learn to let go: You can be a tad possessive of your child, which becomes problematic as they grow older and want to spread their wings. This can feel smothering to them, and lead to you interfering in your older child's life. Allowing children to become too dependent on you can create unhealthy co-dependency. Let them fight their own battles.

Develop your own interests: Be careful not to fall into the trap of making your entire life about your child and/or partner. Don't feign interest in something just for the sake of being together: "We gave my son a bike, but I felt lonely when he went out riding. So I insisted we bought a tandem bike—but then he gave up cycling." Find your own interests, sport, or hobby that doesn't involve others. A good relationship doesn't mean being glued at the hip.

Learn to enjoy being alone: Your love of people means you enjoy socializing, but taken to an extreme it can mean that you avoid being on your own. You may leave the TV on just for the noise, or make yourself indispensable in order to oblige others to spend time with you. Your fear of being alone could mean you fear your child leaving home, because your security relies on them being dependent on you.

Listen rather than give advice: The healthy ability to listen can become a less healthy need to give advice. Remember that, particularly as your child gets older, they may want to figure things out for themselves. It's often good to get your child's input first, asking, "What do you feel is the best way to handle the problem?" before giving your own opinion. This helps your child grow confidence in their own intuition and course of action. Then get permission before giving your input: "I have some thoughts about this. Would you like me to share them with you?"

Don't gossip: Knowing something about someone and being in a position to share this secret to another is false intimacy under the guise of "being helpful." Remember that sharing isn't always caring.

Create boundaries: Twos can also be too permissive, not wanting to rein in an unruly child for fear of losing their love. They can lack boundaries themselves, which can make a child feel less secure. Remember that permissiveness does not equate to love, and setting boundaries does not mean your child will love you less. Not creating boundaries for yourself also sets you up for feeling used and abused.

Fill your own cup: We know what it's like to have someone say, "Don't stress about me. *You* go have fun while I do all the cleaning/babysitting/housework/work . . ." The first part of the sentence seems helpful, but the last part can suggest guilt. Don't be a martyr. Know your worth.

Some Other Twos . . .

In the classic fairy tale *Snow White*:
- *Snow White* cares for the dwarves' needs and is sweet, kind, and gentle.

In *Chicken Run* by Aardman Animations:
- *Ginger* helps Rocky and wants to save the other chickens from becoming chicken pie.

In *Peter Pan* by J. M. Barrie:
- *Wendy Darling* becomes Peter's "mother" and looks after Peter and the Lost Boys.

In *The Giving Tree* by Shel Silverstein:
- *The Tree* gives her whole self to the boy.

In the *Little Miss* books by Roger Hargreaves:
- *Little Miss Helpful,* because she always wants to be helpful.
- *Little Miss Hug,* because she wants to hug everyone.
- *Little Miss Valentine,* because she brings love and friendship.

The Type Two Child
The Little Helper

General Description

Little Twos are wonderful parent- and people-pleasers. They adore social interaction and have a wide circle of friends they want to visit or have round to play. They don't enjoy being alone—how can you fulfil your perceived role of helper if there's no one to help? They need to be needed, so you'll find them assuming the role of teacher's pet, being kind to their friends, and caring for their siblings. Whereas One children like to be given a task to feel a sense of importance, Two children feel needed and loved when they are asked to help. From a young age, having them count the potatoes or stir the cookie mix creates a sense of purpose.

Twos want to be helpful because they want approval. Typically, they find hard to acknowledge that they expect some form of payback: "I'll give you my doll if you become my best friend." They are the friend every less secure child wants, as they mother and fuss.

In the home, young Twos believe that if they help out and don't ask for too much, they are acknowledged and rewarded. They then start to believe that having their own needs is in some way bad or selfish—doing as they please is punishable, while pleasing others is rewarded. They pridefully start seeing themselves as not having needs like other people—this makes them better kids and earns them more love. (Because love is earned by being helpful.)

They have a feeling that they aren't loveable themselves—they have to be kind in order to ingratiate themselves. When other kids or parents don't acknowledge or appreciate their kindness, it creates confusion and feelings of anger and rejection: "What *more* must I do?!" With siblings, this can be particularly hard: "Blake does nothing to help, yet I know he's Mom's favorite." Two kids can become clingy: desperately holding on to friendships and manipulating others using helpfulness as currency.

Interestingly, looking for sweetness in life, Twos often have a sweet tooth, and can use sweet treats and food in general to comfort themselves. Sexual Instinctive Twos (see page 43 for more on the Instinctual Drives) can master the art of being cute or talking in a cutie-pie voice. They can be "Daddy's little princess," who'll charm their way into their parents' and friends' hearts.

When Twos feel unappreciated, rejected, or betrayed, they can shift to their Point of Stretch (see page 38), becoming like little Eights—raging, blaming and plotting revenge on the "enemy" that was once a friend. Mostly, though, they are unaware of their lurking anger and can be shocked if it is mentioned: "Me? Angry?" Because they don't acknowledge their own anger, they may cherry-pick the truth: "No, I didn't throw sand in his face . . . I just had some in my hand and then the wind blew."

Positive Traits of a Two Child

As with adults, the more integrated your child is, the more they can express the unique gifts of their type. A child who is relaxed and happy will be more able to express these traits in a positive way than a child who is stressed and unhappy.

They are helpful: Like Two adults, Two children want to be of service. They are the "Little Helpers" of the world, whether it's being kind to the new boy or helping out in the kitchen.

They are demonstrative: Two children are very affectionate. It's important to know this so you can give them the hugs they crave.

They are friendly: Two children enjoy connecting with others and often hate being alone. Having a special friend can be way more important to them than any school or sporting achievement. They easily slide into the role of mothering other children.

They are extroverted and happy children: Like Sevens and Nines, Twos often display an upbeat, positive attitude in life.

They are supportive: Two children are caring and warm-hearted. They want others to like them, and are supportive as a way to achieve this.

They are generous: Twos will happily share their sweets or toys with a friend. Doing so makes them feel valuable, and they will pride themselves in their generosity.

They are empathetic: While other children may delight in the capture of a small fish, a Two child will campaign strongly for its release so it could be reunited with its mummy. From a young age, Two children can have genuine empathy for friends, family, and animals.

Challenging Traits of a Two Child

As with adults, positive traits can degenerate into their opposite extreme. By understanding these potential pitfalls, you can consciously work with your child to reverse them. Not all of these traits will necessarily apply to your child.

They supress their own needs: Two children want to be indispensable and needed. They pride themselves on being helpful, but often fail to acknowledge they have needs themselves. Any form of self-interest may have been viewed as being selfish and "bad." Wanting to appear kind, they become frustrated at not having their own needs met and repress natural emotions such as revenge or jealousy, which can then emerge covertly.

They are possessive: Little Twos can become very possessive over a parent, sibling, or friend and may not like it if the other child or person displays interest in or shows affection towards another. They may feel: "You *need* me to love you . . . or else!"

They are people-pleasers: In trying to attract praise, little Twos can be ingratiating and insincere as they try to tell you what they think you want to hear. They pick up on and use adult niceties such as, "You look great in that," "I love your hair," or "You're my favorite friend." In relaying information, Twos may tell you what you want to hear rather than what actually happened. Similarly, it can be impossible for Twos to stay neutral when friends or family are in an argument. Little Twos will want to support both parties—which can mean a double betrayal.

They gossip: Kids can say outrageous things in innocence, but Twos quickly learn that trading secrets is a way of creating more intimate friendships: "Chloë told me not to say anything, but because you're my special friend . . ."

They are bossy: Like Ones, Twos (particularly those with a One-wing—see page 35) can become bossy and controlling of their friends, resorting to manipulation if that doesn't achieve the desired results.

Two Preteens and Teenagers

You'll often find Two teens at the center of a group of friends, making sure everyone is happy, caring for broken hearts and supplying information on who likes whom. Twos love having the inside track on intrigues of the heart, and friendships are hugely important. Twos easily assume the role of close friend and confidante, but secrets aren't always kept—instead, they can be traded for "closeness" with another.

They may meddle with the group dynamics to create dependencies: "I'm so concerned about Mia. She likes Jason, but he isn't interested. If I get Jason to change his mind, Mia will realise what a good friend I am . . ." When rejected themselves, young Twos may not accept the rejection: "She really wants me. She's just playing hard to get." Overstepping boundaries can be problematic as Twos try to parent their friends.

Flattery may become a way to maintain friendships, and teenage Twos may flirt in order to get the validation they crave. If they feel it will bring them greater acceptance and "love," they easily slip into relationships that aren't particularly healthy, even giving sexual favors in the process. Because they are demonstrative, a Two's innocent affection can be misread by others as flirting, which can lead to unwanted advances. Twos can also attempt to get their needs met through emotional manipulation or by convincing themselves that a "no" is actually a "yes."

Rather than do everything for everyone, they tend to focus on the person they desire as a friend or a lover, and tend to assume the interests of the other: "Look at all we have in common—we were just meant to be." Rejection reinforces their belief that they are not worthy of love.

Not wanting to display hidden hostility towards friends, they may accuse their parents instead: "You never really loved me!"

Bringing Out the Best in Your Two Child

No matter *your* type, here are some ways you can help your Two child to be the healthiest they can be.

Stress that being able to receive is as important as giving: It can be harder for Twos to receive than to give, so Twos may deny others the joy of giving to them. Allow your child to see that the pleasure they derive from being helpful should be shared.

Ask about their needs: Let them see that caring for others starts with caring for themselves. Only when their cup is full can they give unconditionally to others. Explore their true interests, rather than the interests they assume in order to create connections with others. Help them to see that having needs is part of their human experience, not a sin.

Encourage them to express what they truly feel: Being liked shouldn't come at the expense of their own needs and desires. Ask your Two child each day what they would like to do for themselves—and not what they think you want to hear.

Encourage them to develop a relationship with themselves: Get them to spend time alone being creative, exploring in nature, or doing a fun project.

Teach them about boundaries: Twos need to create their own boundaries, and respect those of others.

Demonstrate unconditional love: Little Twos need to experience that love is not earned, but is their right as your child. Show them often that you love them and are grateful that they are your child. Hug them even when they aren't being helpful.

5

Type Three

The Type Three Parent
The Goal-Setting Go-Getter

General Description

The integrated Type Three makes for a wonderful parent. Not only are you super-organized, you're also fun, enthusiastic, practical, and have loads of energy to keep up with a busy child. You're driven to succeed in all you do, and love to set goals and see them materialize. You value yourself and your contribution to the world, wanting the best for yourself and for your child.

For your kid to be happy, they need to be successful, right? You're a winner and you want them to feel the rush that comes from achievement. And that's what you're here to do—to ensure their top spot. Just as you constantly strive to better yourself so you can hold your own in any company, you want the same for your child. So you'll encourage them to take music, art, tennis, conversational French, or whatever will make them stand out and excel, and you market their abilities to others: "My Sasha is an *incredible* little violin player."

You are task-orientated, and extremely effective when it comes to completing a project. As such, you're a shining example for your child of hard work being more effective than just talent. A natural cheerleader, you're extremely encouraging and will be shouting the loudest from the side of the pitch as they score another goal. Although Threes are part of the Feeling Triad, you can appear to be emotionally cool: "Nothing phases me." You will wait to be alone before you express your bottled-up emotions: "At work, no matter how hurtful a comment might be, I always appear nonplussed."

You're extremely efficient and will happily take on extra activities if your hectic work schedule allows. If you need to bake cakes for the school fundraiser and don't have the time, you'll splash your cash and buy something grand (even if you do mess it up a bit to look homemade!). You're self-confident and able to chat with people at all levels of society.

Like a chameleon, you can change to suit any occasion or company. This malleability means that you tend to over-identify with an idealized version of yourself, and so deny any upsets along the way. For you, failure isn't an option. You can get frustrated with those who you see as lacking ambition or follow-through, or who are slow to grasp a concept.

Threes often report feeling that their lives are a lie or fake: like the writer with three best-sellers who deep down doesn't feel they have any writing talent. With Threes there is often a glossy, sparkly outer shell, but an empty feeling inside.

You tend to place greater emphasis on career than home-life, usually finding yourself in the role of provider. You do well in corporate situations, where your achievements are visible to others. Working alone doesn't allow you to shine, so it's less likely that you'll be a stay-at-home parent (unless you're building a wildly successful online business or busy YouTube channel).

What you may want in your child: You'd like your child to be outstanding at tasks, to fulfil the family's hopes, to seek physical perfection, and be popular—a "little star."

Advantages of Being a Three Parent
When we are healthy and integrated, we are able to share the gifts of our type. These are the advantages of the Type Three parent.

You're naturally organized: You know how to get things done and can easily shuffle office commitments with extracurricular activities and lift-clubs. Your kid knows you'll get things done well, be it baking for the fundraiser or helping with a project. As such, you're also punctual and you do what you say you will, by when you say you will do it.

You're a team player: In a family, this translates into working together to achieve a family goal, such as saving for a holiday or keeping the house tidy, so all can enjoy.

You're an excellent motivator: If your child is lacking enthusiasm for a task, you'll be there giving helpful input and encouraging them to succeed. You want to be the best person you can be, and you encourage your child to be the same.

You're energetic and enthusiastic: You enter tasks with joy and dedication, confident that you'll do a great job, and you instil this confidence in your child.

You're practical: Without being overly emotional, you're good at helping your child negotiate difficult circumstances. If there's a problem, how best are the two of you going to fix it?

You're adaptable: You teach your child to adapt to new people and new situations. This flexibility stands them (and you) in good stead.

You're charming: You're great in social situations and know how to wow a crowd, whether it's on stage, in PR or just working the room. People are drawn to your style, charm, looks, and impeccable taste. You're the yummy mummy or daddy that kids will feel proud of.

Ways to Be a Better Three Parent

You may recognize yourself in the description above. What's not to like, right? Well, when you are less self-aware, stressed, and disintegrated, those ideal attributes can be taken to the other extreme. These represent the opposite of integrated behavior, which in turn prompts us to become healthier. Not all of the following aspects may be relevant to you.

Don't push too hard: A child who doesn't have the same drive as you may be confusing: "How can they possibly succeed with that attitude?" Be mindful that your child may not envisage success the way you do—so what you see as helpful, they may see as pushy. Take care not to confuse your goals for them with their goals for themselves.

Also bear in mind that busy schedules and too many extracurriculars may feel overwhelming to some children. If there is no joy in what they are doing, perhaps they shouldn't be doing it—for example, they may be great swimmers, but they may not feel comfortable being in the swim team.

Don't let your fear of failure stop your child from trying: Children often mimic the behavior they see, so be authentic about your failures and be careful not to overemphasize your achievements. You may sometimes mask your own failures or blame them on others. Your child may pick up on this fear of failure, and be afraid to initiate anything in case it's not a success.

Be more patient: You want your child to be successful *now*. If they're struggling to grasp a concept or complete a task, you can become impatient and irritated. Ask yourself if you're expecting too much of them for their age. This is different from the impatience of a One parent who wants the task done correctly—with a Three, it's about wasting time instead of getting the job done.

Stop being a workaholic: In your desire to succeed, don't make your child feel less important than your work. If you don't make it to the office function, it'll manage without you—but your child may not. Be careful that your child doesn't start to experience you as a well-oiled, highly efficient robot.

Don't emphasize the outer world at the expense of the inner world: While appearance and success are important, don't forget your inner world. Your child's emotional makeup is important. (And so is yours.) Beware of becoming a glamorous but an emotionally empty person who ignores or suppresses their feelings. People are way more important than any work project.

Avoid marketing your child: You want your child to get into the best schools, so there can be a tendency to "sell" them as you sell yourself and your achievements. This can create false expectations, with an inevitable sense of failure when the truth emerges. No matter how amazing your child is, if you say, "James is so brilliant at sports and mathematics—it's hard for other kids to keep up with him," you're setting poor James up for a big fall is he ever has an "off day."

Be authentic: In wanting yourself and your child to appear fabulous to the world, you can gloss over any real or perceived weakness, failures, or vulnerabilities. Your child may come to experience you as artificial, and therefore not to be truly trusted.

Some Other Threes . . .

In *Matilda* by Roald Dahl:
- *Matilda*, the teacher's pet, is "too good to be true," and has many achievements to her name.

In *Gertrude McFuzz* by Dr. Seuss:
- *Gertrude* is vain about her physical appearance.

In the *Little Miss* books by Roger Hargreaves:
- *Little Miss Splendid,* because she enjoys being the most beautiful.
- *Little Miss Princess,* because she likes her royal things and being posh.
- *Little Miss Vain,* because she lives in Prettyville and enjoys having her things match.
- *Little Miss Sparkle,* because she loves to dance and shine.

The Type Three Child
The Little Star

General Description

Energetic Three children are truly the little stars or heroes/heroines of the Enneagram (and often of their families too). They want to shine—on the school stage, in their work, in sport, or whatever else makes them rise and shine each morning. One parent says of her Three child: "She was senior-class president, got a black belt in karate, was awarded "Best Student" in her class at university, and so much more. She appeared uncompetitive, a 'dark horse,' but in her own quiet way, she'd sprint to the finish line ahead of the other kids."

The emphasis for Three children is to be *doing* rather than *being*—because they feel valuable when they accomplish or achieve something. The Three's mantra is "I must do or produce, to be worthwhile," "What I am is not enough," and "I feel loved when I am praised." As a result, young Threes often look to achieve in the areas that will get them the most praise from their prime nurturer, rather than in what interests them. They may take up a sport a parent enjoys rather than play the piano, which is their true love. As they get older, they may become so focused in doing what gets the most strokes that they are unconscious of what they really want to do in life.

Threes enjoy being busy and working on projects—it's how they win approval. Like Twos, you'll often find little Threes as the teacher's pet, because their good behavior is rewarded with praise. They really enjoy being recognized for their achievements—the words "I'm so proud of you" works wonders. With *doing* as their way of being, Three children can get burned out after a period of intense effort—then they'll collapse and want to spend days flopped on the couch in front of the TV.

Little Threes enjoy being the center of attention, so it's common to find them acting in plays and demanding that parents and pals watch them perform. They are constantly seeking opportunities to shine their dazzling light on the world.

Positive Traits of a Three Child

As with adults, the more integrated your child is, the more they can express the unique gifts of their type. A child who is relaxed and happy will be more able to express these traits in a positive way than a child who is stressed and unhappy.

They are good organizers: Little Threes are great at organizing themselves and others. This means there's seldom a problem with getting school projects in on time.

They have varied interests: Threes' desire to improve themselves means they often have varied interests. They want to be accomplished—in anything from tennis to calligraphy.

They are confident: Young Threes speak and act with confidence and seldom shy away from being the center of attention (even if they modestly insist they don't like it).

They can entertain themselves: There's no "I'm bored" here! Because they are always busy, young Threes are great at keeping themselves occupied. They are very self-reliant—a young Three might be making and packing their own school lunches from an early age. They just get on with it—a pleasure for a weary parent.

They are adaptable: Whether at a party, a new school, or a new club, young Threes will be making friends while other types hang shyly back.

Friends are very important to little Threes, and if maintaining a friendship involves changing the way they act, speak and dress, they will morph quickly into what they believe is required of them.

They are practical: I love chatting to my Three daughter about a problem because she's quick to come up with a workable and practical solution. Although they are one of the "feeling" types, Threes tend to suppress their feelings to get the job done.

They work hard: Threes will do whatever it takes to get the desired result. If that means forgoing playtime, it's a sacrifice they'll make. Work is usually prioritized over play.

They are popular: Wanting to feel part of the crew, Three children work hard to be liked.

Challenging Traits of a Three Child

As with adults, positive traits can degenerate into their opposite extreme. By understanding these potential pitfalls, you can consciously work with your child to reverse them. Not all of these traits will necessarily apply to your child.

They are competitive: Threes like to win—it's another way to feel valued. As a result, you'll find them taking part in the sports or academic activities in which they are most likely to excel. This "win at all costs" approach can lead to burn-out.

They set high goals: This would normally be viewed as a positive trait— and it is—but sometimes the goal is simply unobtainable, resulting in a sad and deflated little Three when the feeling of worthlessness arises.

They can be careless: In wanting to get to the goal faster, Three children are inclined to rush tasks, desiring completion over perfection. This can become self-sabotaging: they're the first to hand in an essay, but they lose points for numerous unchecked spelling mistakes.

They can be arrogant: Threes' desire to promote themselves doesn't always win friends: "*I* got 100% for the math test. What did *you* get?"

Their achievement can come across as boastful, especially to other children.

They're overly concerned with outward appearances: Little Threes need to be reminded that it's what's inside that's important. They'll be the child demanding the designer sneakers or feeling bad if they aren't dressed in the latest kiddie's branded fashion item or clutching the most trending toy. Parents need to realize the depth of this desire to impress—which is not to say that all requests should necessarily be fulfilled. The concern with image can extend to choosing friends based on social status rather than personality.

They have trouble accepting failure: We all fail. Often. It's the only way to succeed. But Threes find failure very hard to deal with. As a result, they may resort to denying the failure, or their part in it, or blaming their failure on another child or parent.

They may struggle to make genuine friends: Groups of the "right" kinds of acquaintances may be prioritized over genuine friendships. It's a big step when a Three child drops their guard and lets someone know their real selves (as opposed to the successful outer image). Should the friendship end, or the Three be rejected, it can be devastating.

They subvert their true needs: Like Nines, Threes may try to please everyone in order to win favor—and repress their own needs.

They deal with their emotions alone: A nasty comment may appear not to affect a Three child, because emotions mustn't interfere with the job. But while a little Three on the playground may appear not to be affected by the taunts of other children, they may cry about the issue many days later when they are alone.

Three Preteens and Teenagers

Teen Threes will be shining their success for all to see, so expect class president, team captain, head of debating, or the leading role in the school play. They love being competitive, although Self-preservation Threes (see page 40 on the Instinctual Drives) may be more covert about their goals—they still want to win, but don't want to be *seen* to be wanting to win! Many Threes will be heading to the podium to receive merit awards and cups acknowledging their achievements. If they're not particularly successful themselves, they'll be dating or befriending someone who is—"the power behind the throne." Expect drama when goals are not achieved, or if another child obtains a coveted position.

To connect with a young Three, work on creating combined goals for vacations, the home or specific projects, do a workshop together on a subject you both enjoy, shop together, do an obstacle course, or play group games like paintball.

When it comes to teen romance, some Threes wills opt for a "catch"—the captain of the football team or the teen model. Other Threes will reject all offers, finding them a hindrance in the quest for their own goals, and also because deep down they fear a close connection—they reject a prospective partner rather than face the humiliation of a future rejection.

Bringing Out the Best in Your Three Child

No matter *your* type, here are some ways you can help your Three child to be the healthiest they can be.

Ask your child what's important to them: Remember that in wanting to earn value (praise), they forget what is of true value to them. Be careful not to judge their answers—rather, accept their choices.

Give praise where it's due, but don't overpraise: Performing well is not the same as feeling good. Allow your Three child to see that you love them unconditionally for who they are, not what they do. One parent says: "I went overboard in praising my Three child. As an adult, he now says that it gave him an overrated view of his abilities, which was helpful in some cases but less so in others."

Create a safe, non-judgemental space for them: Encourage them to express their feelings as they come up.

Teach them that failure is a vital step to success: Help them to see that to try is to succeed, because that is where courage lies. Share your own disappointments or perceived failures, and communicate how this helped you to achieve in the end. Real learning comes through trial and error—it's not instant.

Be real: Teach them that external image doesn't last. Being real and authentic does.

Involve them in non-competitive activities: Get them baking or crafting, and let them enjoy the success of their own creative process, rather than winning against others.

Let them just *be*: Be appreciative of their work efforts, but help them to see that true mastery lies in not being a slave to work—it is in being.

Build their self-worth: Teach them to trust their inner sense of self rather than their outward achievements. True winning is about caring for others and themselves, rather than chasing external success.

Extend their vision for themselves: Ask them to imagine how they can use their many talents to make the world a better place.

Reassure them of your love: Make sure you tell them that you love them just for being your child—your love does not have to be earned.

6

Type Four

The Type Four Parent
The Introspective Individualist

General Description

You have many traits that make for being a fantastic parent. You're a creative, empathetic, caring, classy, and expressive parent who, in being introspective and in touch with your own feelings, encourages your child to be the same. Feeling Fours are sensitive to their child's emotions—they can intuit what's happening in a child's mind without the need for words. You enjoy being with your child one-on-one rather than being part of a "mommy and me" group.

You encourage creativity, imagination, and an appreciation of the arts. You enjoy doing and sharing your own interests with your child. You long to express your own individuality—and desire the same for them. As a way of defining your unique sense of self, you love exploring your personal image or how you appear to others—boring and conventional doesn't work! So if your child wants to express themselves by adopting different looks, you'll happily allow them to do so.

Fours are in the Feeling Triad. They internalize their emotions and can spend a lot of time focusing on their feelings and replaying certain emotions. Being melancholy is your way of intensifying your feelings, so when your child seems overly happy, you may mistrust the emotion or see your child as being shallow. You can be past-focused, running current events through your previous experiences.

Fours may envy others and feel a sense of worthlessness: "Why does everyone else seem happier/have a more loving relationship/seem more successful/have better-behaved children . . .?" You long for what you feel you don't have.

Because you value your own freedom of expression, Fours in particular may view the Enneagram as an attempt to "box" you and remove your individuality (see page 17).

What you may want in your child: You'd like your child to be sensitive, artistic, and creative, and to have emotional depth and understanding—a "little therapist" or "little creative."

Advantages of Being a Four Parent

When we are healthy and integrated, we are able to share the gifts of our type. These are the advantages of the Type Four parent.

You're sensitive to your child's needs: Intuitive, empathetic Four parents quickly pick up on their child's feelings or moods. As such, the child feels heard and acknowledged. You feel deeply when a child is sad or experiencing emotional pain.

You're creative: Four parents will relish in exploring their own creativity while allowing their children the same freedom. Shared projects work well with this combination.

You appreciate the arts: With your love of all things refined and beautiful, cultured Four parents instil a love of the arts. Fours are the parents who truly enjoy their children's self-expression, be it writing a poem, drawing a picture, or playing a musical instrument.

You're involved: When healthy, Four parents will throw themselves into their parenting role. Many have experienced unhappy relationships with one of their parents (typically the mother), and they don't want to repeat that experience in the next generation.

You value originality: Fours will encourage their children to express themselves in unique and original ways. Where other parents may encourage conformity, Four parents will do the opposite. This is a wonderful gift for a creative child.

You are honest and emotionally rich: In being self-aware and in touch with their own emotions, Four parents give their children the safe space to be themselves. Four parents are true to themselves and encourage the same honesty in their children. You demonstrate compassion both for yourself and for your child.

You have the ability to renew: As an integrated Four parent, you inspire your child by navigating challenges with humor. You know that there is spiritual gold in even the most painful experiences—like a Phoenix, you're able to rise from the ashes of past experiences, renewed.

Ways to Be a Better Four Parent

You may recognize yourself in the description above. What's not to like, right? Well, when you are less self-aware, stressed, and disintegrated, those ideal attributes can be the other extreme. These represent the opposite of integrated behavior, which in turn prompts us to become healthier. Not all of the following aspects may be relevant to you.

Stop navel-gazing: When in a period of melancholy, you can become overly self-focused. If your own needs seem hard to manage, the responsibility of attending to your child's needs can feel overwhelming. You can stop the cycle by decreasing the time you spend thinking about your feelings—get out and *do* something. Shifting the focus outwards can be healing.

Be aware of being overly sensitive: Four parents are easily hurt, often by things that were never intended to be hurtful. For instance, you can feel rejected by a child when the child simply wanted to go and play with a friend.

Support your "conventional" child: For a Four parent, ordinary equals boring, which is not okay—as a Four, you want your child to be "special." Four parents may see a child who "follows the crowd" as lacking in depth and originality. You may unintentionally make your child feel that unless they are mirroring the depth of your emotions, they are somehow lacking.

Acknowledge your envy: Four parents can feel that other parents have better parenting skills than you, or that the child–parent dynamic in other families is better than your own. You may long for an imagined relationship, focusing on what you feel is missing rather than what is there.

Realize that you can be overly dramatic: Less healthy Four parents can be highly strung, creating dramas from situations that really don't warrant it. As such, you can demand attention, acting the princess/prince. Your child may find your strong emotions overwhelming, or feel that their emotions are minimized in comparison to yours.

Become conscious of how you push-pull: You may draw your child close one day, even to the point of being clingy, only to show up as remote the following day. Similarly, you may idealize them in one situation, only to devalue them in the next. This can be very confusing for a child, who needs a steady relationship with their parent.

Become aware of how the desire for uniqueness can appear as being snobbish: Fours can believe that their sensitivity and taste give them exclusivity—that somehow, they are above the rest of society and its trivial norms. Four parents' desire to be special can make them elitist about their child's friends: "Why would you want to be friends with *her*? She's really not one of *us*."

Don't let your intense emotions become your child's burden: Authentically telling your child how you feel is good, but your feelings shouldn't feel overwhelming to them. Be aware that when you withdraw, you're teaching your kids to do the same.

Some Other Fours . . .

In *Anne of Green Gables* by L. M. Montgomery:
- *Anne Shirley* is imaginative, sensitive, kind, caring, and feels different from other children.

In Disney's *Lilo & Stich*:
- *Lilo* feels like an outsider and believes she doesn't fit in.

In Pixar's *Ratatouille*:
- *Remy the Rat* feels downtrodden, like an outsider, and is rejected for being who he is.

In Disney's *Aristocats*:
- *Duchess,* the white Turkish Angora cat, beautiful and refined, is a music lover who teaches her kittens to sing and play the piano.

In the *Mr. Men* and the *Little Miss* books by Roger Hargreaves:
- *Little Miss Shy,* because she retreats from others.

The Type Four Child
The Creative Child

General Description

Four children are creative, sensitive, and dramatic. When relaying an event, expect to hear all the feelings they experienced ramped up and explained at length. If things didn't go according to plan, temper tantrums can occur. If you're not a Four yourself, their feelings may seem like an overreaction: "Why's she so upset? It was such a small thing." It helps to understand that they take the world to heart. Fours truly feel life.

Little Fours often feel as if they don't belong—as if they are different from you, your partner and/or their siblings. They can feel excluded, or as if they've been born to the wrong parents. Feeling intrinsically flawed makes them feel shame, which they seek to overcome by being unique and special in some way: "How can I possibly belong in this uncouth, coarse family? My real family is in another (more exotic) town." Their hope is to reconnect with the feeling of being loved—something they feel has been lost along the way. The parent who allows them to express their individuality will most likely be the one to whom they form the closest attachment. They are extremely creative and are happiest when they are expressing themselves: be that by dyeing a streak of their hair purple, dressing in vintage clothing, or getting involved in some artistic pursuit. Four children can be passionate about a project or person, often to the exclusion of all else.

Fours want to create an identity for themselves or do something to feel significant in the world. As a result, Four children generally love to play dress-up, as this allows them to explore different roles or characters: "Let's see how I feel dressed as a pirate."

Four children feel as if happiness is always over the hill: never here. They can be nostalgic and yearn for something or someone in the past. To fill this gap, they need loads of love and appreciation from those around them. A calm environment is particularly important, as are regular routines. This creates the stability little Fours need.

Positive Traits of a Four Child

As with adults, the more integrated your child is, the more they can express the unique gifts of their type. A child who is relaxed and happy will be more able to express these traits in a positive way than a child who is stressed and unhappy.

They are creative: Whether it's playing the piano, practicing lines for a play, or creating a fairy garden, your Four child will love being allowed to express their creative selves. The bonus for parents is that creative activities can keep Four children constructively occupied for many hours.

They don't get bored: While Seven children get bored easily, little Fours don't *want* to be bored—or boring. As a result, they can spend lots of time in creating things, or working on changing their appearance (to avoid being predictable!). It's from this desire that new and exciting concepts are born.

They wish to please: For the most part, Four children want to please their parents and friends, so will be pleasant although often shy company.

They are authentic and openminded: Little Fours want to express themselves openly and authentically, and they expect the same from you.

They are compassionate: Because they see beyond the physical into the world of feelings, Four children can show huge empathy for animals and other people.

They are original: In their desire to turn the ordinary into the extraordinary, Four children can be original in all aspects of life. They won't just make you a birthday card—if they care about you, the card will contain fairy dust, a pretty flower, and their own original wording.

They are sensitive: Little Fours are deeply in tune with their own emotions and those of others.

They value aesthetics: Like all Fours, these children have an innate sense of wonder for all that is beautiful. Other children may ignore a pretty flower, but a Four child will truly appreciate it.

Challenging Traits of a Four Child

As with adults, positive traits can degenerate into their opposite extreme. By understanding these potential pitfalls, you can consciously work with your child to reverse them. Not all of these traits will necessarily apply to your child.

They may want what another child has: Envy can rear its head when another child has the toy or outfit that your child desires. What they have never feels quite good enough.

They are emotional: Sometimes, sensitive Four children may appear to overreact, becoming teary and temperamental over the smallest thing. As the parent of a Four, you'll need to understand this and be able to hold space while their feelings dissipate. During an emotional upheaval, Fours can say and do hurtful things, and later feel ashamed.

They can get lonely: Your Four child can feel misunderstood by their playmates, feeling they don't belong in the group. They long for a special friend who really understands them—another pea to join in their pod.

They are easily hurt: Being extremely sensitive can mean that Four children may over-identify with their own emotions and get lost in a world of feelings that emerge from the past and blend with what they are currently experiencing. Retreating into a fantasy world of their own is where they can feel safe.

They make strong judgments: With their One influence (see the connection between One and Four on page 38), Fours can have strong opinions and strong likes and dislikes. If your child decides that they don't like another child, it will be hard to persuade them otherwise. These strong judgments can also emerge in food choices, clothes they do or don't like, and school activities.

Feelings are felt physically: The link between emotional and physical ailments are most apparent in the Type Four: so, if they're anxious about going to school, it could show up as a sore tummy.

They can be shy and introverted: Although they can display extroverted behavior at times, particularly when they're in the pursuit of art, Fours tend to be shyer and more withdrawn than some of the other types. Pressurizing them to be otherwise will only end in tears.

They can be competitive: The stronger their Three-wing, the more competitive they'll be inclined to be (see page 35 for more on the wings).

That's not a bad thing—but tempers can flare if things don't go their way.

They can be sad or melancholy: It can be hard for an upbeat parent to understand a Four's sadness, and they'll naturally want to boost their child's happiness. It's useful to know that most Fours find this melancholy place meaningful. It helps define and intensify their fragile feelings.

They are attention-seeking: In wanting to be seen as special or different, Four children may look for ways to garner attention. They can exaggerate, be overly dramatic, complain, be belligerent, or dress or act in order to shock.

Four Preteens and Teenagers

Adolescent Fours will look for ways to express their individuality because, "I'm not like other kids." They may look to enhance their idealized self-image by getting tattoos, working out to perfect their body (making their body into art), having a quirky dress sense, getting a weird hairstyle or cultivating a taste in unusual music. They may also try to dispel their fear of being boring through dramatic and eccentric behavior.

The slamming of doors and other overly dramatic responses are common when Fours feel hurt, ashamed, or underappreciated. As their hormones rage, so can they. Rather than head into direct conflict, as a parent it is best to empathize with their feelings: "I can see this has upset you. Feeling this way must be painful. Let's see how we can work to improve the situation." Encourage hobbies or activities where Fours can feel significant and special. Allow them to understand that they don't need to try to be special and original—they already are.

Fours want to be heard at a deep level. They want to know that you understand their feelings. As a parent, set aside time to really hear what your teen is saying. Listening to their stories and relationship issues, and reflecting their feelings will go a long way to cementing your relationship.

Bringing Out the Best in Your Four Child

No matter *your* type, here are some ways you can help your Four child to be the healthiest they can be.

Encourage creativity: Creativity is a way Fours can express their unique selves. Repressing their creative drive will only lead to antagonism and theatrics. Let them explore art, drama, music, poetry, cooking, writing, or whatever else rocks their creative boat.

Allow them the space to express their emotions: I watched a video of a young man and his two-year-old, who was throwing a temper tantrum. Rather than get angry, the man simply sat with his distraught toddler, holding a receptive, caring space until anger dissolved into tears and the child eventually calmed down. It was such a beautiful, compassionate gift to the child—and a good way to support a young Four.

Understand their need for time out: Four children need time alone to consolidate and regenerate. They may enjoy visiting a friend for the morning, but then need some time alone. They don't cope well with being constantly on the go.

Appreciate the depth of their feelings: Belittling a Four when they are emotional will only result in their withdrawal. Allow them space and time to discuss their emotions. Reflecting on what they are feeling helps them to feel heard. As a parent, create a safe space for them to express their intense feelings, concerns, and thoughts. Relish their depth and listen attentively to them without judgment.

Allow them to be their true selves: Encourage the idea that they don't need to find ways to be unique—they are already special to you and others. Allow them just to be themselves rather than who they feel they need to be—that's really special.

Encourage their natural desire to care for others: Looking after a special pet, spending time with an attentive grandparent, or serving in the community can all help build a stronger sense of self-worth.

7

Type Five

The Type Five Parent
The Observing Introvert

General Description

As a Five, you may have found it challenging becoming a parent. You value your space, time, and resources because exploring, learning, and discovering are paramount to your happiness—and, let's be honest, it's difficult to work with a screaming baby in the next room. That doesn't mean you're not an amazing parent, just that the idea probably didn't have you saying "Yay, yippee, yay" when your partner first suggested it. You're inventive and innovative—and the fact that you've chosen to have children shows just how much you've been prepared to give up for them. As the child of a Five, your kid will have many opportunities to learn new things, visit and explore interesting places, or experiment with various hobbies and equipment.

As much as you enjoy researching, questioning and learning, traveling to interesting places, and joining the dots between various concepts and discoveries, you encourage your child to do the same. You're the thinker of the Enneagram, which means you're inclined to be cerebral about your emotions: "I think that would make me angry" rather than "I am extremely angry." Your motto is "Knowledge is power" because the more you know, the safer and more confident you feel. You quell your fear by knowing more—but in the quest for information, the heart and body can be neglected.

Most parents find kids' constant questions annoying, but not you—you love finding out and explaining why ice floats, how chickens lay eggs, and why sausages don't grow on trees. As such, while you may find the baby and toddler years a bit tedious, you're a natural teacher for older kids. You don't enjoy *not* knowing an answer, however, and may even concoct one rather than admit you don't know.

You love helping your kid learn, particularly when you're in an advisory capacity. Although you need to be careful about taking over, projects such as building a dinosaur lair or creating a time machine will be right up your cerebral street. Needy, whiney, and emotionally demanding children won't. Fives are open to weird and wonderful ways of thinking. Little shocks you. You're not interested in superficial chitchat and commonly find social functions uncomfortable or even excruciating—unless they're based around a shared interest.

The details that bore others are fascinating to you, and you're intrinsically curious about most things. But heated emotion and demands for attention will have you reaching for your "Do not disturb" sign and withdrawing to your cave.

What you may want in your child: You'd like your child to be independent, studious, intellectual and curious—a "little professor."

Advantages of Being a Five Parent

When we are healthy and integrated, we are able to share the gifts of our type. These are the advantages of the Type Five parent.

You're great with projects: You enjoy sharing hobbies and interests with older children. Birdwatching, photography, taking careful notes on the activities of an ant farm, or researching methods for building a medieval castle are great ways to bond with your child.

You are patient: Fives are generally kind and patient teachers to children who share their interests.

You are observant: Five parents teach their children to be curious, to explore, watch, and observe life, to see the patterns in all things and to find unique solutions to complex problems. You instil in your child a love of knowledge and a sense of curiosity about the world.

You are clever: Intelligent Fives pass on their insights to their children. Their offspring enter the world informed and competent in many fields.

You allow your child the space to grow: Fives are generally no helicopter parents. Being more hands-off, you allow your child to experiment and find their own solutions, gently nudging them towards independence.

You are witty: Children love the weird and wonderful—you're great with puns and you have a playful, dark, and wacky sense of humor that children enjoy. They'll love the stories you concoct or the funny way you read to them. Humor also helps you through the darker moments of parenting: "My toddler had diarrhoea, so we'd been up all night changing nappies. Somehow, some poo had got onto the base of the fan. My Five husband commented drily, 'Well, the shit has really hit the fan.' Suddenly we were laughing again!"

You're a walking encyclopaedia: Fives generally know a lot about a lot of things. Children will seldom need to Google for the answers to their questions!

Ways to Be a Better Five Parent

You may recognize yourself in the description above. What's not to like, right? Well, when you are less self-aware, stressed, and disintegrated, those ideal attributes can be taken to the other extreme. These represent the opposite of integrated behavior, which in turn prompts us to become healthier. Not all of the following aspects may be relevant to you.

Don't get too lost in your projects: As a Five parent, you can become so absorbed that you forget to prepare lunch, collect someone from a class, or see to other practicalities of daily life: "I'd return home to find the children hadn't had lunch. My Five wife was so absorbed in her work that she'd forgotten to feed them." Keeping a schedule or reminder can go a long way to ensuring things don't get skipped. You may also feel annoyed at having to stop whatever you're involved in to assume parental duties, and your bad mood will be felt by others.

Understand why you prefer interacting with older children: Once a child can grasp various concepts, Fives enjoy teaching and interacting with them. You may need to work at spending more time playing with younger children to build the level of communication and intimacy you'll want as they get older.

Be aware of your introversion: Being an introvert means you feel drained by school functions, kids' activities, or going away with other families. Even though you may loath these encounters, you need to remember that children need to be social: "My kids regretted not going camping with other families as that was when friendships formed and fun memories were made," commented the partner of a Five. Fives need to understand this introverted aspect of themselves and find a compromise between their desire to withdraw and their family's need to engage. Sending children to preschool or hiring a nanny who can take kids on playdates may help.

Don't switch off emotionally: Head-centered (Thinking Triad) Fives may find it hard to connect with a more sensitive child's emotional upheavals—you find the drama overwhelming. Your child may experience you as insensitive, when it's just that processing and verbalizing your feelings may be difficult or take time. Getting in touch with your own feelings will help you connect with your child's feeling. Tell them how much you love them, and remember that physical play is also a great way of expressing affection.

Try to be practical: Sometimes, Fives can be so in their heads they lose connection with everyday practicalities—bills that need to be paid, meals prepared, or appointments remembered. You can suggest overly complicated solutions to simple problems. "I know when I help my kid on a school project, I make it way more complicated than it actually needs to be or buy stuff that's not necessary for it. I thought about it and realised that I do so because I want acknowledgement on some level for the ingenuity of what I've created. I want my kid's project to stand out because it's so clever." A caring spouse can help guide you to a more logical approach, be it fixing a vacuum cleaner, or helping a child with a maths sum.

Remember to prioritize: For a Five, the desire to focus on something that currently interests them can mean that paying the bills and spending time with your kid seems less important. Acknowledge that you might sometimes need to sacrifice or curb an intellectual pursuit, hobby or project to avoid withdrawing from your child and/or partner. Similarly, having your child take up time with your partner can feel invasive to you. Put strategies in place so that everyone is given the care and attention they need—including you!

Be aware of age-appropriate learning: Type Five parents need to remind themselves about age-appropriateness: "I took him outside to play ball, and he couldn't kick it back. It was a total waste of time," said a Five about his three-year-old. Remember that the finer points of astrobiology may be fascinating to you but way too complex for a five-year-old, and your obsession with death metal bands from the 80s might prompt nightmares in a nine-year-old. Simplify rather than complicate is key for working with kids—which can be challenging for someone who enjoys all the details.

Don't be authoritarian: You like to be an authority on a topic, but be cautious of moving to your Point of Release at Type Eight (see page 39), where you can become too authoritarian. Know the difference between being authoritative and authoritarian. Take care to show kindness and tolerance towards kids who may not share your interests, but who have interests of their own.

Know that you can be argumentative: Fives can become contemptuous and argumentative with those who don't accept their point of view—so a teenager challenging your opinion or a parent proposing a different perspective may result in a contentious row. If you realize this about yourself, you'll be able to stand back and listen rather than ridicule and destroy.

Be okay with not knowing: Fives like to know stuff. When a child asks a question like "How does the snow get made?", you enjoy answering in detail. But you may find it hard to admit when you *don't* know the answer. Being open about not knowing everything is a healthier approach—and an opportunity for you and your child to find out the answer together.

Understand that parenting can be especially difficult for Fives: I don't need to tell you that children are a major commitment in time and money. Children are noisy and busy by nature, which Fives can experience as draining—as a way of protecting yourself, you may sometimes find yourself wanting to control them, moving towards the less integrated aspect of an Eight. Figure out what works for you. You may find that interacting one-on-one with your child is less overwhelming than interacting with other children at the same time, or that nurturing a love of reading in your child means that they can be with you, but not require your direct involvement.

Some Other Fives . . .

In the *Harry Potter* series by J. K. Rowling:
- *Hermione Granger* is a know-it-all who loves the library, wants to impress the teachers with her right answers, is somewhat reclusive, and wants to study more subjects than is possible.

In the *Sherlock Holmes* stories by Arthur Conan Doyle:
- *Sherlock Holmes'* powers of observation are second to none.

In the *Wallace & Gromit* by Aardman Animations:
- *Wallace* is an inventor . . . who loves cheese.

In the *Mr. Men* and the *Little Miss* books by Roger Hargreaves:
- *Mr. Clever*, because he loves gadgets and has superior intelligence.
- *Little Miss Inventor*, because she invents things and wears glasses as do many Fives.
- *Little Miss Brainy*, because she always says something clever.
- *Little Miss Curious*, because she wants to know everything and loves to ask questions.

The Type Five Child
The Little Professor

General Description

As the name suggests, curious and intelligent young Fives are interested in learning things. Fives are observers and they love acquiring data—those facts that few others find interesting. They are the inventors, scientists, engineers, and IT specialists without whom the world as we know it wouldn't function.

Your little Five will want to understand how things work. They generally have a focused interest—anything from racing cars to dinosaurs to anime to rocks—about which they know a huge amount. Because of their cerebral approach to life, they're often labelled as nerds. Luckily, in today's world, nerds rule—think of Bill Gates, Steve Jobs and the host of IT people who have assumed rock-star status. Although it may worry more outgoing parents, Five kids are happy to play alone and entertain themselves. Fives do enjoy interaction—if it's on their terms. When it isn't, they can find themselves becoming socially isolated.

Little Fives grasp facts quickly and so they may be ahead of the class intellectually but not physically or emotionally, and they may even lag in these areas. Sport is seldom of interest, unless it's in analysing the game—keeping track of batting statistics or who won what when. They can be quite eccentric or quirky, and have little desire to pander to the needs or expectations of others. Sensory overload from crowded places, pushy people, or loud noises can feel extremely uncomfortable for little Fives, who generally prefer playing with a single friend at a time. They are fascinated by the darker, more arcane side of life—knowing what others don't.

When a little Five does share emotionally with you, it shows that they have come to trust you with their secrets. Be careful to respect this trust.

Positive Traits of a Five Child

As with adults, the more integrated your child is, the more they can express the unique gifts of their type. A child who is relaxed and happy will be more able to express these traits in a positive way than a child who is stressed and unhappy.

They are academically successful: It's unlikely that your Five child won't enjoy at least some academic success, although they may perform below their capabilities simply because they get distracted by other interests.

They are innovative: Young Fives can come up with ideas way beyond their years. They are great at joining the dots between diverse ideas. Your Five child may observe the movements of ants and relate this to how to successfully work in a class group, for instance. With their sharp minds, they can be truly original, insightful, and inventive.

They are funny: Fives generally have a playful, sharp, wacky sense of humor and will revel in a good pun.

They're curious and independent: Little Fives enjoy finding out about things, which makes them great at entertaining themselves. This can be very helpful to a parent who needs to work from home.

They are able to focus: Where other kids may be all over the place, young Fives can focus intently on a particular task. Multitasking seldom works for Fives.

They are their own person: Other kids may pander to their peer group or parent's needs, but a young Five can be incredibly determined to pursue their own path.

They are kind to others: Fives can be truly kind when help is needed. Fearing being incapable, incompetent, and helpless themselves, they can relate to a vulnerable child and take action to help them.

Challenging Traits of a Five Child

As with adults, positive traits can degenerate into their opposite extreme. By understanding these potential pitfalls, you can consciously work with your child to reverse them. Not all of these traits will necessarily apply to your child.

They can be "know-it-alls": To other children, little Fives can come across as arrogant about their knowledge, which they might well be. It helps to understand that Five is a "fear" type—underneath the Five's arrogance lies the fear that they don't know enough or don't have the answer, which makes them feel incompetent.

They are creatures of habit: Anxious little Fives may *want* to try something new, but they feel safer with what is tried and tested—doing things the same old way involves less thought and less possibility of getting it wrong. Your child may want to eat the same food every day because that gives them comfort.

They hold on to things: Fives generally feel that there is never enough to go around, which means they fiercely hold on to what they have—be it toys, sweets, or anything else they see as precious.

They hide themselves away: Little Fives can enjoy hiding from others and observing them rather than engaging with them. This can mean that other children experience them as distant and different.

They struggle to share: With avarice as their wounding, little Fives fear that there will never be enough to go around, whether it's ideas, cookies, toys or love. The result is an overwhelming desire to take what they can while they can, and hold on to what they have. They may choose not to share their thoughts with others so they can't be criticized or have someone "steal" their idea. They may find that telling others what they think is like "casting pearls before swine" because, "Nobody gets it—what dorks I have for parents."

They have difficulty dealing with sudden changes of plan: Most Five children are happy to comply with a planned event but take it badly when plans change—when the movie is fully booked, the museum is shut, or the ice creams are already sold out.

Five Preteens and Teenagers

Fives generally have a hard time as teenagers. They can be cynical of their peers' need to follow teen social protocol. Boys may feel intimidated by the class jocks at the same time as they question the need for group behavior. Although Five girls generally have a greater desire than boys to conform, they may feel awkward and isolated, finding giggling discussions about makeup ridiculous and uninteresting. Fives care little for social norms or impressing others, which can mean they are scornful of being part of the pack. Their peers may see them as being outsiders or "weird." Both sexes can feel intellectually arrogant. Being bright, they can become bored in class—because they already know it all.

At the time when other teens are wanting to bond, your Five teen may be rejecting their peers. Feeling like misfits or loners who are different from other kids, they are inclined to convince themselves that they don't need others—"I'm fine on my own"—rather than acknowledge that they feel upset.

Their IT know-how can, however, impress other teens and with so many TV series championing more nerdy characters, Fives are starting to move from zeros to heroes: "When my daughter started dating, it wasn't the jocks the girls were after, but the super-intelligent guys." As ideas about environmental activism, gender rights, and politics become ever more accessible, many Fives are finding niche and increasingly visible spaces in which to channel their intellectual gifts—changing ideas of what it means to be "cool" in the process. Many Fives become skilled in computer games and can spend hours playing   so even if they're not social at school, they may have a network of gaming pals.

Although they can be argumentative, non-assertive Fives don't enjoy confrontation. Remember that inside a Five lurks a possessive and territorial Eight. They may become sarcastic towards a parent, and view themselves as intellectually superior.

It's common for all teens to rebel. One way Fives in particular may rebel against social norms is by ignoring personal hygiene: "If you don't wash your hair, it self-cleans"-type thinking. Teen Fives also don't enjoy being micromanaged or feeling smothered—so parental interest and care can be confused with an intrusion, and a parent's emotions can be felt as invasive or overwhelming. Retreating into their minds, computers, or fantasy world becomes a teen Five's way of coping.

All Type Fives are secretive, so having a parent access their cell phone messages or diary will feel hugely invasive. Often Fives have issues with insomnia, so you may find your teen awake late at night. Self-care can be an issue with all Fives. Watch that they don't start to eat badly, feasting on sodas, fries, and chocolate, or skip meals altogether in favor of some project or game they find more interesting.

Bringing Out the Best in Your Five Child

No matter *your* type, here are some ways you can help your Five child to be the healthiest they can be.

Give reasons for doing things: Five children want to know why something is not allowed. Fobbing them off without a properly explained justification will only frustrate them.

Don't rely on subtext: Be as clear and concrete as you can when giving instructions—Fives don't often pick up on subtleties. It doesn't work to say, "Oh, it would be so nice to have a tidy bedroom ..." Rather be explicit: "Please put the Lego pieces back in the box. Otherwise, I won't be able to cross the room to your bed to read you a story later."

Accept their introversion: Trying to coerce a Five to be more extroverted will generally have the opposite effect—they will only withdraw further. Accept that they are happy as they are: "For years I tried to force my son to be more outgoing. Now he's a really successful software engineer, I realize that all that worry was unfounded."

Encourage interaction with comfortable limits: Fives do need some interaction, so organizing playdates with one child or activities with like-minded friends will be good for them. Encourage them to spend at least some time every day with the rest of the family. Observing feels more comfortable to them than participating, but there is a part of them that enjoys company and they have a lot to share. Finding ways of socialising that suit them, often centers on shared interests.

Don't push them into instant responses: Your Five child will need time to work through a decision or emotion. Trying to force them to respond immediately to something will trigger fear and resistance.

Acknowledge their achievements: This applies to all children, but sometimes introverted Fives' achievements are less tangible than those of some other types. Praising them for knowing the names of 50 dinosaurs helps them build the self-confidence they need.

Work alongside them: A Five once told me that at social gatherings he preferred it when someone came and stood next to him rather than in front of him when starting a conversation—it felt less threatening. The same applies to your relationship with your child. Rather than confronting your little Five with options, find activities you can enjoy alongside each other—it will help build and strengthen your relationship.

Help them connect with their feelings: It's not that Fives don't feel—they feel deeply—it's just difficult for them to connect and express these feelings and communicate them to others. You can help by modeling an emotional language: "I think you might be upset because your sister broke your tower. It's okay to feel like that. If you like, I'll help you fix it."

Help them connect to their bodies: Fives can be so in their heads that they literally don't notice their bodies, and may even actively resist experiencing the world of sensation. If they're involved in a project, they can forget when they're hungry, forget to brush their teeth, or ignore any other bodily need.

Take any opportunity to remind them about their bodies in gentle, non-threatening ways—massage their backs, get them to walk barefoot on the grass, or have them do Tai Chi, play with their cars in a sandbox, or relax in a warm bubble bath.

Demonstrate abundance in their world: Fives often hoard things, fearing that there is never enough, and this makes sharing hard. Reinforce the concept of abundance in nature to balance this fear—point out the number of bees on a flower, or the unfathomable number of grains of sand on the beach. Help them understand that their needs can be met.

Enforce their competence: Little Fives can shift between feeling incompetent in the world and arrogantly inflating themselves to feel better. Help them to understand their value beyond what they do or don't know.

Accept their individuality: Five kids may be idiosyncratic, but their focused minds and ability to be inventive mean their ideas can have huge benefits for society. The hardest thing for young Fives is when their differences are made to seem "wrong." Accept their quirkiness as a strength that allows them to view the world differently.

8

Type Six

The Type Six Parent

The Dutiful Parent

General Description

Being loyal, reliable, responsible, and conscientious sets you up to be a brilliant parent. Your combination of compassion and dependability can make for a stable home environment—and you have a great sense of humor for when things go awry.

For a Type Six, life is full of potential hazards and dangers, so you try to anticipate every possible eventuality what these might be and prepare for each foreseen crisis. If you're on a flight with your child, you'll have taught them the escape drill before the plane has left the runway. You'll be the parent pacing up and down the sports field making sure your child doesn't get hurt (because the grass is still wet from yesterday's rain).

Fear is expressed then both internally ("What could happen to me or my child?") and externally ("How could it happen?"). As you're naturally cautious, you may battle to agree to an away playdate, because you worry about what could go wrong when you are not around. You're a hands-on parent who may not enjoy leaving the care of your offspring to others, because "No one will protect them like I can." This makes you appear suspicious and anxious to others—to you, it's simply what a responsible parent does.

Because of this undercurrent of anxiety, you can appear to others as being on edge—constantly worried, catastrophizing, and expecting the worst-case scenario—and even a tad prickly at times. But you balance your fear with humor. Sixes are often funny, like Robin Williams as Patch Adams in the movie of the same name. Your humor coveys the message, "Hey, you can trust me. I'm not a threat." As you move to your Point of Release at Type Nine (see page 39), you become more playful and accepting.

Trust is a big issue. You may test other parents to see if they are reliable: "Can she be entrusted with my child? Let's see how she reacts." As much as you battle to trust others, you also battle to trust yourself: "Am I up to the task of parenthood? Can I be trusted to raise this precious child?"

At times you can fear authority figures, while at other times you'll rebel against them. The more counterphobic Type Sixes (see page 45 for a description of counterphobic types) will move against their fear to prove to themselves they're not afraid—this type may get involved in bungee jumping, big wave surfing, or adventuring ("fight" as opposed to "flight"). Extreme sports aside, the Six's natural charm, sensible attitude, hardworking approach to life, and good homemaking abilities set you up to be a parenting star.

What you may want in your child: You'd like your child to have perseverance and be dependable, obedient, and trustworthy—a super "little trouper."

Advantages of Being a Six Parent

When we are healthy and integrated, we are able to share the gifts of our type. These are the advantages of the Type Six parent.

You're committed and dependable: Once in a relationship, Sixes are generally 100 percent committed, which makes them good marriage or partner material. Your child will know you are there for them and that they can count on you to protect them.

You're fun to be around: For all their sensible nature, Sixes also know how to ease up and have fun.

You are supportive of others: You're happy to take a back seat and support your child in a venture, help with homework, or organize the school sports event—it doesn't all have to be about you. You are also protective.

You're compassionate and engaging: You're a good listener who can truly feel what the other person is feeling. Because you're good at reading people, you can pick up nuances in your child's mood. You are able to see various perspectives, which makes you understanding of where your child is coming from. With your ability to engage easily, you make others feel seen and appreciated.

You're persevering, conscientious, hardworking, and responsible: You'll make sure your family is well provided for, that your child is always collected timeously from extra-curriculars and that your life policy is paid up. You are able to use thinking and feeling to engage.

You create a warm and welcoming home: Sixes are often good entertainers and you enjoy nurturing others in your comfortable home environment.

You're prepared for anything: Whether it's remembering to pack sunblock for the beach, or providing vast quantities of snacks for the car in case you break down, or doing that first-aid refresher course, you don't enjoy risky surprises and will plan ahead to avoid disaster.

You're a good team player: You're loyal to your community, faith, friends, and family. People know you have their backs. You view everyone in the family as part of your team—your child will feel a sense of belonging.

Ways to Be a Better Six Parent

You may recognize yourself in the description above. What's not to like, right? Well, when you are less self-aware, stressed, and disintegrated, those ideal attributes can be the other extreme. These represent the opposite of integrated behavior, which in turn prompts us to become healthier. Not all of the following aspects may be relevant to you.

Trust your inner voice and instincts: There's spending a lot time fearfully imagining bad things happening to your child, and then there's genuine knowing when something isn't right—differentiating between them is an art. Learn to develop this muscle so that you don't let unchecked fear motivate your decisions. Develop trust in the inner voice that says: "This doesn't feel like a good plan."

Balance fear with faith: Don't allow your own fear to project a world of fear and mistrust onto your child. Try to focus on what could work out well, rather than expecting failure or disaster. Look at ways to build your own confidence.

Be careful not to become overprotective: Much as you'd like to, you'll never be able to protect your child from everything unpleasant in the world. Rather, teach them self-protection and how to make their own decisions. Particularly as they get older, you'll have to let go—you can't always be there, and you don't want to smother.

Learn to trust your child: Allowing your child to take small, age-appropriate risks such as climbing a tree or riding a bike will help them to mature emotionally and become independent: "I taught my children that if they got lost they should find a mother with kids and ask for help. When my three-year-old got lost on a crowded beach, that's exactly what she did. The mother took her to the lifesavers, and thankfully we got her back unharmed. She was relatively unfazed because she knew what to do."

Be aware of your tendency to catastrophize: The cut on your child's arm probably won't result in blood-poisoning. Be careful that you don't overreact—always expecting the worst outcome is stressful for you and those around you.

Accept change and be flexible: The world is in a constant state of change. Digging in your heels and refusing to budge will limit your opportunities and restrict your ability to be spontaneous.

Be careful of not polarising people or groups: As Sixes become less conscious, they can start viewing others as being for or against them. You can accept certain people and persecute those you view as "the enemy" simply because they think, believe, or act differently to you.

Some Other Sixes . . .

In Pixar's *Toy Story*:
- *Woody* is honest, loyal, cautious, and funny.

In the *Mr. Men* and the *Little Miss* books by Roger Hargreaves:
- *Mr. Worry*, because he worries too much.
- *Mr. Brave*, because he bravely overcomes his fear.
- *Little Miss Fickle*, because she can't make up her mind.
- *Little Miss Careful*, because she always watching her step.

In *Wallace & Gromit* by Aardman Animations:
- *Gromit* is the very backbone of society, he's a straight-up, unpretentious, loyal dog who enjoys his tea and newspaper.

In the folk tale:
- *Chicken Little/Henny Penny/Chicken Licken* believes the sky is falling down and the world is about to end.

In Disney's *Mickey Mouse*:
- *Mickey Mouse* is a loveable and honest guy, and an admirable hero when needed.

In Enid Blyton's *Noddy* books:
- *Noddy*, fearful at times, leans on the authority of *Big Ears* for reassurance when he is in trouble.

The Type Six Child
The Super Little Trooper

General Description

Little Sixes are loyal, sensible, compassionate, brave, and responsible. Because they spend so much time worrying and wondering about what could go wrong, it can be hard for them to make decisions. They're a mixture of opposites: the conformist and the rebel, the believer and the doubter, the one who stays and fights and the one who turns and flees. They may act obedient towards one person and rebellious towards another. They can be both fearful and fearless. As a result, together with Nines, they can be the hardest type to identify.

At some early point, Six kids sensed the lack of a strong masculine figure's protection. (Note that "masculine" does not mean male only, but rather the archetypal masculine values.) That parent may not have been around much because they were busy at work or otherwise unavailable, or the child might have felt that this parent was unable to protect them. The resulting message is that the world can't be trusted—and because danger lurks around every corner, the child needs to constantly check who or what does or doesn't feel safe.

While the typical Six experiences a lot of fear, the counterphobic (see page 45) Sexual or One-on-One Six (see the explanation of the Instinctual Drives on page 43) goes against this issue. Unlike the other two Instinctual types (Social and Self-preservation types), Sexual Sixes will attempt

106

to confront their fear by doing scary things: "If I climb higher than the others, then I must not be afraid." All Sixes can be extremely courageous, however: "My 15-year-old son was nervous in the sea, but became a life-saver. When one of the other lifesavers was in trouble in huge seas, my son gave him his own paddleboard so he could get back to shore safely, while he attempted to swim." Stories like this aren't uncommon with Sixes. Their courage means they can act despite their fear.

Little Sixes can be quite authoritarian and may find themselves in leadership roles. They make loyal friends. Their light-hearted banter, humor, and affection, makes them popular on the playground, although they can be quite prickly and reactive when less integrated. Their fear of consequences generally stops them from behaving badly.

Positive Traits of a Six Child

As with adults, the more integrated your child is, the more they can express the unique gifts of their type. A child who is relaxed and happy will be more able to express these traits in a positive way than a child who is stressed and unhappy.

They are good team players: Your Six child will work hard for the benefit of the whole team, either as captain or as a team member. They are cooperative, loyal, and committed participants.

They are caring towards other children: Their affinity and warmth makes them great at taking an insecure or younger child under their wing.

They are honorable and respectful: Integrated Six kids will respect their elders, adhere to the rules, and live by their word. If they accept an invitation to a party, they'll know the right thing to do will be to turn down a better invitation that comes later. It is exactly on these points that they can also rebel!

They like to be prepared: Lord Baden-Powell, founder of the global Scouts movement, may have been a Six. The "Be prepared" motto reads like a Six's mantra:

Being prepared means you are always in a state of readiness in mind and body to do your duty. *Being prepared in mind* by having disciplined yourself to be obedient to every order, and also by having thought out beforehand any accident or situation that might occur, so that you know the right thing to do at the right moment, and are willing to do it. *Being prepared in body* by making yourself strong and active and able to do the right thing at the right moment and do it.

They are affectionate: As kids, Sixes enjoy the security and comfort that comes with being held and cuddled. Then they feel safe enough to reciprocate.

They do things correctly: Sixes want to follow the rules to prevent disaster—as opposed to Ones, who are motivated by doing the right thing. Both types want to do things correctly, but for different reasons. A Six child will want to do his homework because he's worried about the consequences of not doing it.

Challenging Traits of a Six Child

As with adults, positive traits can degenerate into their opposite extreme. By understanding these potential pitfalls, you can consciously work with your child to reverse them. Not all of these traits will necessarily apply to your child.

They don't enjoy change: Generally, Six children prefer predictable and stable environments. They don't travel well, at least until they get used to a new environment and learn they can trust it: "The first few days of a vacation with Rory are hell. He refuses to be anywhere other than next to me. I try take along food that he's used to—although carrying vegetable pie on the plane is sometimes a challenge!"

They are indecisive: Math or History? Football or swimming? Red or green? These can be difficult questions for Sixes who don't trust themselves to make the right choice. In their minds, each answer holds possible danger and they fear having got it wrong. Your child may ask you to decide or turn to their friends or teachers for advice or answers. When Sixes listen to their own inner knowing, it's a sign of integration.

They project onto others: It's easy for little Sixes to imagine things that aren't there, and project their anxiety onto others. Your child may say,

"Jamie wants to hurt me," when in fact it's your child who is angry with Jamie and wants to hurt *him*, but doesn't for fear of being disobedient.

They sweat the small stuff: Sixes can become overly worried about small things, like going to play away from home, or they may imagine that a teacher is angry with them when this isn't the case.

They have random fears: The dark represents the unknown, which can be particularly scary for anxious Sixes: "I used to see this little man in my room at night. Until I was allowed to sleep with a light on, I was terrified." But they can also be scared by sudden or fluttering movements, certain foodstuffs, spiders, frogs, or a host of other things.

Six Preteens and Teenagers

Most teens rebel, but being defiant and rebellious is very much part of the Six experience, particularly when it comes to figures of authority, such as parents and educators. With my own son, I learned that pushing him to study only created resistance and rebellion. I had to stand back and let him find his own way, which he did rather well! Sixes may comply with some people, and rebel against others, and they can act differently towards the same people on different days.

Your Six may go from being polite and well-mannered one day to sarcastic and rude the next, as they swing between rebelliousness and obedience. I knew a Six teen who used drugs during the day but slept in her parents' bed at night—defiant towards the same people from whom she would later seek comfort.

Six teens can easily overcommit to other people—assisting with coaching younger kids, being in too many sports teams, volunteering in the library—which makes them feel burdened. If others aren't pulling their weight in the team, Sixes feel they are being taken advantage of, and this creates anger.

Sixes often test their friends' and partners' loyalty: "If I push him away, will he still be faithful?" As one parent experienced: "When my daughter wanted to debate a rule with me, I had to learn to stand my ground to gain her trust. Later it would become clear that she didn't even want to do the thing she was debating."

In school, Sixes often find they perform better throughout the year than during test time, when anxieties are higher and panic sets in. Being the major fear type of the Enneagram, they can start to imagine failure before they have even started the exam.

Bringing Out the Best in Your Six Child

No matter *your* type, here are some ways you can help your Six child to be the healthiest they can be.

Validate your child's choices: Understand that they may have a cacophony of voices in their heads telling them what to do. "What's the right answer?" When your Six child can't decide which T-shirt to wear, ask them, "What T-shirt do you think works best?" rather than just telling them. Help them learn to trust their own decisions and use you only as a fallback.

Structure your life: Routines generally work well for all children (regular bath-, meal-, and bedtimes) but even more so for Sixes. Routines mean security.

Encourage them to learn some form of self-defense: Feeling physically confident will help to ease a Six's fear of being overpowered: "After an incident on the playground, I was advised to take my son to karate classes. It really helped boost his confidence in himself."

Understand their anxiety: Knowing that they easily feel anxious, try to avoid dropping them off at a new environment if you, a good friend, or sibling aren't around. When they burst into tears over the flutter of a bird overhead or some movement in the grass, understand that they are genuinely afraid. A Six child I knew had such high levels of adrenalin in his system caused by constant fear that it affected his ability to grow. That's extreme, but you can help your child feel safe in the world by taking their fears seriously and allowing them to verbalize their insecurities.

Encourage small acts of change: Encourage them to choose a different pizza topping, play a different game, pick up a different sport or hobby, or invite a new friend to come around. Each small change builds confidence to make bigger ones.

Type Seven

The Type Seven Parent
The Spontaneous Socializer

General Description

You're the cool parent kids want to hang out with. You're fun, adventurous, extraverted, friendly, and creative. For example, in the height of the COVID-19 lockdown, when no one is allowed to leave home except for supplies and medical treatment, there'll be the Seven posting pics on Facebook of her kids on bodyboards in their tiny swimming pool, while she, clad in a wetsuit, makes "waves" for them to ride. Everyone looks like they're having a ball—that's Seven parenting at its best!

As a Seven, you want to grab life and run with it. You love planning new fun activities—with or without your kids. No adventure doesn't excite you, no place doesn't need to be explored, and there are few experiences that you don't want to savor. Sevens are entertaining and enjoy being entertained. You're spontaneous, enthusiastic, and versatile. You think on the move, so you can quickly invent something fun to do or think of a place to go.

You'll take the kids hiking, to paintball, to the theme park, surfing, and on any adventure you can conceive of—all of which makes you perfect for keeping children busy. You take on every adventure with love and enthusiasm.

In contrast, you find predictable and routine everyday chores like helping with homework, cooking meals, shopping for groceries, paying bills, or doing the washing up boring and uninspiring. That being the case, you either ignore them and leave them to be dealt with by someone else, or you infuse them with a sense of adventure—cooking exotic dishes, shopping in the trendiest food shops, or using the latest technology to run your home admin . . .

Even as adults, Sevens often maintain a "Peter Pan" approach to life, never really growing up. Your joy for life makes it easy for you to relate to your kids—and they will always feel like they have a buddy in you.

You also know that bringing fun and cheer to others brings friendships and the attention you adore. Complaining has the opposite effect—so as a child you learned to avoid feeling upset or acknowledging fear. The trouble with this approach is that people may feel that they don't really know the real you. You avoid fear by being busy and planning ahead, but attempting to escape from your own pain through activity can make you feel emotionally unavailable. You're also inclined to *think* about your feelings rather than connect deeply with them.

What you may want in your child: You'd like your child to match your energy levels, to be funny and spontaneous, and to share the spotlight—a "little enthusiast" or "little extrovert."

Advantages of Being a Seven Parent

When we are healthy and integrated, we are able to share the gifts of our type. These are the advantages of the Type Seven parent.

You have a zest for life: You're the fun parent. While others may be more staid or stay-at-home types, you demonstrate the essence of fully living: "Let's try this!"

You're playful and enthusiastic: You're generally a parent who knows how to have fun with kids, particularly older ones. You have a childlike enthusiasm that kids relate to.

You're an optimist: Your glass is always half full. You seek out what's new, fun, pleasurable, and what brings joy and happiness. You look on the bright side of everything: "Okay, so you didn't win this time, but, hey, there'll be loads more chances."

You're flexible and spontaneous: You're happy to switch plans when a more exciting option arises. Taking the kids swimming when you hear that the new skateboard rink has just opened? You'll ditch swimming costumes for skateboards and be off. As long as it doesn't restrict your freedom too drastically, being a parent is also something you can adapt to.

You're imaginative: You can really tap into the rich imagination of childhood—and you're able to relate and engage with kids on that level.

You're adventurous: I met a Seven couple who'd refurbished an old campervan and were planning to drive through Africa with their two young children, despite the risks. Ditto a single mother, also a Seven, who took her son out of school to travel the world for a few years. It's not for everyone, but it can broaden your child's perspective and open them up to incredible experiences.

You're friendly: You'll happily chat to other parents in the playground or to your child's friends. You see everyone as equal and are open to interaction—as long as they're not boring.

You're creative: When it comes to parties, the challenge is on to create the best, most imaginative themes for the kids—that is, unless you're already planning your next adventure.

You're a visionary: And because you have vision yourself, you encourage your child to see the widest range of possibilities.

Ways to Be a Better Seven Parent

You may recognize yourself in the description above. What's not to like, right? Well, when you are less self-aware, stressed, and disintegrated, those ideal attributes can be taken to the other extreme. These represent the opposite of integrated behavior, which in turn prompts us to become healthier. Not all of the following aspects may be relevant to you.

Be present: Real joy is right *here*, not over *there*. You may long for the day when your two-year-old can go mountain biking with you, but don't think ahead so much that you miss their early years. Remind yourself that childhood is short—so use that joyful expressive Seven self to get involved in the game. When it comes to time, quality is more important than quantity if you're truly present.

Be aware that some kids can feel overwhelmed by your energy: More introverted kids who enjoy quiet time can find your activity level and the high pace of your life stressful. You may have difficulty understanding why a child would prefer to build Lego at home than embark on an action-packed day at a theme park. The Enneagram helps explain that there is nothing wrong with them—they just need downtime.

Make yourself emotionally available: What you perceive as fun can feel superficial and emotionally disconnected to some children. Particularly for quieter, more introverted types, make sure to spend one-on-one time with them, not necessarily *doing* but rather just being with them and listening to them. Some children of Seven parents report feeling hurt when a problem is made light of: "Buck up, kid, it'll pass. Hey, how about a game of catch...?"

Offer up the limelight: Your desire for attention can mean your child feels overshadowed or upstaged. Be sure to celebrate them and their achievements.

Remember to engage with your kids: Sometimes your desire for excitement and action can make parenting feel uninspiring. You may have so many projects on the go that parenting gets brushed aside. Remember to connect with your family—they may have more to offer than you realize.

Focus on active listening: Your mind can be so busy that in your haste you assume you know what your child is about to say. To them, this can feel as if you're making assumptions or second-guessing.

Find fun ways to perform everyday tasks: Sevens desire freedom—and who wants to comfort a teething toddler when you could be out on the town? Leaving the mundane chores to your partner can cause relationship strain. Lessen the tension by finding fun in the ordinary.

Learn to focus: Being all over the place—having loads of plans and promises but little follow-through—can be unsettling for children. You start a board game, then decide to head to the park, but, oh wait, how about a burger? Be aware of when your energy becomes scattered. Breathe deeply and focus on the present moment—not on what you're going to do after the board game (or is it a "bored game"?). Feeling distracted or experiencing FOMO because of time spent with your child is a sign that you're shifting to your less integrated side.

Accept responsibility and don't smooth over your mistakes: You've messed up completely—maybe you've said the wrong thing to a teacher or forgot to collect a child from school. In always seeking the positive, you may ignore the actual damage, making you appear insensitive. Sevens can be masters of making excuses and explaining away their behavior, and can deny accountability. You may do or say anything to escape feeling bad: "Doing that was part of the spiritual direction I needed to take ..." Being accountable will connect you to your painful emotions, but in doing so you can move beyond your need to escape.

Some Other Sevens . . .

In Roald Dahl's *Fantastic Mr. Fox*:
- *Mr. Fox* is a charismatic, funny, loveable rogue.

In *Peter Pan and the Lost Boys* by J. M. Barrie:
- *Peter Pan* is free-spirited, doesn't want to grow up and accept responsibility, and he loves adventures.
- *Br'er Rabbit* in stories from the oral tradition: he's a trickster who uses his wit rather than brawn to succeed, all while provoking figures of authority and bending social norms.

In the *Nancy Drew* series by Edward Stratemeyer:
- *Nancy* is an accomplished and somewhat unruly all-rounder who paints well, speaks French, and loves travel, cars, and boating in between conducting her investigations.

In *Winnie the Pooh* by A. A. Milne:
- *Tigger* bounces around with joy.

In *Pippi Longstocking* by Astrid Lindgren:
- *Pippi* is independent, outgoing, free-spirited, playful, and unpredictable. She embellishes stories and makes fun of pompous, unreasonable adults and their social conventions. She is kind and clever, yet can at times be self-centered.

***Oh, The Places You'll Go!* by Dr. Seuss:**
- This is a very Sevenish book.

In the *Mr. Men* and the *Little Miss* books by Roger Hargreaves:
- *Mr. Rush*, because his job is being fast and he is always in a hurry.
- *Mr. Adventure*, because he just loves to travel and see the world.
- *Little Miss Daredevil*, because she feels the need for speed (some may argue she's a counterphobic Six).
- *Little Miss Fun*, because she loves to party!

The Type Seven Child
The Enthusiastic Extrovert

General Description

Idealistic Seven children laugh often, enjoy new friends and experiences, and are generally upbeat and energetic. If you're not a Seven yourself, their energy levels can be exhausting. You've no sooner sat down to work than your Seven child is saying: "I'm bored. What's next? What can we do?" Little Sevens need excitement and entertainment—TV, PlayStation won't hold their attention in the same way it might for other children. With all this daytime activity, if you manage to keep them calm at bedtime, they tend to collapse into an exhausted sleep.

When a Seven kid visited me the other day, he was like a puppy on steroids, investigating everything, running round in circles—completely wired. It is understandable how Seven children could be prone to disrupting a long lesson by becoming the class clown or the daredevil just to liven things up. They're creative and have wonderful imaginations and vision—little Sevens enjoy seeing the bigger picture and possibilities: "What if . . .?"

Being busy is their way of avoiding painful feelings, and no matter how tough things are, little Sevens will generally put an upbeat spin on things. Unlike Eights, their fear has them avoiding fights with humor, charm, or guile—but Sevens with an Eight-wing may be more confrontational (see page 35 for more on the wings).

Positive Traits of a Seven Child

As with adults, the more integrated your child is, the more they can express the unique gifts of their type. A child who is relaxed and happy will be more able to express these traits in a positive way than a child who is stressed and unhappy.

They have a wide variety of interests and talents: One day they'll be in the swim team and the next they'll be wanting to take up drama. They want to experience *everything*, so new and varied interests are common. You're going to have to be flexible to be able to accommodate these changes of plans and interests.

They are resourceful: Seven kids think big. If they can't get the cash from you to buy that toy they're after, they'll find another way—be it buying colored pencils in bulk and selling them individually at school (the Seven I know who did this as a child is now a wealthy businessman), trading cards for a profit, baking cookies to sell, or organizing parties and selling tickets.

They are charming and charismatic: Sevens are generally popular with peers, and charming to adults—they're great to be around.

They treat work as play: If a Seven child is enjoying what they're doing, then they'll be more prepared to do mundane tasks. Washing the car can mean playful fun with foam. If doing homework offers some fun reward, then the anticipation can make the task bearable.

Rather than have your child repeat the same household chore daily, you may get better input if you vary the tasks from time to time.

They are bright: Because they're so open to learning new things, Sevens are often intelligent and can easily learn things, such as a new language.

They care for the planet: Sevens, particularly the Social Instinctual types (see page 42), can have a strong desire to make the world a better place. You'll find little Sevens happy to spend time recycling plastic, or doing a beach cleanup.

They are joyful: Integrated young Sevens can bring great joy into the world. They sprinkle happy fairy dust around them, and leave everyone feeling better about themselves.

Challenging Traits of a Seven Child

As with adults, positive traits can degenerate into their opposite extreme. By understanding these potential pitfalls, you can consciously work with your child to reverse them. Not all of these traits will necessarily apply to your child.

They don't want limits imposed on them: Little Sevens don't enjoy being told they can't do something, so discipline can be tricky. It helps to get your child's buy-in and make them feel part of the decision rather than subject to authoritarian law. When it comes to tidying a room, try: "Hey, you'll probably not want to do it, but if you help tidy your room now, then we'll have time to grab an ice cream and head to the park later." The "probably not want to do it" bit gives them a sense of freedom to choose, which Sevens of all ages love.

They can be insecure: While little Sevens enjoy their freedom, a lack of boundaries can make them feel insecure. Remember that as Thinking types, they experience deep-rooted fear, even though they attempt to disguise their fear with activity. Their points of Stretch and Release are Five and One (see page 39), making them want some containment and order respectively.

They have a short attention span: It can be exhausting trying to keep pace with a Seven's busy mind and body. They enjoy dabbling in things rather than exploring them in depth as a Five might do. If learning something new requires effort, Sevens can easily get bored. This also means that new toys are exciting today but forgotten tomorrow. This desire for novelty can become almost addictive. Their need to move quickly to the next thing can have them eating too fast or skipping meals simply to speed things up.

They are garrulous: Young Sevens can talk nonstop, and they'll often embellish a story (because the actual event is less exciting . . .).

They are excitable: This can be challenging for parents! Take your little Seven to the store and the fun of being in a place with so many tantalizing goodies can have them going wild. You're going to need to set firm boundaries.

They fear missing out: Wanting to be at the center of all things fun, it can be particularly difficult for a little Seven if they're left off a party guest list—although they'll seldom show it.

Seven Preteens and Teenagers

If all teenagers are prone to rebellion, and young Sevens are all about freedom, then it's clear that a Seven teen is not going to enjoy having rules imposed on them. Curfew? Clearly something to be broken. School dress code? Let's see how far we can push things. Repetitive class- and homework at school or college can put a huge damper on a Seven's excitement, and could lead to skipping class and doing what interests them or, more painfully, lying about what they've been up to. Unlike many teenagers who may feel awkward and embarrassed, these self-confident teens enjoy being the center of attention. They're funny and often extremely cool in the way they dress and the things they do, which makes them very popular. They love organizing social events, going to parties, or just hanging out. Teenage Sevens can find being in a family of introverts frustrating.

Teenagers are known to be experimental, and for young Sevens trying new (and sometimes illicit) things holds particular fascination: "I wonder what would happen if . . . ?" Allowances slip quickly through their fingers: "It's only the 12th and I've spent it all. Can I have a loan till the end of the month?"

Young Sevens are astute and relentless about using their sharp intelligence and charismatic charm to persuade an unwilling parent: "Can we have a party here Saturday? I'll clear up afterward. It'll be fun." If you thwart their plans without a reason that they understand, they may become rude, critical, or sarcastic in order to gain the upper hand. They may also provoke your anger by deliberately trying to shock you: "I was angry with my parents, so I bought a pack of cigarettes and smoked one in front of them, even though I don't really want to smoke. Their shock made me feel I'd won."

They're often late—there is so much to do on the way to where they are meant to be. If they get detention, they'll generally laugh it off. They need educators who make learning fun and interesting, with plenty of choices. Be aware that in their pursuit of freedom, Sevens may leave home sooner than their peers. Ironically, avoiding painful feelings can make them less emotionally mature. More authoritarian parents may despair over their Seven teen's lack of focus, but Sevens are often very successful, particularly later on in life.

Bringing Out the Best in Your Seven Child

No matter *your* type, here are some ways you can help your Seven child to be the healthiest they can be.

Get excited about their plans: Seven children just love it when you get equally enthusiastic about their dreams and ideas. Don't get stuck on "how" and "why"—it's the possibility that's exciting, so just go along for the ride. Tomorrow will bring a different idea.

Assure them you're there for them: Because Sevens are fear types, underneath their bravado is a child wanting to know that you'll look after them.

Make them feel appreciated: Your child puts a huge amount of energy into spicing up life. Let them know how much you appreciate the rays of sunshine they bring to you.

Help them to face their pain: Sevens are generally not happy working through feelings of sadness, rejection, loss, and disappointment. In avoiding emotional pain, Sevens may not learn how to cope with difficulty, and denial becomes their go-to response. Something may have happened at school, and your Seven might avoid telling you rather than admit it has upset them. Gently help to draw out these feelings, saying things like: "I guess having your best friend go away is tough. You were such good buddies. How are you feeling about it?"

Help them push through their boredom: Help them to find joy in the project, not just the planning, and encourage them to go the distance. I taught art to a Seven child. No sooner had we started one project than he wanted to move onto the next. It was disruptive, and I quickly learned to maintain firm boundaries in the lesson. When he learned to stay with a project, he was able to explore his art in greater depth and achieved deeper satisfaction.

Channel their energy into healthy activities: Encourage them to join a hiking club, learn how to surf, go climbing at an indoor climbing center, or take up a sport or martial art.

Type Eight

The Type Eight Parent
The Assertive Adult

General Description

Your assertive, protective, big-hearted, and strong presence makes you an ideal protector and parent. On your watch, nobody's going to mess with your kid. When you walk into the PTA, it's clear you know what you're about—it's in your charisma, the way you stand, confidently, chest out. You easily assume the role of leader and will probably be directing the meeting by the end of the evening.

As an Eight, you're strong-willed and even tough. Your philosophy is "Only the strong survive"—and you intend to survive, even when the odds are against you. No matter your gender, on the Enneagram, Eight represents the archetypal male. You love a challenge and enjoy being in charge, hence the name "The Boss" or "The Challenger" in some Enneagram schools.

You're self-made and you expect your child to be the same way. You have a high level of energy and drive, and you're generally a hard worker—you get things done. You also play hard.

You'll make rules for your kids, but you're a rulebreaker yourself—a rebel of sorts. You're straight-talking and can get impatient with people who don't say it like it is. You don't enjoy being dependent on anyone but yourself, but unlike Five (your Point of Stretch—see page 38), you're generally happy to have others be dependent on you.

Eights sit in the Instinctive Triad (which involves anger/the gut). They project their anger outwards, and as such are not afraid to confront others, take action, and wage war. As an Eight, you may have a huge fight with someone, but will have forgotten about it a few minutes later, provided you don't feel that you have "lost." If you do feel that the other person has got the upper hand, then you'll be planning revenge. If you "won," then you may be confused as to why others can't move on with the same ease you do.

Justice is very important to you. If someone upsets your child and you feel it was unjust, then they'd better beware! You like standing against the world—it makes you feel more alive. You're fiercely protective of those you love, but if you take this too far, they might experience this as being controlled and dominated by you. You go after what you want in life with lusty vigor. As strong as you are, you enjoy feeling the support of those for whom you care. Many Eights report having had tough childhoods where they had to assume the role of protecting themselves or their siblings because the person who played the male or protector role was either missing or abusive. As a result, they grew up quickly—life was kill or be killed. Behind that rough-and-tough exterior is a soft, generous, loving, sensual, warm-hearted person who doesn't enjoy exposing their vulnerability.

What you may want in your child: You'd like your child to be independent, know how to take care of themselves, talk straight, and succeed in business—a "little entrepreneur" or "little boss."

Advantages of Being an Eight Parent

When we are healthy and integrated, we are able to share the gifts of our type. These are the advantages of the Type Eight parent.

You're protective: You protect the weak and innocent, and your child will feel that you've got their backs—no one will mess with them while you're in charge. Your discipline may feel harsh at times, but you impose it to teach them how to survive in the world—it's done from a place of love. You will help them be successful in whatever way you can—that's where your magnanimous heart arises.

You read people well: You have excellent gut instincts and no one pulls the wool over your eyes. You intuitively know when someone is not to be trusted. As a result, you may be intimidating to educators or parents who you don't respect or trust.

You assume responsibility: You're probably a leader or boss in some way, and are inclined to run your home the same way as you run the office—although Eights with a Nine-wing can be gentle and supportive in one environment and more ruthless in the other. You teach your child to take responsibility for themselves and their lives.

You're good at making decisions and taking charge: You can think on your feet and act fast, making you a great parent when things go awry. If someone gets injured on the playground, you'll quickly take charge.

You have a big, warm, and generous heart: When someone feels loved by you, it's an incredible feeling. You love with the openness and innocence of a child, and you will go to the ends of the earth to protect and support those you care for.

You're courageous: You're not afraid to stand up to those you see being unjust. If a teacher is giving your child a tough time, you'll march into the school to deal with the problem, and you won't back down until the issue is resolved.

You teach your child to be strong: You were raised tough, and you expect your child to be tough too. Cowboys don't cry. Challenges are there to be overcome. It's a hard world out there, and you want your child not only to be able to cope with it but conquer it.

You have firm boundaries and are a good disciplinarian: Your child knows where they stand with you, which creates security. You won't tolerate any nonsense, yet you aim to be fair.

Ways to Be a Better Eight Parent

You may recognize yourself in the description above. What's not to like, right? Well, when you are less self-aware, stressed, and disintegrated, those ideal attributes can be taken to the other extreme. These represent the opposite of integrated behavior, which in turn prompts us to become healthier. Not all of the following aspects may be relevant to you.

Stand back sometimes: Children may find it hard to step out of your shadow, and at times may feel as if your will overrides theirs—as if they have no say. Allow more withdrawn children to find themselves as individuals with their own desires and personalities rather than be extensions of yourself. One mother explains: "One of my sons has always been able to stand up to his Eight father, which won his respect. My other son can't. I could see that the potential was there for him to be crushed, so I made the decision to send him to boarding school, away from his father, where he could find his own personality. It was the right choice as he excelled at school, and as such gained his father's respect."

Become aware of your power: To children, particularly more withdrawn, sensitive children, your strong energy can be experienced as intimidating, and even frightening. Anger may not concern you, but a small child can be very frightened when you blow your cool. Eights are often surprised by their own power—you just don't realize how strong your presence can be.

Allow your child to have their own views: Don't take it as a threat to your authority if your child doesn't comply with your views. Accept that they have the right to their own opinions. They may not want to wage war simply because they don't agree with you, and that doesn't necessarily mean they don't respect you. Listen to their views while containing your anger—you brought them up to obey you, but you don't want them to be "yes-men" as adults, do you? You want them to be independent, right? They are thinking for themselves. Crush their opinions, and they're more likely to become followers than leaders.

Don't be too harsh and restrictive: "Shape up or ship out" is an Eight's view of parenting, "my way or the highway." If your child doesn't follow the expected regime, you won't be shy to show your anger. While some discipline is good, if you are overly strict or harsh your child will either defiantly rebel or fearfully withdraw.

Allow your child to see your vulnerability: You don't enjoy revealing the softer side of yourself, but your child needs to experience you not only as a force of action, but also as someone with feelings. Similarly, be careful not to dismiss sensitive, emotionally sharing children as being weak or needy. Rather see their development of this "feeling" center as a strength. In a sense, they are doing what is difficult for you—revealing their softer side.

Be aware of your competitive nature: Eights are very competitive. Be aware of this when you share a sporting interest with your child. Allow your child to win occasionally.

Some Other Eights . . .

In Enid Blyton's _Noddy_ books:
- _Big Ears_ is Noddy's guardian and authority figure, rescuing him from various scrapes. He has an intimidating presence and is much feared by goblins.

In _Chronicles of Narnia_ by C. S. Lewis:
- _Aslan the Lion_ is a wonderful example of an integrated Eight. Aslan is the wise king of the beasts and a guide and protector of the children. He is both powerful and potentially dangerous.

In _The Wizard of Oz_ by L. Frank Baum:
- _Dorothy Gale_ is forthright, takes charge, and shows no fear, whether she's slapping the lion or confronting the Wicked Witch of the West.

In _Yertle the Turtle_ by Dr. Seuss:
- _Yertle_ lusts for more power and as a disintegrated Eight he isn't concerned about literally standing on people to get it.

In the _Mr. Men_ and the _Little Miss_ books by Roger Hargreaves:
- _Mr. Strong_, because he's tough, robust, and red, the color of anger.
- _Little Miss Bossy_, because she loves giving orders and bossing people around, letting everyone know that she's in charge.

The Type Eight Child
The Bossy Boots

General Description

It is generally easy to spot Eights on the playground, because they're the kids in charge. Not in the rule-following way of a One (in fact, Eights are probably breaking the rules), but in the powerful presence of natural leadership: "I've got this!" Eight kids are in-your-face personalities who can't (and won't) be ignored. One moment they're fighting, and the next they'll step in to protect another child from being bullied. They love and fight with equal intensity, and justice must rule.

Little Eights are strong-willed, confident, fearless, and have huge hearts. Their security comes from being in charge and in control. They can't allow themselves to be seen as "soft" or "weak," yet beneath their assertive and abrasive surface lies a softer, more vulnerable side.

Everything Eights do, they do with passion and as such they aim to live life to its fullest. They're very much their own person and they desire autonomy. As a parent, raising this forceful child isn't always a smooth ride.

As much as they lust for life, they can also lust for what nurtures them—food. They generally have healthy appetites that match their high energy levels. Frilly and fancy doesn't work—they want big flavours and simple, tasty options.

Positive Traits of an Eight Child

As with adults, the more integrated your child is, the more they can express the unique gifts of their type. A child who is relaxed and happy will be more able to express these traits in a positive way than a child who is stressed and unhappy.

They are confident: While other types may feel unsure of themselves, Eights are generally confident in themselves.

They assume leadership roles early: Because of their strong physical skills and ability to influence and take the lead, they are generally looked up to by their peers and easily win votes for leadership roles like team captain or youth leader. They are also generally responsible when charged with caring for a younger sibling.

They are generous: A healthy Eight child can be warm, supportive, and caring to their friends, and generous with their time and resources.

They're their own person: Independent Eights don't bow to anyone, no matter the consequences: "Gorilla snot to you," says the young Eight as he is sent to his room as punishment. They will respect a coach or educator who treats them fairly and is straight with them. Wanting others to trust them, Eights see through people who are fake.

They have enormous energy and enthusiasm: Sitting still holds way less appeal than being physical—Eights are action types and enjoy contact sports. They go after what they want with a passion and with the ability to persuade others to join them in their quest. There's nothing that will stop them when an idea springs to mind.

They are noble: There is something very noble about Eights—it's as if they are heroes and heroines on a quest.

Challenging Traits of an Eight Child

As with adults, positive traits can degenerate into their opposite extreme. By understanding these potential pitfalls, you can consciously work with your child to reverse them. Not all of these traits will necessarily apply to your child.

They have anger issues: As a result of feeling less refined than their peers, Eight children can develop a chip-on-the-shoulder experience of the world, becoming overly reactive to what they see as a slight or to other children making fun of them: "If you're not with me, then you must be against me." Other children may provoke them to see what the result will be, since Eights tend to respond with angry action. Being body-centered, this may mean a physical fight, which, because they're generally strong, little Eights often win.

They are overly independent: While raising an independent child can have many advantages, some Eight children may reject parental support when in reality they still need it, insisting on leaving home when they are too young, for instance.

They are authoritarian: Eights aren't inclined to be democratic. If they want to play a particular game, then that's the game that needs to be played, no matter other children's opinions.

They seek intensity: Eights want their intensity to be matched. If you're not able to stand your ground, they become frustrated and can lose respect for you.

Eight Preteens and Teenagers

You probably know this already, but bringing up an Eight child is going to be as challenging as it is rewarding. If you're an Eight yourself, then it will be less daunting—you know what you're dealing with. If you're not, then you'll learn fast! Your preteen or teen will have loads of energy to test your parenting skills. You're going to need to be firm and talk straight to remain in charge, because your child won't be afraid to voice a strong opinion. Be aware that any punishments you dish out can result in revenge being quietly plotted against you. Your Eight child might be thinking: "I'll play the long game and win." Eights don't enjoy losing a fight, even when clearly at fault—instead, they'll blame, name, and shame. After an explosion, while you're still picking up the pieces, they quickly move on, showing you the warm, loving heart that is at the core of their being.

Your Eight teen will stride into the fire of life. They seek intensity—it makes them feel more alive. They can be fiercely noble and protective of you one moment and vilify you the next. More fragile teens will enjoy their protection.

As hormones rush through their bodies, Eight teens may become grouchy and refuse to comply with the niceties of life. Eight boys particularly feel unrefined in themselves—they may express this by farting in company (letting off offensive steam /anger), belching loudly, talking in monosyllables, or being generally antisocial and aggressive. They want to rile you. The saying "Manners maketh the man," does not apply in their case—being resilient does. They're cocky, confident, and self-assured, meaning they may end up attracting more dates than their peers. Many Eights report losing their virginity earlier than other teens—particularly boys.

As hard as they work, teen Eights will expect to reward themselves with play. They are eager for parties or nights out. Getting them involved in sport is a healthy outlet for their energy and anger, as it gives them a chance to win. The more academic side of school or college may be less interesting to them.

Being fearless, they have the potential to create mischief—they're not afraid of being caught. Chores may prove a battleground. Don't back down, as they need to understand the importance of contributing, but it's more in keeping with their personalities to give them physical tasks such as mowing the lawn, raking leaves, or dog-walking.

Bringing Out the Best in Your Eight Child

No matter *your* type, here are some ways you can help your Eight child to be the healthiest they can be.

Talk straight: Eights understand justice so don't beat around the bush. If your Eight child is offsides, tell them—they would not expect less. But never impose unfair punishment. That will seriously upset them.

Help them manage their anger: You may need to teach them healthy ways to control their rage, such as counting to ten before reacting to a perceived slight.

Don't be reactive: Reacting strongly when your Eight child unleashes their anger will only add fuel to their fire. Try to remain steadfast and calm until they have simmered down.

Encourage them to share their vulnerability: Many Eights are fiercely protective of their sweet, softer sides—the side that is more Two-like (their Point of Release—see page 39). Create a safe space for your child to show their vulnerability, then let them see that sharing it shows real strength and bravery. It's very important for them to feel that the trust they've put in you will not be betrayed.

Find positive leadership role models for them: Identify inspiring leaders—from religious leaders to the football coach—and discuss what makes them good leaders.

Listen to your child: Sometimes in the heat of the moment, you may not see the reason behind the fight. Let your child know that you understand their frustration—this will cool things down. You may say: "Tom, I understand the situation has made you mad. Would you like to chat a bit about why?"

Get a pet: Generally, Eight children like animals, so having a playful pet to romp with can help with high energy levels. Plus, little Eights normally respond well to the responsibility of caring for a pet.

Meet them energetically: To feel loved, little Eights need to feel that your physical intensity matches theirs (in the same way that Fours need emotional intensity and Fives need intellectual sparring). They want you open, honest, and straight so they can trust you and feel supported.

11

Type Nine

The Type Nine Parent
The Accepting Adult/Patient Parent

General Description

You're patient, up-beat, accepting, receptive, and unflappable—all of which make for brilliant parent material. When someone falls, gets into a scrap, or is feeling down, you're there to calmly pick up the pieces with easy-going reassurance. With your nurturing nature, you commonly put others first.

You're creative, self-aware, and open, with a wonderful ability to unselfconsciously engage with children at their level. You have a tendency to "merge," confusing and feeling responsible for your child's feelings, thoughts, desires, and needs as if they are your own.

Most Nines report having had a happy childhood. As children, they feel good and accepted for not rocking the boat or being needy. They learned from a young age that going along to get along is the best way to be, and because no one seemed interested in what they wanted, they learned not to take notice of their preferences, needs, or feelings. Over time, this habit becomes so ingrained that much of the time they don't know what they want or feel.

Nines enjoy feeling part of a group. Waving flags and drawing too much attention to yourself carries the potential of upsetting others (and falling from grace)—as a result, you remain humble, no matter how much you achieve. You also know that voicing your opinion may create disagreement in a group, and so you find it best to remain silent. In failing to express how you really feel, you can be indirect or evasive with others and so avoid imparting your truth, while convincing yourself that everything is just grand.

Nines can at times be lazy—sometimes physically lazy, but more commonly lazy to show up and care for yourself. You may deny yourself physical care, or items you need or may enjoy, because deep down you wonder if you're worth it.

Being the peacemaker of the Enneagram, you just want things to be nice and harmonious. When the world isn't the peaceful place you'd like it to be, you swallow any anger or uncomfortable feelings: "Why can't everyone just be happy and nice?" To this end, you avoid conflict. When others push you too hard, you won't say anything but will stubbornly dig in your heels. At some point, repressed anger may be sparked and you can explode, only to quickly regain your usual calm and friendly disposition.

Nines are often hard workers, provided the work environment allows them to manage their own time. Work can be soothing for them, especially in the creative fields. When Nines move to their Point of Release at Three (see page 39), they can be ambitious and widely accomplished leaders, particularly if they have an Eight-wing (see page 35).

Being in the Instinctive Triad, Nines are an action type, yet taking action can frequently be challenging, and even upsetting—you'd rather make a nice cup of tea and focus on more pleasant things. If you are unhappy with certain aspects of your life, you may nevertheless procrastinate and do little to change them. As Nines become more integrated, they're more inclined to take action.

What you may want in your child: You'd like your child to be gentle, easy-going, receptive, and have very few needs or demands—a "little angel."

Advantages of Being a Nine Parent

When we are healthy and integrated, we are able to share the gifts of our type. These are the advantages of the Type Nine parent.

You are tolerant: Nines are exceptionally tolerant of other people and their foibles—unless it affects their child (and particularly if they have an Eight-wing). Mess with a Nine's child and all that nicey-niceness can disappear in the blink of an eye—the protective he- or she-bear emerges, swatting off the "enemy" with impunity. For the rest, Nine parents won't stress if there's some mess in the home, as long as the child is happy.

You're intuitive, perceptive, and understanding: Nines are generally good listeners. They can intuitively understand a child's problem, can empathize deeply, and aren't likely to dive in and judge—so the child of a Nine feels heard. If two of your children are at war, you're able to understand each child's perspective and find common ground to broker peace. You also bring a lightness and sense of humor to situations, which helps to ease the tension.

You are childlike: Nines have an open and unselfconscious approach to life. This allows them to really connect with children. They may be found waddling across the garden pretending to be a duck or swinging with gay abandon from a tree with a trail of happy kids in tow.

You are easy-going and accepting: The paint has spilled onto the floor. The cookies are burnt. Nines are seldom fazed—they'll just clean up the mess or whip up another batch of cookie dough and let the kids help. You're fine with it, as long as everyone's happy. As a Nine, you create a supportive environment where children feel able to explore, create, experiment, and most importantly, be themselves. You can see each child's perspective and are accepting of each view. You're guileless and allow your child's friends to feel safe, accepted, and relaxed.

You are nurturing: Nines are nurturing and warm parents who give generously of their time and energy to their child.

You are patient: Nines have incredible patience with their children, which creates a feeling of safety and security—particularly good for more fear-type children.

You create healthy routines: Nines are happy to follow regular weekly or daily routines, like meal- and bedtimes. For most children, this regularity helps create a safe and stable environment. Structure works for you because well-worn routines feel comfortable.

You are funny: Nines often use their humor to diffuse tense or emotional situations, or even to solve problems. When kids are laughing together, they don't get into conflict.

Ways to Be a Better Nine Parent

You may recognize yourself in the description above. What's not to like, right? Well, when you are less self-aware, stressed, and disintegrated, those ideal attributes can be taken to the other extreme. These represent the opposite of integrated behavior, which in turn prompts us to become healthier. Not all of the following aspects may be relevant to you.

Be aware when you're sulking: When things don't work out as planned, your natural response is to withdraw and ruminate over what has upset you. Others can experience this as sulking or even passive aggression. Communication is the key here—let your child know if they've upset you and why. Very often voicing your hurt rather than mulling over it clears the air.

Don't let passive aggression interfere with your parenting: Nines seek autonomy and don't enjoy feeling controlled. This can be a problem with young kids, who naturally control their parents' space and time. If a partner isn't available or willing to help, Nines may become passive-aggressive and just "forget" to do certain chores.

Notice how you merge with others: To feel engaged and connected, Nines will emotionally "merge" with those close to them. So if their child is upset, the Nine will feel upset themselves and find it harder to be objective about the situation. This mom explains another effect of this tendency to merge: "When we went on vacation, I wanted the family to be happy and have a good time. If they weren't, I took it personally, as if the entire weight of their happiness was my responsibility. I've since learned that other people's happiness cannot be my responsibility."

Find out what you want out of life: Understand that in merging with your child's life, you have created a void in your own. At some point, your child will leave home, and with that break comes not just an empty nest, but a large gaping hole where you thought your life was. This can also make it more difficult for them to make the break. So, start a practice of asking yourself daily, "What do *I* want?" and then set boundaries or deadlines to act.

Step out of the role of peacemaker: Although this comes naturally to you, always playing peacemaker can be exhausting—and sometimes the situation requires something different. As this Nine explains: "I had always taken on the role in my family of negotiating truces between warring parents, siblings, and extended family. It's a heavy and exhausting role, and doesn't necessarily serve the best interests of all concerned. Eventually, I advised those involved to seek joint therapy. Did it work? Not really—they left before the work was completed. But it did help me to understand that if a professional couldn't solve things, then neither could I. When I learned to step back, I found my strength."

Work at being more direct in how you speak: In not knowing what they think or feel, Nines can speak indirectly, making communication confusing. It's hard for a five-year-old to understand: "Yes, you could possibly go to play with Susan, but it might be hard for me to collect you because I'm taking Brian to tennis lessons. But I could ask Jill, although I think she might be busy." Be aware of this tendency, and try to firm up in your own mind what it is you're wanting to do.

Learn to say no: Nines can be accepting of behavior that's not acceptable. In wanting to please everyone, your child included, you can be overly accommodating and allow them to behave in antisocial ways: "He pulled his tongue at me and gave me the finger, but he is only six and I'm sure he'll grow out of it." Pets may also be overindulged to the point of being spoilt and demanding.

Create healthy boundaries: Even though you tend to avoid it, kids need discipline and the security of firm boundaries. Being too permissive can be as devastating to a child as being too harsh, as children who don't have boundaries may struggle in later life. You are a parent, and sometimes that means not being your child's best friend. Be careful of accommodating your child's needs while suppressing your own, and don't be afraid that you'll lose their love if you lay down the law. Do so with compassion: "My children always demanded sweets at the cashier counter at the supermarket. I always refused because I knew that if I gave in once, they'd push every time. There were initial temper tantrums, which I hated, but those stopped pretty soon." You might need to ask your partner for help.

Some Other Nines . . .

In *Jungle Book* by Rudyard Kipling:
- *Baloo* the sleepy bear, a sloth, he doesn't sweat the small stuff, is even-tempered and friendly. He shirks responsibility and enjoys a happy, carefree lifestyle.

In *Harry Potter* by J. K. Rowling:
- *Hagrid* is huggable, likable, lumbering, compassionate, and loves the exotic creatures he looks after. He assumes a nurturing role to Harry and friends.

In *Winnie the Pooh* by A. A. Milne:
- *Winnie the Pooh* is kind, friendly, loveable, optimistic, and is a reliable friend and leader of the group (probably a Nine with an Eight-wing).

In Enid Blyton's *Noddy* books:
- *Tessie Bear* is kind and loving towards all her friends and neighbors, and you can't help but like this gentle soul.

In the Disney Cartoons:
- *Goofy* is an endearing, inherently good, loveable goofball.

In *Horten Hears a Who* by Dr. Seuss:
- *Horten* forgives the nasty kangaroo and the two become friends (he's also an elephant, which are often associated with Type Nines).

In the *Mr. Men* and the *Little Miss* books by Roger Hargreaves:
- *Mr. Daydream*, because he's pleasant but distractable.
- *Mr. Happy*, because of his positive disposition (Sevens might claim this title as well).
- *Mr. Sleepy*, because he's an escapist who enjoys sleeping (his town of Sleepville only has four hours of daylight per day).
- *Little Miss Yes*, because she's calm, likes to agree with everyone, and doesn't express her own opinions.

The Type Nine Child
The Chilled Child

General Description

Little Nines are calm, patient, and forgiving. They enjoy having a comfortable routine and they don't enjoy confrontation. They're unselfconscious, funny, creative, warm, sensual, and often have good imaginations. Nine children can be hard to detect because they easily merge with the personalities of friends, parents, or siblings. As such, they may develop interests in several areas but will seldom explore any in great depth.

Putting a positive spin on things is natural for them, even when the situation is far from happy. They are often (but not always) "middle child syndrome" kids, feeling overlooked because of an achieving older sibling or a demanding younger one. Nine children are intuitive and often pick up on issues of which others may be unaware—because having an early-detection system for potential disharmony is a way of keeping the peace.

Animals are generally less threatening than humans, and Little Nines love them. They enjoy caring for pets or growing plants, and will thrive in nature or on a farm. Board games are typically enjoyable pastimes for little Nines, as is anything creative and crafty, and they love spending time in nature. If they misbehave, it's generally at another child's suggestion.

Nine kids enjoy daydreaming and can detach into their own little worlds. Other kids can easily dupe them because they approach life naively and expect honesty from people (because they are honest themselves): "My older brother told me to ask my mother what a certain swear word meant, and I dutifully did so. The consequences were not good! It never occurred to me that he was setting me up."

Little Nines have learned to appear relaxed and easy-going in the world: "If I don't make a fuss, everything will be fine." Sometimes this can be taken to extremes, as with the Nine man who recounted how he'd broken his leg while on vacation as a child, but didn't want to upset his parents by complaining. Not realizing how serious his injury was, the family drove home with him in silent agony instead of taking him to a local hospital.

Fading into the background may seem like a safer way for a Nine to be, but it creates the problem of not feeling heard. In a large family group or classroom, little Nines can get overlooked: "I'm the third of four children. When I was five, we went on a family picnic and afterwards I got left behind. No one noticed that I wasn't in the car until they were home."

Because young Nines just get quietly on with it, they are easy children to raise. Parents may see this as being a big plus, but being seen but seldom heard is going to result in an adult with little self-worth. Getting angry and having and expressing needs is normal; when a little Nine sees this as a problem, they can turn their anger inwards, disassociate themselves from their legitimate needs, and lose themselves in the mundane. The result is low energy levels because everything seems like too much effort.

Positive Traits of a Nine Child

As with adults, the more integrated your child is, the more they can express the unique gifts of their type. A child who is relaxed and happy will be more able to express these traits in a positive way than a child who is stressed and unhappy.

They are easy-going: Raising a Nine child is generally an easy task. They want to please and don't want to confront, so they go along to get along and very little seems to faze them.

They are popular: They tend to be liked by other children because they'll happily play whatever games are suggested rather than insisting on their own choice. They also create a relaxed space for their friends. Because they are able to see others' perspectives, they are open to friendships with children from all walks of life.

They don't show off: Boastful children will enjoy the Nines' humility and modesty as they don't feel they are in competition with them.

They have a calming presence: Nines are quietly comforting and have a natural ability to help others relax.

They are happy to let others be themselves: Little Nines don't try to force other children to be who they are not. They accept everyone at face value and are quick to forgive.

They are happy to entertain themselves: Nine children can move easily between playing with others and playing alone: "As a child, I spent hours watching clouds and the images they formed. I found it soothing."

Challenging Traits of a Nine Child

As with adults, positive traits can degenerate into their opposite extreme. By understanding these potential pitfalls, you can consciously work with your child to reverse them. Not all of these traits will necessarily apply to your child.

They can be indirect: Nines find it a challenge to say things directly, particularly when they are contentious or emotional. They may go off at tangents, disappear into drawn-out stories or deflect. This can mean they're either not sure what they think or feel, or they're afraid the truth may offend you.

They are indecisive: They may base their decisions on what they believe will please you, rather than what they want or need. They may also examine several different options and be unsure of which is the right one for them. Choosing a way forward can become problematic.

They zone out: When your child doesn't want to hear what you're saying, they can zone out—there, but not there. You may think they've heard you, but they haven't.

They procrastinate: Their homework may be due, but your child has wasted hours playing Candy Crush. The more you push, the deeper they dig in their heels—leading to panic later because they don't want to get into trouble.

They over-adjust: All Nines have a childlike resistance to growing up and taking accountability for their feelings and actions. This is acceptable when little, but as they become older it starts becoming more of an issue. What do they want? What do they feel? Going along to get along starts to become a giving up of self to keep the peace.

They can be passive-aggressive towards their friends: Young Nines do tend to decide who they want to be friends with—and not everyone is welcome. If they feel that they have not been seen by another child, their repressed anger may emerge as ignoring the other child: "I don't care if you don't notice me."

Nine Preteens and Teenagers

When your adolescent Nine doesn't get round to doing a chore despite numerous requests, chances are you're encountering the passive-aggressive behavior of a Nine who feels unheard or unimportant. See this as a sign for you to step in and engage—encourage them to share their dreams, goals, and plans. You may be surprised at the depth behind their nonchalant attitude: their typical "No worries," "It's fine," "I don't mind," and "No problem" will indicate the opposite.

They may seem complacent and easy-going, but push too hard and they'll stubbornly refuse or even rebel. That's when the anger that's been suppressed for so long explodes, followed by a feeling of, "Oh hell, what have I done? I've upset everyone. Will they leave me?" As a result, they'll quickly withdraw and revert to their peaceful selves.

Procrastination is a common Nine trait and may show up in adolescence as a way to rebel. It can also result from them getting stuck—they may mean to start a chore, but then stop to play with the dog, answer several messages from friends, and then see something interesting on social media. Hours may pass and the original task will be forgotten.

They generally do their homework because not doing it will make a teacher angry: "I got into the habit of doing my homework as soon as I got home. That way I never got stressed about it." Nines can abdicate responsibility by switching off, retreating into their own candyfloss worlds, or even blaming others.

Most teenagers experience fluctuating energy levels, but for Nines this can exacerbate their tendency to be unresponsive, self-neglecting, and indolent. They may spend days mooning around, not getting out of their pajamas, not getting off the couch, or taking a shower. If they're angry with you, they will sulk or speak in monosyllables rather than expressing the cause of their anger. Cell phones provide a great way for them to withdraw and lose themselves.

Bringing Out the Best in Your Nine Child

No matter *your* type, here are some ways you can help your Nine child to be the healthiest they can be.

Listen to them and just be with them: Nines feel unimportant and overlooked. You can help your Nine child by spending quality time with them and listening to what they have to say. Ask for their opinion, but don't demand it—if they feel threatened, they'll respond merely with what they think will make you happy. Give feedback to show that you've heard them—they're often surprised by having had your attention. They'll generally enjoy doing simple tasks with you, because they're looking for connection. Value their contributions and be as accepting of them as they are of you.

Let them know they're important to you: While Threes may wave flags about their achievements, Nines are often very self-effacing and easily diminish themselves. They'll appreciate your acknowledgment—it makes them feel seen and that they do count. Seek them out. Let them know you value them.

Help them learn to assert themselves: Encourage them to stand up for themselves and to have their own opinions. Afraid of upsetting others, Nines can fence-sit—if I don't have an opinion, then it can't be wrong can it? Creating a safe space for them to speak up for themselves or make decisions, even if you don't always agree, can go a long way to boosting their sense of self. Realize that often with Nines, a "Yes," can actually be a "No." Your needs feel way more important than theirs, so they respond with what they think you want to hear.

Encourage them to journal their thoughts and feelings: Being able to express themselves without fear of conflict is a great way for young Nines to acknowledge themselves. Because they are so perceptive about people, Nines are often good writers and storytellers—encourage them to take advantage of this skill.

Ask them what they want: Have patience as they mull over the answer and avoid judging their decision. When they are younger, limit their options to: "Would you like the burger or nuggets?" Giving them too many alternatives can be stressful as they will second guess themselves in looking for the "right" one. Help them learn to make decisions without being overwhelmed.

Help them to focus and prioritize: Nines can easily focus on non-essential tasks, whilst avoiding essential tasks, such as forgetting to do homework, while spending ages collecting leaves for a future project. Becoming absorbed in non-essential tasks can also be a way to avoid confronting uncomfortable feelings.

Encourage them to be more spontaneous, take risks and make changes: Little Nines may fear shifting out of a routine that works for them. This is not necessarily a bad thing, but can mean that they seldom explore new possibilities. Risks can equate to feeling upset if things don't work out, so they'd rather avoid. Help them to see that taking on a challenge is the success, regardless of the outcome.

Merging: Nine children can often merge with a parent. It feels safer to be an extension of you. But, when problems occur, they easily fall into blaming you. "You said we should go this way!" Encourage them to be their own person and to find self-worth.

On Being Stressed

In the following section I provide an overview of each parent/child combination. Ideally, we would all be healthily integrated, at any given time. However, as we all know, that's not the reality. As a result, I look at how our relationship gets affected when we find ourselves under pressure and stress. To empower ourselves to change, we need to bring awareness to our less integrated behavior.

It's not always pleasant or easy to face these less integrated aspects of our personalities. These less healthy aspects are not intended to be judged or condemned. But, for the keen Enneagram student, through self-reflection we can achieve growth. However, both require emotional intelligence so that we do not see these behaviors as who we are, but simply as vestiges of our ego-driven personality. Be kind to yourself, and remember, it's only through having the courage to see the shadow or darker sides of ourselves, that we allow the great lightness of our being to enter.

PART 3
Parent–Child Combinations

Type One Parents
and Their Children

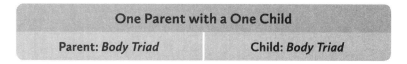

One Parent with a One Child	
Parent: *Body Triad*	Child: *Body Triad*

What Your Relationship Is About . . .

Together, you make the perfect parent–child combination. You both want to make things right in the world and in your home, and you treat each other fairly. You'll both put others first, firm in the belief that it's the right thing to do. As the parent, you understand the responsibility and commitment that goes with childrearing, and you try not to have favorites in the family.

Your relationship involves telling each other how to be better, while signaling your own moral standing: "If I didn't love you, I wouldn't care how you dressed, would I?" Because you both understand the importance of a neat and tidy home, your child will be doing chores from a young age, which will take precedence over playtime.

But life is also about letting go and having fun—it's not all about hard work. Being serious personality types, both of you may need to learn to lighten up occasionally. Going on holiday or to the park, watching movies, or eating pizza midweek (no, it doesn't have to be a wholewheat base with organic tomatoes!) can be a great way of showing your more upbeat side—that's when you shift to your lively, joyful Type Seven, your Point of Release (see page 39).

You will seldom need to encourage your child to be truthful and to play fairly. It comes naturally to them, a trait you admire.

When You're Getting Stressed . . .

Be aware that your similarities can exaggerate the less healthy elements of your type. You may start to form a mutual bond of disapproval: "That Smith family always looks like such a mess," or "Amanda and her mother

145

were late again for the party. Typical!" or "Those people have no manners whatsoever. Aren't you glad I raised you so well?"

You may clash when your idea of what is right differs from your child's. This can occur more frequently as children mature and start developing their own views on politics, clothing, or religion. You can start viewing each other as needing to be "fixed." Given their fear of messing up, One children may be afraid to take on a task if they don't feel they can complete it to your and their own (high) standards. Be careful not to push your child beyond their capabilities.

Being anger types, you will both be inclined to suppress your rage, but it emerges in your high expectations of the other—and an explosive showdown can occur after months of suppressed anger and resentment. Alternatively, it can emerge as snippy, sarcastic, or hurtful comments.

Both of you would benefit from removing the word "should" from your lives and learning to follow your hearts, not always your sensible heads. Because acting like a child isn't always acceptable, and because of the desire to improve and be perfect, your One child may act like a mini adult. I'm reminded of seeing a group of kids playing in the mud, while a One child stood back watching sadly but spotless. The mum was also a One.

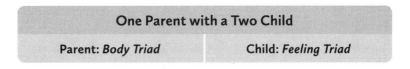

One Parent with a Two Child

| Parent: *Body Triad* | Child: *Feeling Triad* |

What Your Relationship Is About . . .

Your cooler One personality meets the warm and generous Two child. While you are practical, your child can be a praising, possessive, and affectionate child. You are the North Star shining the way to a better world, but your little Two may feel the need for more demonstrative love. You will thoroughly approve of your child's need to be helpful. United in the cause of making a positive difference in the world, you can bond well.

Your steadfastness can be comforting to your more emotional child. Both of you believe that your lives should be about helping others, yet you both tend to deny your own needs—because having needs would be selfish, right? Be aware of this, and teach your child that both their needs and your own are valid.

Your firm boundaries and committed parenting will make your child feel safe and supported. Two children can help their One parents experience greater warmth and feeling. Both will believe that love is earned: for the One through hard work or self-discipline, and for the Two through being helpful. Your child brings an example to you of a more sentimental, people-orientated, and personal approach to others.

When You're Getting Stressed . . .

Twos are more expressive and extroverted than Ones, and their demonstrability can clash with your more formal and constrained approach. One parents can even be embarrassed by the exuberant love shown by their child. Your Two child may want to attend to your needs, at the same time as you feel shame or guilt for even having needs at all.

You tend to be committed to your work, being an active member of your community, or volunteering. Believing that you're more concerned with being socially responsible than parenting them, your child may feel rejected as you rush out the door to your next appointment: "Mummy loves you, but I have to make soup for the homeless shelter ..." Feeling neglected can be particularly hard for a Two child, as they want your attention as payback for the way they've stroked your back, helped with dinner, and baked your favorite cookies.

As one Two recalls: "Both my parents did a huge amount of good in our neighborhood. Yet as their children, we often felt neglected—as if the needs beyond the family were a more noble focus of their attention."

One Parent with a Three Child	
Parent: *Body Triad*	Child: *Feeling Triad*

What Your Relationship Is About . . .

Both of you want to make the world a better place, and you will thoroughly approve of your child's commitment to hard work and goal-setting, and their striving to be the best they can be. As a result, your child will feel affirmed and supported. You're both sensible, capable doers, and value the importance of getting the task finished—and as such, you're both welcomed onto any committee or task team. Your child wants to shine, and you want to be seen to be socially responsible and doing things the right way. When it comes to organizing a school function, you'll tackle it efficiently. Both you and your child are motivated by how others view you: "What will the PTA think?" "What will my teacher think?"

As a family team, you are both accomplished and competent in all you do. Excellence is your motto—from the way you present to the board to how your child goes about a school project. You both appear confident (at least to the outside world). As a parent, you enjoy being able to present your successful child to others: "Heidi works so hard at her swimming lessons, and she's the youngest in the team." (It's a fact, so not bragging, right?)

When You're Getting Stressed . . .

Expressing and working through your feelings are stumbling blocks for both of you. You'd both rather follow your compulsive need to be active than show your emotions.

Your desire for absolute truth can make it hard for you to deal with your child's tendency to falsify the facts in order to appear not to have failed. Your child longs for acknowledgment and praise for their efforts, but you see praise as an indulgence. Doing things well is a given—it's a duty and responsibility, rather than an achievement. Boasting is not acceptable to you, and you find it distasteful when your child brags to get the praise they desire.

Your strong ideals may have a Three child trying to fulfill *your* desires rather than their own. They have a great need for your praise—and when it's not forthcoming, they may try harder by choosing hobbies and interests that they think will win your admiration.

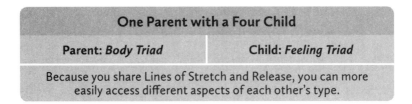

One Parent with a Four Child

Parent: *Body Triad*	Child: *Feeling Triad*
Because you share Lines of Stretch and Release, you can more easily access different aspects of each other's type.	

What Your Relationship Is About . . .

When integrated, you're an idealistic pair who can harmonize and work well together. Your One serenity meets the strong emotions of your Four child, and you balance each other. At times, your child will mirror those emotions you have suppressed.

You strive for perfection and your child strives to be unique. You help your child to be more grounded, sensible, and practical. Your child can teach you to open up to your feelings, trust your intuition, express yourself creatively, and be more spontaneous. As a result, your child can open up a richer and more exciting world to you.

You meet in your mutual intensity and belief in high standards. Nevertheless, your "right" way may differ from what your child sees as being right—this can appear in your ideological or spiritual choices.

Your child's fears of being abandoned are lessened by your steady presence—even if there is a fight, they know you'll forgive them. While you're inclined to focus on what's not perfect, they look for what's missing. Together, you can work to see that everything is perfect the way it is and nothing is missing.

When You're Getting Stressed . . .

When less integrated, your emotional detachment combined with your child's intense emotionality can cause problems. They can experience you as cold, while you experience them as moody and melodramatic. You may want to restrain your Four child's creativity: "Accounting is a far more sensible profession than being a musician."

Both of you can feel superior to the other. While your child believes their desires should be indulged, you believe strongly in discipline: "Spare the rod and spoil the child." Your child can feel misunderstood and unheard. Guilt and the fear of being flawed arises in your child as you accuse them of being self-centered and needing to be special: "Don't be so selfish—you should be more concerned with the needs of others."

Your child may find you too strict and rigid, and can throw tantrums in frustration. In an argument, both of you will remember old slights and past events, which you'll haul out and throw in the other's face.

One Parent with a Five Child	
Parent: *Body Triad*	Child: *Thinking Triad*

What Your Relationship Is About . . .

The need for perfection meets a little professor's focus on knowledge—both of you have a more serious approach to life. From a relatively young age, your child will enjoy discussing "sensible" topics with you, and you will both value each other's wisdom and intelligence. For your little Five, a conversation about how the weather works will be a happy substitute for a bedtime story. Although you enjoy working and playing alone, as a parent you will happily experiment with ant farms or build a solar-powered engine because you enjoy the mental stimulation and getting it right. You are both equally happy to get on with your tasks alone.

While your child may have a quirky sense of humor, neither of you spends much time being frivolous—there's work to be done. Your little Five may, however, enjoy computer games—which meets your disapproval, since their time could be better spent on more productive activities such as helping others and self-improvement.

Your Five child is a fear type, and will enjoy your steady presence. A lack of focus on emotions suits you both, as you both prefer feeling in control.

When You're Getting Stressed . . .

Problems can arise when you and your child get locked into your own worlds. With little emotional connection or expression, you can both become distracted and removed. Experiencing you as distant and critical, your child may withdraw to their own room, finding it hard to engage, while you experience them as detached. They no longer seem to care what you think or feel—for example, they may stop recounting the events of their day, letting only small pieces of necessary information slip.

A danger is that your relationship may become too adult too soon. With their serious nature, you can sometimes forget that you are still dealing with a child. Keep this in mind when choosing points of discussion or activities.

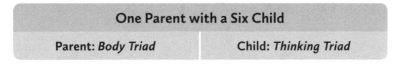

One Parent with a Six Child	
Parent: *Body Triad*	Child: *Thinking Triad*

What Your Relationship Is About . . .

One parents and Six children share a mutual belief in hard work, logic, responsibility, and commitment, understanding too that work comes before play. You both believe in supporting those less fortunate—you because it's simply the right thing to do, and your child from an empathetic viewpoint. You also share a "glass half empty" view of life. They doubt and question, while you worry about what is wrong. As a result, both of you find it difficult to view things as being okay. You both like order—you because it's right, your child because it feels safer.

Seeking security, nervous little Sixes feel they can rely on your steadfastness. You respond well to your child's loyalty, and your focus on truth allows them to trust you. Being the authority figure that Sixes seek (at least while they are still young!) and because you hold strong opinions, you are able to guide your ambivalent child towards making decisions. Your child, being engaging and funny, can lighten up your serious nature.

Like Fours, little Sixes like to explore their creativity, which allows you to explore yours. If your child has a Seven-wing, it helps to create moments of fun and frivolity—something you both need. (For more on the wings see page 35.) Both of you can be tense and uptight. Recognize this in times of stress (like school exams) and look for ways in which you can both relax.

When You're Getting Stressed . . .

Both of you struggle with procrastination, albeit for different reasons—you because of your need for perfection, and your child because they find it difficult to make their own decisions.

Sixes have a relatively low sense of self and may find it hard to bear your tendency to criticize and attempts to improve them. At times, your child may feel as if they are not able to meet your high expectations. They may nervously scan the horizon, looking for what could upset you, avoiding potential criticism, and unconsciously creating the very scenario they fear. Given their tendency to project their feelings onto others, a Six could imagine that you're angry with them even when you aren't. Be aware of this tendency and the need to assure them of your support and love.

In reaction to the One's tendency for rigidity, Six children can become reactive and rebellious, wanting to destroy the very authority figure they once admired. You may not understand the degree to which your child worries about things and may get irritated with them: "Pull yourself together!" Be aware that minimizing their anxiety only makes it worse.

As a Six child, it can be scary to express anger, while a One believes that it's just not right. There is potential for resentment to build on both sides, which can be expressed in sarcastic or punitive ways.

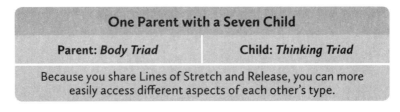

One Parent with a Seven Child

Parent: *Body Triad*	Child: *Thinking Triad*

Because you share Lines of Stretch and Release, you can more easily access different aspects of each other's type.

What Your Relationship Is About . . .

Sevens represent the shadow or disowned self of Ones. Not wanting to own the Seven aspects in themselves, Ones make them "wrong," yet inside the One lies a wild, rule-breaking, pleasure-seeking Seven who, rather than seek perfection in all things, is greedy for all life can offer—and vice versa. This dynamic has the potential to ignite your relationship in both healthy and unhealthy ways.

In this relationship, seriousness and perfectionism meet exuberance. Your Seven kid can stimulate you to move beyond your own limitations. In the best case, you enjoy the opposite personality expression of the other—you providing order, boundaries, and stability, and your child opening you up to a world of spontaneity, possibility, and joy. You meet each other in that you both enjoy being busy.

You see detail and your child has broad vision—aspects that complement each other. Taking holidays, going on outings and visiting theme parks are great ways for you two to have fun and feel adventurous—your child enjoys new thrills while you learn to let go and enjoy yourself.

When You're Getting Stressed . . .

There's a case of opposites at play here: you are the most rigid of the types, and your child is the type most desiring freedom. Having a One as the parent can be hard for young Sevens—your child may experience you as restrictive and bossy. Meanwhile, your thrifty and sensible self may frown at the way their allowance can slide so swiftly through their fingers as they go all out for adventure.

Wanting to break free, your child can get bored of the rules and routine you impose. While you demand perfection and completion of tasks, your child is always keen to try something new—when something interesting catches their eye, they'll be off in that direction, leaving a trail of tasks done below your expectations.

When less integrated, you may become disapproving and attempt to reign-in your wild child. As you become more focused, your child becomes more scattered. Your child may rebel and become more demanding, while you tend to become more critical and punitive.

One Parent with an Eight Child	
Parent: *Body Triad*	Child: *Body Triad*

What Your Relationship Is About . . .

Both of you are high in energy. Your common desire for fairness, justice and taking a stand for a cause can bond you. Both of you are hands-on, hard workers who believe in getting the job done—be it building an empire, or doing the washing up. Your Eight child will respect your forthrightness and ability to call a spade a spade.

The difference is that while Ones see themselves as being good, Eights see themselves as being badass (an attitude you secretly admire). They are what you'd seldom allow yourself to be— unashamedly focused on their own needs and unconcerned with what society thinks or believes.

When anger arises, as it inevitably will, you won't be judged for letting loose—at least not by your Eight child. They teach you not to get bogged down in details, that expressing anger is okay, and that it's okay to enjoy what life has to offer.

When You're Getting Stressed . . .

Both of you believe you're right and both are inclined to be reactive under pressure. You attempt to control while Eights fear being controlled— making for a potentially fiery combination. As you demand control, your child can rip it away, wanting to be in charge. Both of you have strong wills, which can lead to angry outbursts and a vying for leadership in the family unit. Your child will resist your commands of "Make your bed!" "Cut the apple this way!" "Don't answer back!" and confront you in turn with "You can't tell me what to do!" "You're not the boss of me!"

Criticism becomes a red rag to a bull. Little Eights will enjoy the fight, but you will recriminate yourself afterward for such base behavior. Particularly in their teens, Eight kids can delight in provoking you. The One parent is left seething. Neither of you will back down, which can lead to days of hostile stepping around each other. Finding you small-minded and hypocritical, your child will seek revenge for what they feel is punitive discipline. You see them as loutish and selfish.

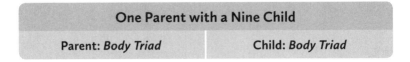

One Parent with a Nine Child	
Parent: *Body Triad*	Child: *Body Triad*

What Your Relationship Is About . . .

This combination, particularly if you share wings, has many commonalities. You both have problems expressing anger. You both work for the greater good, sacrificing your needs for others. As a One, you do so from an idealistic perspective, while your Nine child does it to make the world a happier place. Both of you seek autonomy and enjoy time alone. You typically both enjoy having pets, although One's may dislike it when pets mess and shed fur.

You give direction and order to your child, while they provide you with acceptance and calm reassurance. A Nine child's chilled approach to life can be soothing to the more uptight One—though it may also infuriate.

Your child may merge with you, believing in whatever you believe. It may take years for them to have a firmer sense of self.

When You're Getting Stressed . . .

Nines are often slow to initiate action. If they are afraid that whatever they do will be wrong in your eyes, they may find starting projects or making decisions even harder: "I want to surprise Mom by laying the table, but what if I do it wrong and make her angry?" "I want to make Dad a birthday card, but he might criticize my untidy writing." To an opinionated One, the Nine child's reticence to voice an opinion or stand up for themselves can be viewed as being insipid: "Get a backbone!"

Nines have a tendency to accept the blame and apologize even when they are not at fault. When under pressure, Ones can do the opposite. The angrier an intolerant One parent becomes, the more their comfort-seeking Nine child will withdraw, creating yet more frustration and anger.

Your child's desire for peace has them accepting some of your more controlling or critical aspects, denying the hurt they are feeling. A harsh comment or criticism will be swept aside or even denied in their desire to keep everyone happy: "It's no big deal." One parents often don't realize the extent to which their Nine child suppresses their anger. Instead, the Nine child may passively-aggressively resist being pushed around. As you become more intent on fixing them, little Nines become more stubborn about not colluding.

Type Two Parents
and Their Children

Two Parent with a One Child	
Parent: *Feeling Triad*	Child: *Body Triad*

What Your Relationship Is About . . .

As a Two parent, you bring warmth and love to serious little Ones. You forgive easily, allowing your child see that they are loved even if they don't always do the right thing. As a pair you are happy to help—if a stray kitten is found, both of you will believe it's your duty to take care of it. Two parents are commonly very involved in the community through churches, school committees and volunteer groups and your One child will feel proud of your commitment.

When inviting a friend to play, your child can rely on you to be welcoming and nurturing—you're the kind of parent who, remembering that someone enjoyed green jello the last time they came round, will make some for that child again. Two parents will often be the ones to organize activities—having so much adult involvement may be a novel experience for children of other types. Even little Ones can be nervous about entertaining correctly—"Should we have had less cake and more salads?" In contrast, you emphasize the pleasure of socializing, helping your One child to simply enjoy themselves.

Your child believes that if they do what they imagine is the right thing, then they'll be good and everything will be fine. You believe that helping others is your path to being okay. Your caring nature helps your child express their feelings, while they bring a more logical and practical approach to your life.

When You're Getting Stressed . . .

Problems arise when you or your child negate or deny your own needs. Both of you believe that expressing needs is somehow selfish or wrong—

Twos feel that other people's needs are more important than their own, and Ones want to be seen as being selfless and doing the right thing. If you see your child as an extension of yourself, you may find that your social roles start to take precedence over child-rearing—and your child can become resentful. When a Two parent is a teacher or closely involved with other children, a One child can find sharing their beloved parent hard to deal with, even if they see it as the right way to behave. You, in turn, can become possessive and angry as your child withdraws: "After all I've done for you!"

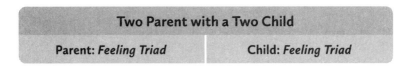

Two Parent with a Two Child	
Parent: *Feeling Triad*	Child: *Feeling Triad*

What Your Relationship Is About . . .

Both of you will engage in loving, open displays of affection. You both love to love. The little Two helper fulfills the Two parent's needs for reciprocation: "I'll help you with your homework and you'll help me make supper." Two kids will be mothering their group of friends, while you nurture all of them! Both of you can tap into how the other feels, so you both feel heard. Integrated Two parents don't smother or manipulate their kids. Integrated Two kids aren't needy or possessive.

Both of you want to feel indispensable to each other or other members of the family. You're good listeners who love to compliment and care for others. You support each other and happily praise each other's successes. You have a bond other parents and kids long for. Sounds perfect—and it can be, much of the time.

Encourage your child to express their needs, while doing the same yourself. Let them see that they won't be less loved for doing so. Realize that if your child doesn't text you several times a day, it's not because they don't love you—it's just because they're caught up in other activities, which is healthy.

When You're Getting Stressed . . .

Both of you are natural givers, but it can be frustrating when neither of you are able to receive: "I know just what you need," you both pridefully feel. When your child is little, they have to receive, but as they grow up they'll be wanting to give to you more. As a result, you'll feel obliged to give more back ... and on it goes!

When less integrated, the issue of "Am I lovable?" arises in the Two. Both of you may compete for attention from the other parent, becoming jealous and demanding in the process. A Two daughter may become quite coquettish, wanting to be "Daddy's princess" and showering the non-Two parent with love, while ignoring you. Or little Twos can become ferociously jealous of a sibling who seems to be getting more attention. If they feel they have lost the attention of their parents, little Twos may seek comfort from sweets or junk food, which becomes a substitute for love.

If the parent has learned that illness gives them the attention they crave, a Two child may easily slip into this same pattern. This begins something of a competition: "I've got a cold, Mom. I can't go to school. I need to stay home with you."

"But honey, I'm *really* sick with bronchitis."

"No, Mom, I'm really, *really* sick . . ."

Each may feign deep concern for the other. This can become a codependency, with both desperately needing the other, yet secretly resenting their need. This Two pair may text each other frequently, send each other numerous heartfelt Instagram quotes, and soppily declare their mutual love on social media—yet behind the facade lurks blame, frustration, loneliness, and resentment.

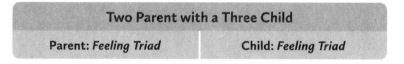

Two Parent with a Three Child

| Parent: *Feeling Triad* | Child: *Feeling Triad* |

What Your Relationship Is About . . .

Two parents make the ideal support system for ambitious little Threes. While Two parents may enjoy a spot of social climbing, their Three child likes to climb the ladder of success. You aim to achieve self-identity through relationships, while Three kids find themselves through acknowledgments from their achievements and performance. Your child wants your recognition, whether it's winning a race or being top of the class. Twos are usually very involved parents, so will be happy to encourage and support your little Three.

Two parents will bask in the glory of being the mum or dad of the kid getting the prize. Your child enjoys doing what it takes to make you proud, and as such feels proud of themselves. Both of you enjoy being the focus of others' attention, and you thrive at social events, where you enjoy mixing with different groups of people. You both charm and disarm others with ease and are popular and people-orientated.

You can both stand out on the school grounds. Chatting to teachers, working extra hours to help at the bake sale—you'll both do whatever it takes to get acknowledgment and appreciation.

When You're Getting Stressed . . .

While you express your feelings outwardly, your child both expresses and represses their feelings—they may put their feelings on hold, expressing them later when alone. Twos deny having needs, while Threes can refrain from expressing authentic feelings. Twos can feel unworthy of being loved, while Threes believe they have little internal value.

Two parents can see child-rearing as a project to nurture success: "I'm doing all this for you, darling, so you can be successful." As a result, Two parents can take it very personally if the child "fails," and can get resentful if their little superstar doesn't appreciate their efforts. Little Three stars like to shine alone, and they may not enjoy having to attribute their hard-won success to a parent. In retaliation, you can start to threaten your child's success: "I haven't got time to take you to riding lessons anymore," "I'm too busy to help with your project."

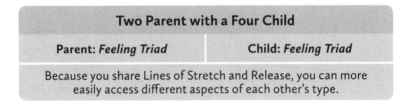

Two Parent with a Four Child	
Parent: *Feeling Triad*	Child: *Feeling Triad*
Because you share Lines of Stretch and Release, you can more easily access different aspects of each other's type.	

What Your Relationship Is About . . .

Your Four child will love the warmth and care you show them. They will feel heard and their feelings will be authenticated. Both of you openly express your emotions. As a Two, you enjoy the buzz of connecting, so you can help your shy little Four to be more outgoing and confident. Twos feel they have much to give, and Fours are happy to receive the support their parent so freely offers. You enjoy feeling indispensable and your child makes you feel needed.

Your child teaches you to acknowledge your own needs and learn how to be yourself, rather than being what you feel others want you to be. Through them, you learn that your needs are just as important as those of others, including your child. Your child also helps you to develop an appreciation of beauty and creativity.

You enjoy making others feel special, and your child wants to feel special. You demonstrate to your child how caring for others can lessen their tendency to become self-absorbed. While you understand their need for melancholy, you encourage them to become more joyful and outgoing.

When You're Getting Stressed . . .

Fours can represent the disowned aspects of Twos and vice versa. Depending on how integrated you both are, this has the potential to cause problems, because we dislike what we have not acknowledged within ourselves. Stressed Twos become like the stressed aspect of a Four—angry, self-focused, belligerent, and demanding.

You can try to earn your child's love through being helpful. If your child retreats, they can appear unappreciative of all you do for them. They may feel you lack the emotional depth to fully understand them. When you assume the role of rescuer, your child can easily become the lost or rescued child. Both of you can vie for attention from the other parent, setting up unhealthy competitiveness, particularly if either of you have a Three-wing (see page 35). Fours can feel like outsiders in their parent's socially focused lives.

Twos are irked by their Four child's self-focus, believing that they should be more focused on others' needs—like they are. To a pouting Four, their Two parent's sugary sweetness can feel false and hypocritical: "You're so busy trying to save the world, you don't care about me!" Both of you have a Type One aspect (you as a wing and your child as their Point of Release—see page 39), so you can both become critical of the other while feeling hurt and misunderstood. You may focus more attentively on another child, leaving the Four feeling helpless and unlovable.

Two Parent with a Five Child	
Parent: *Feeling Triad*	Child: *Thinking Triad*

What Your Relationship Is About . . .

To an exuberant, outgoing Two parent, having serious, cerebral offspring can be something of a mystery: "I don't get it . . .he's happier working alone with his microscope than playing with the other kids!" Little

Fives want information—"How? What? Where?"—while you want an emotional connection. You want to be needed, but your child appears self-sufficient—even emotionally detached. You look on the bright side, while your child has a more pessimistic view of life.

Fives who battle to nurture themselves will enjoy being nurtured—even if they feign the opposite. Respecting their need for space will endear you to them. They'll appreciate your interest in their projects—listening to their theory on space-monster time travel or answering tricky questions about polyamorous fish species. Learning things together, dismantling the toaster to see how it works, or hunting for bugs are great ways to connect. Twos, who typically enjoy food, may be confused by their Five child's apparent contentment with eating an unadventurous daily menu or their tendency to skip meals when they're involved in something.

You can teach your child to express and value their feelings and to create the ability to think beyond themselves. They can teach you containment and inspire you to learn more. They balance your need to please others with their need to please themselves. You teach your avaricious child to become more generous with their resources and time, like you are.

When You're Getting Stressed . . .

Fives want strong boundaries. Twos often lack boundaries. Fives can experience a sense of being smothered—of being loved, but not really understood. They may experience your parental attention as intrusive, which creates the need to batten down their bedroom hatches. They can also start to think that you meddle too much in their lives. Reading their messages or diary feels hugely invasive and will provoke anger.

You may feel that you need to fix your child socially. Most Twos abhor being alone, so you see wanting to be alone as somehow wrong: "Wouldn't you rather play with friends?" Your little Five may want to play with one friend, but asking them to attend a function to appease your social needs could meet with resistance or disgruntled withdrawal.

Two parents will want to hear all about their child's camp stay or the party they've been to, and may experience their child's lack of response as a withholding of love. Your child feels that you are interfering. You get frustrated when your demonstrative affection is not reciprocated—as a parent, you feel diminished or rejected. As they grow up and value their privacy more, Five teens may withdraw more, become secretive, which leaves you feeling rejected. Both of you feel alone.

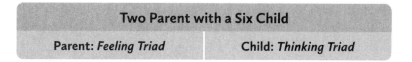

Two Parent with a Six Child	
Parent: *Feeling Triad*	Child: *Thinking Triad*

What Your Relationship Is About...

Little Sixes will welcome falling into the loving and protective arms of their Two parent. Two parents provide a safe space for Sixes to express their feelings, helping them feel calm and positive. Sixes also enjoy the consistency of Twos: "You've got my back, Dad, right?" With you, your anxious, worrying child feels safe and secure.

You both can be compassionate and empathetic. Your child is more reserved and emotionally cooler, which can frustrate you at times, while you're generally warmer and more demonstrative. Both of you will work hard to meet the needs of others.

Both of you feel that love is earned—you through doing for others, your child through being loyal. Generally, you both enjoy family life and doing things together, such as playing sports, baking, hosting get togethers, or having picnics. When it comes to chores, Twos are helpful and Sixes are dutiful—so you both understand the need to work for the good of the family.

You may gush at your child's artistic endeavors or school marks, which helps their self-esteem. But bear in mind that trust is an issue for Sixes. Your child may start to doubt or question your sincerity: "Is she just *saying* she likes my painting?" "Can I trust his word?"

When You're Getting Stressed...

To your Six child seeking autonomy, you may start to feel like an authority figure—not one they feel safe with and admire, but someone to rebel against. If you try to push your child towards a particular subject, sport, friend, or musical instrument, you could meet with resistance. Best is to get their buy-in.

Your child is generally unsure of their choices. As a parent, under-mining them makes things worse. Six children may be afraid to act without reassurance: "Should I have Sue or Sandra to play, Mom?" They may ask for validation yet resent you for giving it. If you are to nurture them into healthy adulthood, your role is to encourage them to make decisions themselves. If they don't, Sixes never learn to trust themselves and their intuition.

As they move into their teens, Sixes may start to feel controlled, or even manipulated by you, which sparks more rebellion. Their ambivalence can come to the fore—one moment rebelling and the next seeking safety with you. Your fear of not being needed arises as your child pushes your sensitive rejection button. You attempt to gain control while they retreat. Both of you can become reactive.

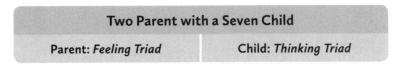

Two Parent with a Seven Child	
Parent: *Feeling Triad*	Child: *Thinking Triad*

What Your Relationship Is About . . .

Little Sevens want fun and Twos need love—you just can't help adore your energetic, sharp-witted, happy little Seven offspring. Both of you see the sunny side of life, quickly brushing away any negatives: "Pity the party got rained on, but the kids had a good time playing in the mud."

This friendly and upbeat pair loves socializing—your home will be filled with guests and you'll often be involved in party planning. This combination will provide a warm and comforting space that other kids want to hang out in. You will enjoy making sure everyone is happy and your child will have loads of fun planning games and activities (but may change plans when something better arises). Both of you are generous with your possessions and time. Both have an idealistic view of life, particularly the Social Seven, who like you, wants to help others.

Twos are happy to play the role of the adoring parent to their center-stage child: "Our boy Adam is such a hoot!"

When You're Getting Stressed . . .

Trouble in paradise can occur when young Sevens get older and want more space and freedom. Your desire for closeness can begin to feel smothering. Being a Fear Type, Sevens enjoy the security of home but can rebel against the constriction at the same time. Finding their own identity may involve them pushing away from the parental shore. You may want your child to spend more time at home—but that's boring to your child, who's looking for their next adventure.

Fearing the loss of connection, you may not want to let go. You may even hang around, trying to be part of the school outing or teen party. For a Seven, this can feel invasive. Fun activities you used to enjoy together no longer spark excitement in your child—for you, the juice is drained from life. As the child pulls away, you are inclined to move closer. Manipulation may arise: "But you said that you wanted to come for a walk with me. We'll get waffles afterward."

You can rage, feeling unappreciated and used by your child: "I've driven you all around town and what thanks do I get?" With teenagers particularly, fights can ensue as you shift to your Point of Stretch at Eight (see page 37) and want to assume control. They react badly to having their freedom impacted and become sarcastic and confrontational.

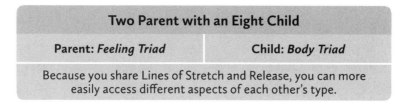

Two Parent with an Eight Child	
Parent: *Feeling Triad*	Child: *Body Triad*
Because you share Lines of Stretch and Release, you can more easily access different aspects of each other's type.	

What Your Relationship Is About . . .

With this pair, the archetypal female (Type Two) meets the archetypal male Type Eight)—irrespective of your actual gender. Here, love meets power. As a result, little Eights can be very protective of their Two parents: "I'll take care of you, Mom/Dad."

The Two and the Eight have much in common. Both have high energy levels and enjoy life's comforts. Both of you are affectionate and easily assume caring and providing roles. Both are generous. Your softer nurturing and sentimental side sits at the hidden core of your Eight child, who will enjoy your expression of inner gentleness.

You want to please your child and will sacrifice your own needs to do so. Eights, however, demand that their needs are met (or else). When integrated, little Eights are able to access greater empathy while their Two parents can be more direct and open about their own needs, which makes for a loving combination. Healthy Eights are more able to do things for the parent instead of it being a one-way street—then you as the parent get the appreciation you desire.

When You're Getting Stressed . . .

Whereas Twos tend to gravitate to others and often don't enjoy being alone, Eights want their independence. Your child may not always want a parent hanging around: "I can take care of myself. I don't need you."

Your child can be angry in their desire for independence while you, feeling you're losing them, become increasingly possessive: "I've sacrificed so much for you!"

Both types are strong-willed and may butt heads when each wants something done their way. The Two parent will use guilt and manipulation, the Eight child blunt force and a refusal to back down. Twos tend to skirt around an issue, which may be frustrating for Eights, who need direct instructions: "Just say it like it is!"

Twos enjoy schmoozing with other parents and being seen to be socially acceptable. Being more self-focused, Eights are less inclined to be influenced by others. For example, they may want to change friendships: "I'm done with Pam." The Two parent may respond: "But how can you ditch her? You were good friends. How am I going to deal with her parents now?"

As the child acts out more, you cover up and apologize: "I don't know what's got into her." The child starts to lose respect for the parent, who they see as weak and inauthentic. Both of you vie for control of the other. If you don't actively work to heal the relationship, feuds can last for years, with both seeking revenge.

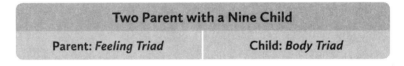

Two Parent with a Nine Child	
Parent: *Feeling Triad*	Child: *Body Triad*

What Your Relationship Is About . . .

Both the Two and the Nine are caring and nurturing types who put other's needs above their own. As a result, these warm types can be confused. Yet you care for others in different ways. Both of you are optimistic.

You're both happy entertaining, and friends are welcome to your comfortable home—you'll be baking the cookies, which young Nines will happily share out. You're more outgoing and energized than your child, and are more likely to do the inviting, welcoming any strays (both people and animals) into your home.

Easy-going young Nines will enjoy being "seen" by their parent as their needs frequently get overlooked—yet you're able to sense what it is they're after. You calm each other and can be each other's shelter from the storm of life. You're both sensual, affectionate, and adept at nonverbal communication. You both enjoy creature comforts, such as watching a movie on the couch together surrounded by pets and snacks.

Two parents will encourage their child to find something that elevates them. As their child achieves, they can pride themselves on being the force behind their success. But a lack of success can become a source of frustration: "Why didn't you do better? I worked so hard to help you." This relationship works best when each creates their own identity by having some separate interests and hobbies.

When You're Getting Stressed . . .

You have a great need for being appreciated and having the gifts you offer reciprocated. Your pride in what you do for others contrasts with your child's natural humility. Both of you can merge with each other's emotions and the child may internalize a difficulty the parent is experiencing: "I'm sad, but I don't know why."

When stressed, Twos start to believe they know what their child wants: "I don't need to ask, I just know." But you may not, in fact, know—which leaves your child feeling frustrated and unseen: "He just doesn't get me." Both of you have problems saying how you really feel. You may resort to manipulation to get your child to do what you want.

Twos take pride in the fact that they believe they are indispensable to their children. As your child matures, they may find this isn't necessarily true. Some children enjoy your involvement, but Nines enjoy autonomy, and may experience your efforts as meddling. If you start to become stifling and controlling, your child can become passive-aggressive, stubborn, or sabotaging. As they pull away, you become angry and push for attention. At this point, the Two's lack of boundaries becomes more apparent, leaving the child feeling awash in a huge scary ocean: "If there aren't any boundaries, how do I know if I'm breaking them? Better not to move (inertia) than run the risk of making Mom/Dad angry."

Type Three Parents
and Their Children

Three Parent with a One Child	
Parent: *Feeling Triad*	Child: *Body Triad*

What Your Relationship Is About...

Both of you want to make the world a better place—your child by improving themselves and others, and you by improving yourself. Both of you are good organizers, are responsible, and can put aside personal issues to get the job done through hard work and efficiency. Doing homework will seldom be an issue: "I don't think I ever had to tell my child to do her homework. She just got on with it. When I had a second child who was less motivated, it came as a bit of a shock."

Both of you are sensitive to failure and familiar with success. You do a good job. So, while you are organizing the school committee, your child is ensuring they're doing their bit to help. This combination of talents, self-confidence, and the desire to be better sees your child hopping up to the podium to receive awards and you, the accomplished parent glowing in their success. You both love being acknowledged for your achievements as you rely on the outside world for approval. You enjoy recounting each other's successes: "Mom got the office award for the best marketing plan!" "Cilla's just been made sports captain."

When it comes to household chores, you'll be practical and fair about whose responsibility it is to do what. You become role models for each other—you demonstrate a less perfectionistic approach, while your child teaches you how to set more realistic goals.

When You're Getting Stressed...

Your image and brand-consciousness may not be appreciated by your practical child: "Why would you pay more just for a label?" As a truth-seeker, your child could criticize your tendency to obfuscate or actually lie about issues. When tension rises, both of you will try to resolve your issues, but the Three's tendency to disconnect from their feelings can be problematic.

Both of you can attempt to outdo each other to be the "best," particularly if one is acknowledged more than the other. Whereas your child can get lost in the details, you are caught up in the desire to succeed. Your child may accuse you of being devoted to work.

You want acknowledgment from your child. If it's not forthcoming, you can be left thinking: "What's the point? I've tried so hard." You can feel under increasing scrutiny as they tell you, "You aren't doing it correctly." You find your children's judgment hard to bear—they start to feel more and more like a disapproving parent. You may turn your attention to another child or to a project that will get you the praise you're after. Your child feels abandoned and resentful. Further criticism ensues.

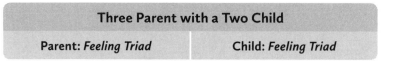

Three Parent with a Two Child	
Parent: *Feeling Triad*	Child: *Feeling Triad*

What Your Relationship Is About . . .

You are both social, good entertainers, and fun to be with. When you put on the party of the decade, your engaging child will be winning over the guests with their charming cuteness. You want the party to be a major success—you shine your glowing light to the world in exchange for recognition. Your child wants approval and reciprocal love for all they do. While you tend to hide your feelings, Twos are more expressive, though they often avoid deeper hurts.

Two children want to feel proud of their parents and their achievements, and you enjoy basking in their adoration. Twos can brag: "My dad is very clever. He made that billboard." It's the parent's achievements that tend to get the spotlight rather than the child's. You enjoy the care and attention your child foists on you. You're an attractive pair, dressed in the latest trendy gear. Both of you know how to get others to like you. Wherever you go, you'll delight and charm your way to achieving your goals.

When You're Getting Stressed . . .

Little Twos may find it hard to cope with the time you spend working—they want to be included. For you, "doing" is an expression of love, while your child wants physical and emotional connection—so your dedication to your career feels like rejection. Your child fears not being lovable and needs assurance that you are emotionally available, if not physically. Being late to collect your child from school because you got caught up in the marketing meeting is hard for little Twos. This can also be difficult for you, because you are working hard to provide: "I'm doing this for the family!"

Threes want their child to shine and can get annoyed when their child behaves in a way that detracts from them, such as failing. The child gets tired of taking a back seat to their parent's work and social activities. They try to manipulate you to get their needs met. You distance yourself. Their possessiveness and neediness increases: "Mom, I want *you*," they whimper. "I have a tummy ache. You have to stay at home with me." You feel guilty yet overwhelmed by work and your child's needs: "Can't you see I'm working hard for us?" The child retaliates with: "You're never there for me!" Both feel increasingly unlovable.

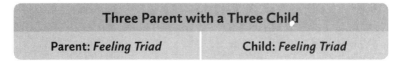

Three Parent with a Three Child	
Parent: *Feeling Triad*	Child: *Feeling Triad*

What Your Relationship Is About . . .

Ta da! Enter the stars! This pair shines their way into any company with confidence and charm. Both being the same type makes them blind to their foibles—no one wants to see the denied aspects of yourself mirrored in your child. Particularly with this pair, integration is the key to being friends or foe.

Both of you understand your need for success and ambition and will work hard to make something of your lives. You both enjoy being in the spotlight and want the other to recognize and admire your achievements. You take huge pride in seeing your child succeed—they're an extension of your success as a parent.

While your child will be offering to host the class party, you'll be doing the same for the office. Threes know how to work the room and can connect with people from all strata of society. You both put effort into your appearances and enjoy the favorable responses you get as a result. If this pair can appreciate each other internally and externally, that lays the foundation for a solid relationship: "My dad just gets me."

You'll work hard to make your home an efficient, trendy, and desirable place to be. You'll be an excellent motivator and support for your child, inspiring them to greater things, be it in sport, art, school, or any other interest: "You can do this."

When You're Getting Stressed . . .

Threes are competitive. As a result, you can start to compete with each other in your looks, achievements, popularity, sports, or even for the attention of the other parent. As they age, parents can feel threatened by their successful child—just like the queen in Snow White, when the mirror tells her that she is no longer "the fairest of them all." Life is no longer about support, but an attempt to outdo: "At your age, I was valedictorian." The parent may start to feel that the child and their needs are a stumbling block to their success. Neither can discuss their feelings, instead: "I wait until I'm alone in the car before I cry or show an upset." This is justified because "My feelings get in the way of my work." They can become apathetic about the relationship: "It's too much effort and a waste of valuable time."

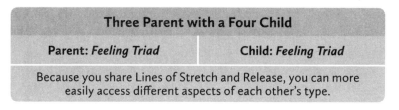

Three Parent with a Four Child	
Parent: *Feeling Triad*	Child: *Feeling Triad*
Because you share Lines of Stretch and Release, you can more easily access different aspects of each other's type.	

What Your Relationship Is About . . .

The Three's desire to achieve meets the Four's need to be unique. As a parent, you're probably more interested in goals and external success. Your child is more focused on feelings and the depth of interactions. You're inclined to hold back your emotions—introspection is common in your child, but you seldom have time for it. So what can you teach each other? If you're open to it, your child can teach you greater self-awareness and authenticity. You can contain any emotional fall-out with your ability to be diplomatic.

Together you can explore the arts—you to feel more accomplished, and your child because the appreciation of beauty is a driving force. As your child becomes older you'll enjoy the better things in life—fine dining, fashion, or art-house movies.

Your older child can help you with all things aesthetic. Both of you want to be seen to be stylish—you because it goes with presenting a successful image, and your child because it offers the potential of being different. You teach your child practical ways to succeed, the ability to organize, set goals, and reduce their moodiness in a work environment.

When You're Getting Stressed . . .

When you get stressed, your inclination is to withdraw and find solace in work because it calms you. Your child, however, will be inclined to ruminate on their feelings, particularly in the moody teen years. Your child may long for more time with you, yet be unable to express their need except in temperamental outbursts, which can become hard to deal with. Work seems a calmer space to be, so you take on more commitments.

Your desire for recognition is not dissimilar to your child's need to feel special. You're both wanting to be noticed, albeit for different reasons, and being dependent on others for self-worth results in a low sense of self. Getting recognition from others can become a competition, and could mean you both vie for your partner's attention while undermining the other.

Both of you have an idealized version of who you feel you should or who you want to be. As tension rises, the distance between you feels like it's increasing, so you both try harder to get more strokes. You start to become the ice queen or king, and both of you and your child may resort to sarcastic interchanges and full-blown anger.

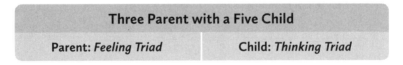

Three Parent with a Five Child	
Parent: *Feeling Triad*	Child: *Thinking Triad*

What Your Relationship Is About . . .

You are an achieving, goal-orientated, extroverted parent with an introverted, quietly observing, studious child. The big difference here is confidence. Threes just exude it, even if it's not genuine, while little Fives generally only feel confident in something they've specialized or taken an interest in. As a result, you can teach your Five child how to be more confident and less introverted, while the child guides you into having a richer internal world. While Threes go after success, Fives pursue their particular (specialized) interest.

You enjoy the recognition you receive as the parent of a child who may be exceptional in some way—the chess expert or science prize-winner. Fives are happy to play alone, which suits you because it allows you to do what you enjoy most: work. Neither of you wants to dwell on your feelings, you both prefer to work through them alone in your own time. You enjoy socializing and know how to work a room, so your child's dislike of large crowds may be confusing. Social events energize you, while they drain your child. Your child is contemptuous of the outer world, while you see its potential.

When You're Getting Stressed . . .

There is homework to be done, but little Fives will um and ah and take their time to finish it: "I just need to do a bit more research . . ." You just want the homework supervision to be over so you can get back to work. Your child dillydallies, lost in their thoughts. Inaction clashes with action—it can be very frustrating. Your child can't understand the rush: "How can I do my homework properly if you don't let me prepare?" As they become argumentative, you become icy, even sarcastic: "What's wrong with you? Why can't you just be like other kids?" No longer is your child someone you can proudly present to the world. Your child sees their parent as superficial and lacking real knowledge.

If a project is successful, fights can erupt over whose idea it was. Fives resent the parent using their success to enhance their status, yet both seek recognition. The child may resent the intrusion on their personal space by the parent. Be respectful of the "Do not disturb" sign on the bedroom door.

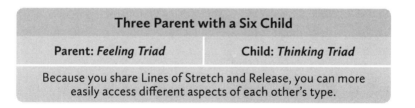

Three Parent with a Six Child	
Parent: *Feeling Triad*	Child: *Thinking Triad*
Because you share Lines of Stretch and Release, you can more easily access different aspects of each other's type.	

What Your Relationship Is About . . .

The Three's desire to achieve meets the loyal, responsible "Little Trooper" Six. You make a great parent–child team as you're both hard-working and practical, and you want to make the world a better place. Your natural self-confidence inspires it in your child. Your optimism and drive can help your self-doubting child to believe in their potential.

The major way you relate to each other is through your ability to get the job done, whether it's cleaning the house, organizing the school sports day, or helping at a charity drive. Your child's loyalty will mean a lot to you, since you may be accustomed to the business world, where backstabbing is the norm. This is a child who has your back.

Whereas you enjoy riding the wave of your success, your child is inclined to negate theirs, so it's important to remind them of what they have achieved. Your child will develop your compassion for others and understanding of what it means to be a well-rounded human being. From you they will learn how to acknowledge their achievements, doubt themselves less, and look beyond achievement as being the sole indicator of self-worth. From your child, you can learn to help others, to be more comfortable with internal reflection, and to put less emphasis on an external image.

When You're Getting Stressed . . .

Your shadow side—the unclaimed or unacknowledged aspects of yourself—is mirrored to you by your child, which is difficult for you. You want to be the star but your child gets anxious when they are under the spotlight. Their insecurity, anxiety, self-doubt, indecisiveness, and fear is what you avoid acknowledging inside yourself—because what if you aren't quite as confident as you believe yourself to be?

Your child starts to question whether they can trust you. All that self-aggrandizement feels problematic to them, as if you're not someone to be trusted: "Successful today, but what about tomorrow?" Being an achiever sets you up for their attack. Social media posts showing the latest goal you have reached can invite their sharp criticism. They start to experience you as inauthentic and self-inflating, while you experience them as reactive and self-deflating.

Dealing with these feelings is uncomfortable—you prefer to avoid them. You can become irritated with a child who displays little of your drive and ambition. You both reject the other or seek out the other parent as a mediator in your silent conflict. To the outside world, things appear okay, but you both know differently.

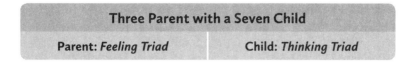

Three Parent with a Seven Child

Parent: *Feeling Triad*	Child: *Thinking Triad*

What Your Relationship Is About . . .

Wow! Watch this combination go! You're both energetic, fun, and fabulous! As a busy and driven Three, you've met your match in your energetic, upbeat, excitable child. You share many commonalities: you're both assertive, confident, optimistic, energized by others, and able to see the broader picture. You both enjoy social activities and are able to plan ahead. Neither of you enjoys quiet introversion—you'd rather engage with the world head-on: "Life's too short not to have fun, right?"

You are both great ideas people who know how to get your needs met. Both of you enjoy being seen as cool and fashionable. You both enjoy trying out new things, being adventurous, and you delight in the good things that life has to offer. You'll vie to be the center of attention—you through promoting your successes and your child through entertaining others with stories and infectious enthusiasm.

You teach your child the value of completing a task (Sevens can become scattered), a greater ability to tune in to others, and the need for limits, social norms, and being practical. Your child teaches you spontaneity, that there's more to life than work, and that failure is not a catastrophe but a stepping stone to success. Together you bring joy and sparkle to the world.

When You're Getting Stressed . . .

As a Three, you could find that your child's need to interact with others impacts your already hectic schedule: "Why can't you sit still for a moment? I need to finish this report." Their busy schedule of sports, play dates, and extracurriculars can have you feeling resentful if it's up to you to cart them everywhere—whose schedule is more important?

Having so much energy has the disadvantage of you both not knowing when to stop. You can exhaust each other with the need to project a busy, upbeat, successful image.

Little Sevens can feel neglected if you become immersed in work: "Where's the fun in that?" They will not take kindly to promised excursions being canceled, but you feel justified: "I'm doing this for you, so you can get a better education!" As a parent, you may feel irritated by how the things you worked so hard for come so easily to your child. Your child just doesn't seem to take things like a career and achievement as seriously as you do. If you both avoid facing issues such as failure or hurt, nothing gets resolved. It is difficult to admit to the fact that your relationship with your child is troubled. Work becomes a seemingly legitimate place to escape.

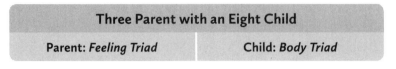

Three Parent with an Eight Child	
Parent: *Feeling Triad*	Child: *Body Triad*

What Your Relationship Is About . . .

Both of you are assertive, confident types with high energy levels. You set goals, while your child sees what they desire and goes after it with immediacy. Winston Churchill's famous line "we shall never surrender" is apt for both of you. Neither of you takes kindly to not getting what you want. You both are charismatic and can be confrontational. You can assume a leadership role, but leadership is not as important to you as it is to your child. While you see your role as that of provider, your child feels the need to protect those they care for—you, their other parent, or their siblings.

You each have an outside persona that belies your softer interior—you are more concerned with pleasing others while your child is more focused on pleasing themselves. While you tend to be more diplomatic, your child is straightforward. The best things happen in this relationship when you feel your child loves you for all that you are, not what you do. Your child's strength allows you a safe space to reveal yourself emotionally. They are able to show their more vulnerable side when they know you've got things under control and are protective of them.

When You're Getting Stressed . . .

Vulnerability is an issue for both of you. Neither of you enjoys exploring feelings and so both tend to avoid going there. You numb your feelings while your child denies them: "I'm tough so don't mess with me." Your child demands your emotional support, yet you'd rather use your time and energy to acquire the finances to support them physically.

As a pair, you're the most competitive types in the Enneagram. When you're on the same "team," all is well, and you tend not to compete with each other. Should you find yourself in a family feud, such as a divorce, where your child sides with your partner, things can get messy.

You are both A-Type personalities who drive yourselves hard to succeed—but you are the one more likely to reach burnout. You are less controlling than your child, but still can attempt to pull strings behind the scenes. As your child feels more out of control, they may become jealous of you, possessively fighting off other siblings for your exclusive attention. It all feels too much as if you're just an extension of your child's will—you respond by wanting to pull away and will likely head to the office.

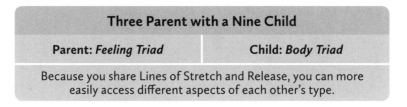

Three Parent with a Nine Child	
Parent: *Feeling Triad*	Child: *Body Triad*
Because you share Lines of Stretch and Release, you can more easily access different aspects of each other's type.	

What Your Relationship Is About . . .

You want to project a positive image while your child is naturally optimistic—it's not the same thing, but you both have a need to focus on the good. Your little Nine will easily merge with you and your goals, and as a result can feel a part of your success. Your child will give you recognition and appreciation for your efforts: "My mom's so brilliant, she's the boss of marketing." They'll also encourage you to take time out and smell the cookies you're baking together or enjoy time in nature.

Threes generally enjoy children—their own or others. Because of their easy, accepting natures, little Nines are generally popular with other kids. Both parent and child will be happy at intergenerational parties and family gatherings. You both enjoy the material comforts of the world and can work hard to achieve material security and provide for others. While you aim for an impressive, beautiful home, your child prefers a secure, comfortable, and relaxing environment.

The Nine's acceptance allows you to open up emotionally without fear of judgment. While you want to shine, your child may fear that doing so may make them more vulnerable to attack—"Uneasy is the head that wears the crown." You can demonstrate how to develop yourself, which Nines find difficult. Your confidence is inspiring to them.

Nines sometimes live in a cotton-candy world and can lack direction. You can guide and motivate your child to focus and find direction—they'll benefit from seeing how you set and achieve goals.

When You're Getting Stressed . . .

You share a desire for comfort and stability. You want others to admire and desire the ideal relationship you project as having with your child. Because Little Nines don't enjoy conflict or anything that disrupts their peace, they will seldom voice what's upsetting them, except in the occasional angry outburst. They also fear being separated from others, particularly you, so it's unlikely that they will choose to raise a sensitive issue for fear of sparking anger. Instead, they hope that things will sort themselves out naturally.

As a Three parent, you also don't want to create a war zone at home—it doesn't look good. Like your child, you keep quiet about what's bugging you for fear of being rejected and having to admit that you don't have a wonderful relationship. As a result, issues can fester. Your child can withdraw into passive aggression and become increasingly stubborn while you try to put a positive spin on things: "Oh, that? That's just the hormones raging."

When Nines feel unheard (because it's all about the Three parent), they can dig in their heels. Their parent may find them indecisive and be frustrated by their procrastinating: "Just do it already!" Threes can also experience their child as clingy, which makes them impatient—feeling overly controlled inhibits their autonomy. In this situation, Threes can become anxious and stubborn, and angry outbursts can be followed by hostile silence.

15

Type Four Parents
and Their Children

Four Parent with a One Child	
Parent: *Feeling Triad*	Child: *Body Triad*
Because you share Lines of Stretch and Release, you can more easily access different aspects of each other's type.	

What Your Relationship Is About . . .

Sharing your Lines of Stretch and Release (see page 39) means that your shadow aspects are reflected in your child and vice versa: when healthy you understand each other, but when disintegrated you confront in the other what you reject in yourself. Underneath the Four's creativity, originality, expressiveness, and unconventionality is the perfectionistic, self-controlled, conventional, controlling, and critical tendency of the unhealthy Type One.

You help your One child become more expressive and emotionally warm. You also encourage them to be more imaginative and creative, helping them to experience life on a deeper level. You're a brilliant support when your child is going through a trauma: a broken relationship, being bullied or rejected by a best friend. You can be with them in their pain, making them feel truly heard. As such, you help them become more emotionally articulate and aware. You can also demonstrate spontaneity and an ability to enjoy the moment. You'll be saying: "Come on, let's have a fun time out today." Your child will be saying: "Should we really be doing this on a Tuesday?"

You both meet in your idealism and desire to improve the world. Because of this, you both enjoy beauty, conservation, and ecological issues and enjoy working together as a team: "While we're on this lovely walk, let's collect all the garbage that's lying around."

Your child helps you to experience the benefits of structure and discipline—if you're an artist, for example, you can enhance your career by getting better at administration. A little One can balance your moments of irrationality with their logic: "Mom, should you be spending money on that?"

When You're Getting Stressed . . .

You may find yourself becoming melancholy or depressed and withdrawing from everyone, including your child. Steady young Ones will find it confusing that you withdraw only to move towards them later. They believe that consistency is the key and can judge you—you were the perfect parent and now you're just "wrong." Feeling hurt, they move to the more critical aspects side of the One—and your "ideal" child doesn't exist any longer.

When your connection is gone, it is replaced with judgment on both sides, and a sense that the other is not living up to expectation. The Four parent can be left thinking: "Where did I find such an unfeeling, emotionally inhibited child?" Meanwhile, the One child is thinking: "I can't believe he still hasn't learned to control himself! And he's the adult here!"

As you become less integrated, you can both become intolerant, critical, self-righteous, and unbending (the low side of One) and overly emotional, depressed, and self-focused (the low side of the Four). You feel flawed while your child focuses on your flaws. It can make for an uncomfortable situation.

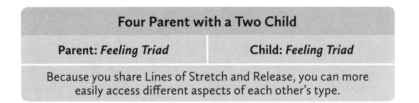

Four Parent with a Two Child	
Parent: *Feeling Triad*	Child: *Feeling Triad*
Because you share Lines of Stretch and Release, you can more easily access different aspects of each other's type.	

What Your Relationship Is About . . .

Sitting opposite the archetypal male Type Eight, you both carry feminine, nurturing energy. You enjoy feeling connected to each other and the intimacy and comfort this brings. While you may be more emotionally aware and honest about your feelings, your child encourages you to be more outgoing and active. Both of you care about people and share a desire to make the world a better and more loving place. You teach your helpful child that having needs of their own is perfectly fine.

You also demonstrate that it's okay to put your feelings first sometimes. You both enjoy sharing information about yourselves. You enjoy it when your child understands you, especially since others often don't seem to. Your child will enjoy feeling essential to you and will love working with you on a project, rather than being given instructions to work alone. Together you can create a connection where you both feel safe enough to be and express yourselves. Your child will reward you with a practical approach to tasks and inspire you to action. Doing creative crafts together will see you both having fun. You'll appreciate their care and loving help, and they'll appreciate your ability to nurture and listen to them.

When You're Getting Stressed . . .

When less integrated, you want to be rescued, while your child acts as a rescuer, and could want or feel obliged to parent you. If you weren't a parent and child, this combination of types works well, but it can be trouble when the parent is the one needing to be rescued.

You may feel burdened by the needs of your child. You can find your child's desire to create a pleasing little persona inauthentic and annoying: "She has none of my depth and authenticity. She tries too hard to be someone she's not." Meanwhile, they are thinking: "Mom's way too focused on her needs. She never cares about mine!"

As your child gets older and finds more friends, you may feel a sense of abandonment. You could start resenting your cute child's popularity, wondering: "Why don't they like me?" Your child can start to feel that nothing they do for you is appreciated. Neither of you seems to be able to satisfy the emotional needs of the other. You both need to be needed and want to feel close to someone. If it's not from each other, you may vie for the attention of the other parent: "I'm Dad's favorite person."

You need to assure your child that when you do become moody, they are not the cause. Children inevitably see themselves as being the problem. Be careful not to nudge your child into being your confidant and therapist or don't attempt to be theirs.

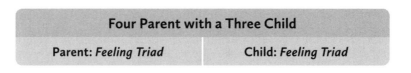

Four Parent with a Three Child	
Parent: *Feeling Triad*	Child: *Feeling Triad*

What Your Relationship Is About . . .

To your little Three, you may feel like a beautiful, mysterious, exotic creature they desire to emulate, while their efficiency, ambition, and practical approach to life can be a source of inspiration for you. Although your approaches are different, you connect in a desire to make the world a better place.

Your individuality meets their desire for achievement—one is internally focused, the other externally orientated. You are connected to your feelings, while your child tends to delay or deny painful feelings. You can help them to express their feelings authentically as you do by drawing on your natural ability to listen deeply—this allows them to go within and discover their own inner beauty.

You both want external recognition: your child for their achievements, and you for being special in some way. Your child will enjoy your creativity and enhanced sense of style. Chances are you'll both enjoy spending time on your physical appearance. You look cool and that makes them feel good—holding your hand allows them some of the recognition they desire. You'll help your child to see that there's more to life than hard work, and that there is beauty to be enjoyed—an exquisite piece of music, a sunset stroll in dappled autumn light, the taste of a meal cooked with care ... As your child gets older, these are important self-improvement lessons they'll enjoy.

When You're Getting Stressed . . .

Your child's inhibited emotions may be something you find hard to understand. You're so expressive and in touch emotionally, yet your child seldom reveals their true feelings. You may start to feel that your child is shallow and insincere while they become contemptuous of your drama, which they find equally insincere. Your child may also at times feel overwhelmed by your emotions.

They crave your approval for their achievements. You can start deliberately withholding praise. You may find it frustrating that your child is preoccupied with projects when you're wanting a deeper connection. They ignore you, which ignites your need to be noticed. This becomes a powerful tool, as you pull on each other's image strings. Starting to feel envious of your child's achievements, and even a bit competitive, is a warning sign that you're stressed.

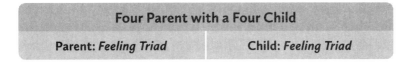

Four Parent with a Four Child	
Parent: *Feeling Triad*	Child: *Feeling Triad*

What Your Relationship Is About . . .

Being the same type offers an opportunity for deep understanding and connection. At its most positive side, this relationship offers you both the chance to connect deeply and become good friends when your child gets older.

You can openly share because your familial bond creates a mutual acceptance of each other, perceived flaws and all. Your desire for a soulmate may feel like it is being met with this child: "We've lived together in past lives. We complete each other." Society may not get you, but your child does. Other parent–child relationships may feel empty and lacking the depth that you experience.

You can be a very accomplished team, bringing your unique creativity to all you both do, be it the school play, or a dress-up party. Neither wants to be seen as ordinary and you respect each other's right to be an individual. You permit yourselves to fully explore your personas.

You both enjoy beauty, the arts, fighting for a better world, dressing well but differently, and being creative and unique. You both accept each other's emotional fluctuations without judgment. There can be a sense of "us against the world—we're different." No one else understands things as deeply as you both do. Each is sensitive to the other. You can fight, scream, and then quickly forgive and make up, bringing humor to your foibles.

When You're Getting Stressed . . .

With added stress comes a creeping concern: "Is my relationship with my child really that good? Jenny and Sam seem much closer. Perhaps my child needs to be more special. . . then things would feel better between us." Your child may experience the same sense of doubt: "The way Mom dresses is really boring. If only she was more like Sam's mom."

You both blame each other for what you perceive is lacking or missing in yourself. You then feel: "What happened to my perfect child?" They are feeling: "What happened to the mother I thought I had? She really isn't a good parent. If only she were more fun." You draw away from each other and yet both fear being abandoned by the other.

Parenting seems like a heavy burden as you start identifying with depression. As you both become increasingly self-absorbed, there's the feeling that you both want the focus to be on yourself. You both want a rescuer—can your partner rescue you both simultaneously? You withhold your attention, so your child feels abandoned. You both become overly sensitive, lashing out at the other. You both can say things that sting. Hurt festers. You withdraw further. Your child moves towards you, only to withdraw as your need for connection has you moving towards them. This will draw you close again, but the push-pull relationship may become a pattern.

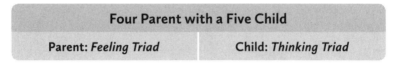

Four Parent with a Five Child	
Parent: *Feeling Triad*	Child: *Thinking Triad*

What Your Relationship Is About . . .

The sensitive, feeling-orientated parent meets the cerebral, serious, intellectual child. Having each other's type as your wing could draw you closer to each other's worlds (see page 35). As the two most introverted Enneagram types, chances are good you won't be signing up to join the "Parents-and-kids afternoon-fun Society." Neither of you feels part of the mainstream and it will be comforting for your child to feel that you stand together in this.

Neither of you enjoys superficial chitchat. You seek emotional depth while your child wants knowledge: "How do engines work, Dad?" It makes for an intense connection. You balance your child's cerebral nature with your creative flair, aesthetic appreciation, and openness to feel. Helping your child connect with their Heart/Feeling center will be very beneficial.

Your child is also creative and enjoys joining the dots between different concepts to create a new idea. Their observation of the way birds build nests may be the precursor to a unique style of architecture later in life. In them, you find a curious, inquiring mind that pushes you to explore life further. As such, you both inspire each other. You enjoy your child's ability to see the world differently.

You are happy to allow your child the time they need to focus on their interests alone. Your combined humor can be dark and quirky, and you both love word puns. Neither of you is afraid to delve deeper into the esoteric or darker side of life. While you see yourself as different, your child can be seen as eccentric, making for a nonconformist parent–child duo who are accepting of each other's quirks.

When You're Getting Stressed . . .

You long for the juiciness of connection but your child holds back, valuing their personal space. Particularly as they reach puberty, your child wants to keep some things secret, which you find frustrating.

Their desire to detach sparks your fear of abandonment: "How can you be so unfeeling? For once just feel rather than intellectualize." The more emotionally demanding you become, the more likely your child is to withdraw behind a "Do not enter" sign. They can experience you as being too intrusive and energetically draining: "Just leave me alone!" The feeling of emotional severance is painful. You may have pushed them away, but now you demand them back. In their rational response, your child starts to feel more like the adult in the relationship, at least to them.

Four Parent with a Six Child	
Parent: *Feeling Triad*	Child: *Thinking Triad*

What Your Relationship Is About . . .

You're both compassionate, empathetic, intuitive, and emotional. You're both sensitive and can listen deeply to each other. Your child may feel like your soul-mate—one of the few people who understands you. Should you fall into a sad space, your child will typically be able to show understanding, which boosts their own sense of self. Your child may use you to help them make decisions, while you enjoy their loyalty: "At least my child would never abandon me."

Mistyping Fours and Sixes is not uncommon, because you share many similar characteristics. Neither of you is afraid to voice an opinion. Both of you can feel unsafe in social interactions, can be reactive and reckless, can feel self-doubting, oppose authority figures, and make problems larger than they are. You can both be very creative, yet you're more likely to be original in approach. While your child may be happy to perform on stage, you prefer to express your creativity alone.

While you are motivated by the desire to be unique, your child wants safety and security. You're a feeling type and your child is a thinking type, and this is where the difference lies—you have a deep longing for intimate connection, while your child fears becoming bogged down in uncomfortable feelings. Their focus is on what could potentially go wrong and how to deal with that danger. Yours is on what is missing from your life—everyone else's life seems better. You teach your child how to connect with their feelings on a deeper level, while they bring a practical, hard-working, and steady approach to the relationship.

When You're Getting Stressed . . .

You can share a sense of gloom, doom, and fear for the future. You both can see yourselves as not belonging—the underdogs of the world, though you are better equipped to take on the world together.

Things fall apart when you feel criticized by your child. You can become reactive; they assume the opposite stance to you. You withdraw your attention, sparking your child's belief that no one can be trusted. Yet even as they slam their bedroom door, you start to feel abandoned: "What's the point of even trying with you?"

Pessimism prevails, and possibly projections too. You can both get caught up in games of rejecting the other rather than being rejected: "You were never really there for me." In your mutual hurt, you both can blame and become critical. The relationship that felt so close drifts apart. Your child feels boring, conservative even: where's that sense of possibility and the little free spirit you loved? To them, your emotional behavior and temper tantrums make you feel more like the child.

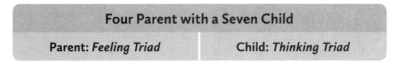

Four Parent with a Seven Child

| Parent: *Feeling Triad* | Child: *Thinking Triad* |

What Your Relationship Is About . . .

Having many opposite characteristics, this relationship can be a dynamic pairing in which you both learn from each other. You can find your child's differences interesting. Your deep capacity for feeling meets their quick thinking. Their optimism balances your tendency towards pessimism. Your little Seven will keep you busy and encourage you to be more confident as you move out into the world, trailing them to parties and new experiences. You are both spontaneous and know how to have fun and find humor in the absurd.

Despite your different personalities, you can share many common interests, particularly as your Seven gets older and starts to enjoy fashion, the arts, fine dining, or art-house movies. You bring the potential for your child to connect with their feelings so they won't feel compelled to run from anything that feels painful or like failure.

Your garrulous Seven's conversation can keep you entertained, and they enjoy being the center of your attention. You fear being boring, while they fear being bored. In your desire to be different and your child's need for entitlement, you can feel that you are removed from the drabness of ordinary life. You are inwardly focused, while your child is focused on the exterior world—another way you bring balance to each other.

When You're Getting Stressed . . .

The aspects that attract when you are both integrated can repel when you are less healthy. Your child starts to feel as if they lack emotional depth and authenticity. Their energy becomes exhausting: "Can't you sit still for a moment?" "Just be quiet for an hour and give me some peace so I can focus on my writing." Your mutual need for attention feels overwhelming. Once a source of intrigue, their excitement feels boring and their response to you feels insensitive and uncaring. They pull away to find stimulation. You withdraw to your inner emotional sanctuary.

You start to envy their friends and accomplishments: "Why doesn't anyone notice me? What's so special about him?" Your child feels that you are pulling back, creating anxiety and frustration. You become more critical (Type One) and both of you can throw tantrums. Neither takes criticism well. You may want to discuss the problems, but they've disappeared into escapist activities. Little is resolved.

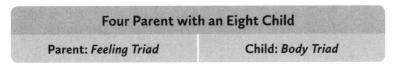

Four Parent with an Eight Child	
Parent: *Feeling Triad*	Child: *Body Triad*

What Your Relationship Is About . . .

The feeling, watery parent with the action-orientated, fiery child makes for an intense, exciting combination. Life will not be dull. Your child wants to step into the fire with you, and you provide that intensity and feeling they seek of being fully alive. Their bold energy feels thrilling and you can both incite each other to be impulsive. Neither of you is afraid to voice an opinion and you hold strong, passionate views. Your vulnerability is mirrored in the shadow side of your child. While you're at home in your emotional world, your child rules the outer world. As your child becomes older, you may feel that they are your protector and even provider: "I'll take care of you, Mom." This can be an endearing attitude. You have each other's backs, and seem to have life sorted.

Your love of aesthetics meets your child's blunt, rough-and-tough attitude. They display the solid, strong, courageous self-confidence you feel you lack. You're the sensitive, creative, emotional, cultured, refined parent your child finds intriguing. You magnify each other's strengths: your emotional depth and creativity, your child's determination and strength.

When You're Getting Stressed . . .

Some say that depression is repressed aggression. You are the paradox of each other's wounding: the water (of sadness) versus the fire (of anger). As such, your child may find your depressive periods hard to deal with. Your child's nature is to take care of you, rather than the other way around, which can be tricky for them.

Neither of you holds back when angry. Huge fights can happen, which have anyone around you heading for the hills, only to find you hugging and making up a short while later as if nothing ever happened. The drama makes you feel alive. The confrontation does the same for them. You both dislike feeling controlled by the other or backing down. As a consequence, things can get out of hand, even to the point of becoming physical. Both of you seek vengeance and may plot revenge.

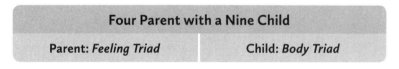

Four Parent with a Nine Child	
Parent: *Feeling Triad*	Child: *Body Triad*

What Your Relationship Is About . . .

Despite your many opposite traits, you can be a harmonious pair. You share things like wanting privacy, being good listeners, needing autonomy, and having empathy. Both of you are extremely creative, although your approach to creativity differs. Your child can merge with you, meaning you both see the beauty in things, become mutually supportive of each other's creative endeavors, and combine to enjoy the good things in life.

You want to go deeply into your emotional world, in contrast with your child, who can be slothful when it comes to their inner growth. You seek to nurture your inner world while your child nurtures others. You're comfortable with feeling sad at times, but your child identifies with being upbeat. You don't mind a heated interaction, but your child finds it upsetting and wants peace. You'll both be quite happy being at home working on whatever creative project inspires you, knowing you're there for each other.

Your Nine child will accept you completely, which in a lifetime of feeling flawed is very comforting. You, on the other hand, draw out your child and show them a shinier approach to life, getting them to connect with and more accurately verbalize their feelings. Life becomes more vital and is lived with greater passion. With you as the role model, your child awakens.

When You're Getting Stressed . . .

Neither of you deals well with criticism because you both can lack self-esteem. Both of you tend to blame the other. Your child doesn't respond well when pushed to change. You can become irritated with this contented little soul who appears to lack the intensity and emotional depth you desire. Is your child ignoring you or simply lost in their own world? The angrier you get, the more they switch off: "Hello, is anyone home?"

Your Nine's steadiness contrasts with your push-pull approach to relationships. When they don't show up emotionally, digging their heads ever deeper into the sand, you get frustrated. You increase your provocation and volatility simply to get a reaction. Your child stubbornly refuses to react—to them, you're starting to feel like a spoilt child who isn't getting its way. Your anger disrupts their peace. To you they feel boring; frustratingly wasting time on superficial activities while avoiding the real issues.

Type Five Parents
and Their Children

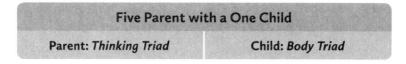

Five Parent with a One Child	
Parent: *Thinking Triad*	Child: *Body Triad*

What Your Relationship Is About . . .

You share many similarities. Both of you see yourselves as a rational voice of guidance and you both enjoy mental stimulation—facts, research, political opinion. Although you can challenge each other's viewpoints, neither of you enjoys confrontation. Neither of you is comfortable showing your feelings and prefer a more detached, factual approach. Essentially, you'll focus on thinking through problems while your child spends more time doing things to overcome them. Both of you are cooler types when it comes to displaying emotions—believing that feelings interfere with logic.

You may be happy helping on a school project if it's in an advisory capacity. Your child has a practical approach to all they do, whereas you're more fascinated by the idea or concept than any practical implementation. You'll be comfortable doing tasks separately rather than working as a team. Both of you seek independence—you'll enjoy your child's ability to get on and entertain themselves without putting too many demands on you, while they'll enjoy your lack of interference. You both can have many interests and share a quirky sense of humor.

When You're Getting Stressed . . .

Your child holds strong opinions while you enjoy challenging opinions or arguing against their more rigid thinking—not because you don't agree, but because you enjoy the mental sparring. This can become contentious if you attempt to prove your perceived superior intellect. While your child is certain of their viewpoint, you may be less so of yours and can change tack more easily. They will see this as a weakness in your rationale.

Your child creates rules, but as an iconoclast you criticize the rules your child wants to uphold. They want to conform. You don't. They care what others think. You don't. They may cringe on your behalf if you don't follow the rules—like arriving at the PTA in jeans when semi-formal was requested or not noticing the spill mark on your blouse.

In this pair there's the One's self-righteous, strongly held beliefs (the "Truth") versus the Five's nihilism and belief in many truths. Both of you can become cynical of the other's beliefs—so expect heated debate around the supper table. Your child wants to be right, while you want to be intellectually superior and to rattle their ridged cage.

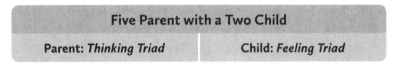

Five Parent with a Two Child

| Parent: *Thinking Triad* | Child: *Feeling Triad* |

What Your Relationship Is About . . .

They say opposites attract. This can be the case in this pairing, where differences create a unique bond. Your rational, cerebral thinking will be balanced by your child's emotional and sentimental approach. You say: "I think . . ." They say: "I feel . . ." You detach from your emotions; they can be overwhelmed by what they feel. When this relationship is at its best, you can heal the missing or less expressed parts in each other. At lower levels of integration, you may battle to understand each other.

The second area in which you differ is in the way you interact with others. Being a loner for the most part, you'd rather lessen your need for interaction, while your child just loves people. You'll cringe at the request for a big party, preferring to do nothing, or something in a small group, whereas your child will be inviting rent-a-crowd. As withdrawn as you can be, you do desire connection—you'll enjoy your child's attempts to do things to please and nurture you, yet you may find their emotional demands exhausting. You just want to be alone and have peace and quiet.

Your third big difference lies in issues around boundaries. Yours are very firm, while your child's are very loose. Being the calm in their emotional storm, you assume the role of the parent well and can be a sage advisor and listener when problems arise.

When You're Getting Stressed . . .

Remember that Twos are trying to help so they can receive the love they're not sure they have: "Am I lovable?" When Fives withdraw into their mental or physical "caves," it can trigger their child's fear of not being loved. How many more cups of coffee do they have to make for you before you'll acknowledge them and give the attention they crave?

"Come and play ball with me, Dad. Please?"

"Not now I'm busy filing my bird photographs."

Your child may try to get your attention by being cute, asking your opinion, helping, acting out, or trying to engage you in a lengthy conversation—all of which feels intrusive on your precious time: "Why can't they just entertain themselves like I did as a child?"

While your child is concerned about other people's feelings, you may hold contempt for what others think: "I don't give a damn what the other parents are wearing—I'm not getting out of my track pants for the PTA." This could cause conflict between you.

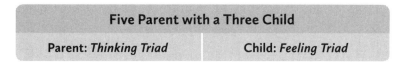

Five Parent with a Three Child

| Parent: *Thinking Triad* | Child: *Feeling Triad* |

What Your Relationship Is About . . .

This can be an outstanding pair. Your knowledge and desire for competence meet your child's efficiency and success. An added benefit is your child's ability to focus on their projects and work alone, as you covet your time.

You relate best when you're doing something together such as researching the origin of a particular dinosaur or walking in nature. Your child's gift to you is their successes; your time is what you gift them. Although you both feel deeply, you're both happy not to go there—work or your current project takes precedence. Simply committing to staying with your child is in itself a gift.

You're detached from the outcome, while your child wants to succeed and be acknowledged—you'll need to understand this and give them the praise they desire. Young Threes enjoy being taught skills and acquiring knowledge to improve their social standing. You teach your child the value of research and going more deeply into things, as opposed to rushing to the finish line. Your child demonstrates the confidence and competence you desire and brings a more practical approach to a problem. Being introverted and more cerebral, you're happy to have your extroverted child take center stage as long as others recognize your part in their intellectual prowess.

While your child puts time and energy into looking good and wearing the right brands, you may view your "fashion slave" teen's delight in acquiring the latest brands as superficial.

When You're Getting Stressed . . .

Having a child can be challenging for independent, loner Fives. Children use up so many resources—time, cash, and space. While your child adores parties and being in the spotlight (such as being the lead in a play), you loathe superficial chitchat and being the focus of attention, unless it's to impart your knowledge. You fiercely protect your time, so having to chauffeur your popular child to parties and extracurriculars can feel like a huge invasion of your resources. If you aren't able to offload much of this responsibility onto a partner, your frustration can increase. You may decline offers to go camping with the other parents and their kids or refuse to attend PTAs. For your child, this can feel as if you don't care.

You get annoyed when your child takes the fastest route to completion and find their push to market themselves cringeworthy. You both tend to avoid dealing with emotional upsets directly, so things can build and be expressed in cutting wit or hurtful sarcasm. You withdraw or resort to your intellect to belittle. They numb themselves through work or social activities.

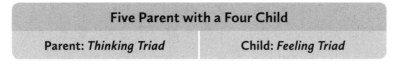

Five Parent with a Four Child

| Parent: *Thinking Triad* | Child: *Feeling Triad* |

What Your Relationship Is About . . .

This can be an interesting, intense, quirky pairing. While others consider you a bit of an eccentric, your child wants to be different and special. As a result, you both feel like outsiders. You both also lean towards introversion. Your child will enjoy how unafraid you are to explore the arcane and esoteric, and will enjoy how you march to the beat of your own drum.

You're both happy in your private worlds and will tolerate each other's quirky behavior while enjoying sharing a clever pun or a dark joke. Although you are both creative, you approach things differently. Your child has a more spontaneous approach while you have probably observed, researched, and thought about the project before starting. Still, both of you can inspire and encourage the other, and enjoy discussing your projects together. You have a cooler, more intellectual temperament than your child, who may feel needier and overly emotional.

"I don't feel I belong in this family," your child may say while you stare in wonder at this emotional being you've co-created and wonder where they've come from.

"Is it normal to be so emotional?"

You traverse very different perspectives: feeling versus thinking. A combined wing helps bring better understanding. (See page 35 for more on the wings.)

When You're Getting Stressed . . .

Your child's frustration with what they perceive as your unavailability and lack of emotional depth can ignite conflict. They may want more than you're able or willing to give.

Fours are prone to abandonment issues and may take your need to be alone as rejection: "You don't care about me!" They may feel unheard and that you lack empathy, while you can find them moody and demanding. To your intellectual mind, displays of unbridled emotion feel childish: "Pull yourself together." As you pull away, they run after you, which feels intrusive. Their neediness feels overwhelming. To get a response, your child may deliberately bait you into being more reactive. Realizing their feeling is butting against your thinking approach to life may help broker peace and understanding.

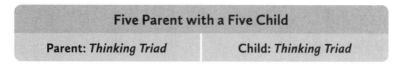

Five Parent with a Five Child	
Parent: *Thinking Triad*	Child: *Thinking Triad*

What Your Relationship Is About . . .

Your curious minds will bond delightfully as you explore a variety of interests. You feel safe together: neither of you will impinge on the other's space, as you both value privacy and independence. You stimulate each other's thinking and are very comfortable not having emotions interfering with your intellect. You'll love it when your child excels and you'll respect that they don't care what their peers or society thinks. Together, you're not afraid to explore the dark and the deep and to share your findings: "What makes psychopaths commit murder?" "How did a meteorite kill off the dinosaurs?" Your focused and intellectual child can feel to you like the perfect child to raise.

Watching a factual show on Netflix will be sure to start an interesting conversation or debate. You both belief that being secretive is natural and logical: "Why would anyone want to gush about their life on social media?" Much of your communication may be nonverbal—so you may feel a comforting sense of togetherness while focused on different tasks in the same room.

When You're Getting Stressed . . .

When you are less integrated, what connected you to your child can start to repel. All thoughts and no feelings can make for a potentially cold relationship: "We're happy doing our own thing and don't enjoy much social interaction. If we have to attend a school function, we both tend to hang around the exit and observe."

Both of you withhold aspects of yourself and your life from each other—it feels safer that way. Your relationship becomes distant and may disintegrate without either of you noticing until it's too late. Then you'll typically convince yourself that you never really wanted the dependence of a child, and that being alone and disconnected feels better because there's no one to make demands on you.

As your child gets older, another area of potential disharmony is your intellectual sparring. You both want to win the argument so the other is forced to acknowledge your intellectual superiority: "Really, Dad? I don't think so, and here's why . . ." "Don't forget I received straight A's when I was your age."

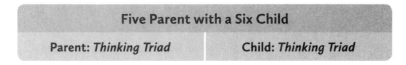

Five Parent with a Six Child	
Parent: *Thinking Triad*	Child: *Thinking Triad*

What Your Relationship Is About . . .

You offer a sense of calm security and steadiness to your more fearful and anxious child. You're both cooler types who enjoy discussing philosophy, details, and facts because you both admire intellectual prowess. Sixes seek authority figures (although they can also rebel against them)—you can fulfill this role for your child because you do well as an advisor. You're surer of yourself (at least you appear to be) than your child is, which helps your child to trust you. You enjoy each other's company while not necessarily having to interact verbally. When integrated, you both respect each other's boundaries. Your child brings a certain warmth to the relationship, and a compassion that matches your kindness.

You're more open to exploring new ideas while your child tends to stick with tried-and-tested thinking. Both of you can be creative, although in different ways. You can both get by with less and have the ability to endure hardship. As your child gets older, you are tolerant of them stepping out into the world only to retreat back into the safety of the family space.

When You're Getting Stressed . . .

Trivializing your child's anxiety or providing lengthy factual reasons as to why they shouldn't be afraid is only going to cause them to worry more. Detaching too much from your child you can spark trust issues, making your child insecure and demanding. Not enjoying being imposed upon, you may disengage further, creating a feeling of rejection.

Your child can be emotionally reactive while you can be argumentative. You may be able to deal with their reactivity in infancy, but if it continues you may begin to lose respect for your child. When you escape to your office or "cave," doubt arises in your child—they feel you no longer love and care about them. They project their insecurity onto you. At the same time, your child can become indecisive, constantly needing your input before acting, which can feel draining to you. Nevertheless, your ideas, once intriguing and stimulating to them, can start to feel bizarre and impractical.

Your interest in the arcane can spark further doubts and fears in your little Six: "Can Dad be trusted? He's so weird. Then there's this obsession with death and the darker side of life." As a Five, you need to know everything—when you don't have the answer to a question, you can fudge around for something to say. This makes your child feel less sure of you: "How can I trust her when she doesn't tell the truth about not knowing something?"

Five Parent with a Seven Child	
Parent: *Thinking Triad*	Child: *Thinking Triad*
Because you share Lines of Stretch and Release, you can more easily access different aspects of each other's type.	

What Your Relationship Is About . . .

You help your child by being grounded and steady and showing them how to focus. They help you become more outgoing. Both of you find stimulation in new ideas and concepts, and your child helps broaden your interests.

Both of you want independence—your child because dependence of others curtails their freedom, and you because it spares your (perceived) limited resources. Both of you are intellectually quick. While you have wacky, whimsical humor, your Seven child's is cruder.

You're both fear types. You tend to internalize your fear through acquiring knowledge: "The more I know, the safer I'll be." Your child externalizes their fear by running away from pain and fear through heightened planning and activities.

There are many, many ways in which you show up as opposites. You are very focused while your child is scattered: "I'll play this game . . . Oh wait, let me try this . . . or this . . ." You're introverted and for the most part you find being social draining, while your child is energized by being with others. (They'd love a surprise party; you'd be horrified to find a large group of people in your home waving balloons.) You hold on to what you feel are your limited resources and minimize your needs while your child has a gluttonous need for experience and always wants more. You want depth while your child is happy to skim the surface of things. You seek knowledge while they seek joy. You battle with confidence while they're very confident. You don't enjoy sudden changes in plans or surprises while your child loves spontaneity. You hold on, while they let go—be it with resources, control, or cash. You're happy to be a bright nerd while they want to be cool.

When You're Getting Stressed . . .

When under pressure, you withdraw and become emotionally detached—it feels safer. Your child, on the other hand, becomes busier. You take them to a ball game, but they're asking to go play paintball before the game has even ended. Nothing seems to satiate their desire for experience, but you can get by with very little and all you want is time alone. Your tight control meets their out-of-control activity. They feel manic, and too demanding. To them you feel boring, cold, and without passion.

Their desire for confrontation meets your need to argue. Trust is lost in the fallout. For you, analyzing the situation masquerades as feeling. Running from pain into a life of pleasure convinces them that they have the answer to everything. They feel they have the upper hand, which can be infuriating when it is clear they don't.

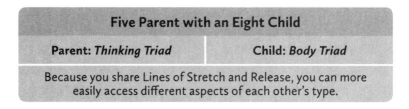

Five Parent with an Eight Child

Parent: *Thinking Triad*	Child: *Body Triad*
Because you share Lines of Stretch and Release, you can more easily access different aspects of each other's type.	

What Your Relationship Is About . . .

You enjoy and admire your child's ability to go after what they want, be direct and assertive, and take risks, as well as their sensual enjoyment of life—things that come less easily to you. You both enjoy independence and privacy and have strong boundaries. Neither of you enjoys intrusion on your space. Your cool cerebral space meets their intense fieriness.

While you are introverted and unassertive, your child is the most assertive of the types, and doesn't back down from a fight. You are contracted, while they are expansive. They go after what they want with an immediacy, while you attempt to minimize your needs. You feel good about avoiding needing stuff, while your child feels good acquiring it. While you inspire them to think before acting, they will help you develop your mind–body connection.

You feel relatively powerless in the world while your child feels powerful. Your child can become your natural defense against the world, while you provide careful thought since you can foresee the consequences of rash action. As such, you become a brains–brawn pair—that's not to say that Eights lack brains, but rather that their persona is more identified with the body and being tough.

Neither of you feels like you really belong in society, and while you use intellect to hide your vulnerability, your child uses a "take it or leave it" approach to hide theirs. Your child is a doer while you are a thinker. They are pragmatic and practical while you are more about thoughts and observation than direct action. You were probably a late developer when it came to love relationships, but your child may be the opposite of you.

When You're Getting Stressed . . .

It's not inconceivable that as your child gets older, they will attempt to gain the upper hand in the relationship. You may have created the family rules, but they have created their own, which they expect you to follow while seeing no need to comply to yours. Your backing down can have them losing respect for you; backing off creates frustration. They are challengers—they need someone to step into the arena with them.

Eights have high energy levels, which can feel invasive and even overwhelming for you at times. Sometimes they suck the very air from the room, dominating the space you share. Typically, you withdraw to your own space. For a child wanting to feel connection and who has issues with rejection (as you both do), this triggers anger and aggression. Life feels unsafe as they roar and rage. Both of you can retreat after an argument to plot revenge and find ways to control the other. Life becomes a series of retaliatory actions. Your child attempts to intimidate, while you become uncommunicative. Both of you convince yourselves that you don't need the other.

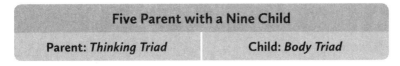

Five Parent with a Nine Child	
Parent: *Thinking Triad*	Child: *Body Triad*

What Your Relationship Is About . . .

You'll find your laid-back, easy-going, accepting, and undemanding child easier to manage than many of the other types. They're happy to get on with it and not rock your boat, meaning you have more time to do what inspires you. Much of what transpires between you may be nonverbal: as your child merges with you, they just sense what you need. You're both undemanding of the other, and your child learns quickly to entertain themselves, something you enjoy and admire. They're not dramatic and emotional, aspects that you view with contempt. Neither intrudes on the other. Your Nine child wants you to spend time with them—they just won't demand it.

Both of you can be intelligent, although you put more emphasis on knowledge and want to dig deeper than a Nine is inclined to do. As your child gets older, you'll enjoy being able to share your knowledge with them. While they tend to get caught in a fog of possibilities, your thinking is clear.

You're happy to allow your child the freedom to be what they want to be. Both of you can be patient and kind with the other, and you enjoy your child's nurturing qualities. You're often tense, but your child has a natural ability to help those around them feel relaxed.

When You're Getting Stressed . . .

You are self-focused, while your child is focused on others to the point of neglecting themselves. Their merging with you that you may have enjoyed (since it serves you to have your needs understood) can start feeling claustrophobic. They feel emotionally dependent and needy, which has you panicking: "How much do they want from me?" "I'm not geared for parenthood." As one Five told me: "I'd like my own apartment, away from the family, so I can visit when I feel like interaction." Having kids seldom involves this option!

Your need for space can make your child feel abandoned. They experience you as indifferent—on your own cerebral planet. You're happy to be an authoritarian, aloof advisor. Their desire to merge creates your desire to withhold of yourself. Frustration results, but little is expressed. Neither of you is good at discussing your feelings, although your child is more emotional than you are. You become cool, thinking through your feelings, which take time to surface. Your child may bury their hurt and anger in pleasantness or becoming stubborn. They become numb, engaging in other activities to avoid feeling. Huge issues can fester with neither of you confronting the problem. Conflict, which neither of you enjoys, is avoided at the cost of open expression, and you can drift apart.

Type Six Parents
and Their Children

Six Parent with a One Child	
Parent: *Thinking Triad*	Child: *Body Triad*

What Your Relationship Is About . . .

This pair dreams of a perfect world, where everyone follows the rules and is safe. Both believing you're on earth for some reason greater than yourselves, you're dutiful, hard-working, and responsible. You are both able to negotiate tough times, pulling together to help where you can. There is a desire in both of you to help the underprivileged, although you do it for different reasons—you because you identify with the underdog and your child because it's the right thing to do.

You both take life seriously, although you bring greater warmth, amiability, generosity, compassion, and demonstrative emotion to the relationship. Your lighter, more playful nature allows your child to take life a bit less seriously. You are happy to work hard provided others work alongside you, so you appreciate your child's help and commitment to getting chores done.

Your child's high integrity and desire for truth makes you feel they can be trusted. Together, you're an asset to any community.

When You're Getting Stressed . . .

Whereas you tend to be uncertain, indecisive, and ambivalent, your child is decisive and has strong opinions about everything. While you have a buzz of voices in your head instructing you on what to do, your child has an "inner critic" who points out what they are not doing perfectly. As a result, both of you can be hard on yourselves: "Did I mess up again?"

You can be reactive and suspicious of others' motivations. Your child controls their emotions but their anger emerges in resentment, indignation, snippy comments, or the occasional fallout. Being security- and safety-focused, you are anxious. Projection is common: your project your fears onto your child, believing they are your child's own fears. Your child worries about correct procedures—the right way to be and do. You're inclined to be less orderly and logical than they are.

Both of you look at what's wrong rather than what's right. You doubt things will be okay while your child looks for where they are not. You can both procrastinate—you're unsure of the direction to take while your child is afraid they're going to mess up. Different ideologies or religious beliefs could cause friction later in life.

You work exceptionally hard, but you do like to have fun—your child makes you feel like this is an unnecessary indulgence: "Grow up, Mom!" You resent being told off and retaliate, then worry and feel bad: "Did I do the right thing? Have I failed them?" You become more defensive. They judge: "Honestly, Mom, I expected a lot more from you." It's one thing having a partner judging you—it's another when hurtful criticism is lobbed by your ten-year-old. You start to wonder who's the adult here. There's an icy atmosphere in the home. Criticism meets blame.

The One's tightly controlled emotions clash with the Six's reactivity. Nothing you do seems good enough, and you find it exhausting. The way to heal is to share openly and honestly how you feel before anger and resentment build.

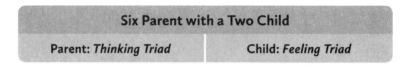

Six Parent with a Two Child

| Parent: *Thinking Triad* | Child: *Feeling Triad* |

What Your Relationship Is About . . .

You're both warm, helpful, and good at listening. You're happy to focus on others, helping and supporting where needed, being responsible and dutiful. You both want connection and a sense of belonging—you for the security it offers, your child for intimacy and to feel loved. You both enjoy playing the host or hostess. Your home is important to you; you enjoy entertaining and having friends and family around. You both tend to have a wide circle of friends, even if it's based on the organizations where you help out. You appreciate how kind and generous your child is, while they see you as loyal and committed to others as they are.

You can be overprotective, but this may not pose a problem to a child who loves attention—at least when younger. Whereas you doubt life will work out for you, your child has a more positive outlook. Their warmth and affection bring out your lighter, warmer, more playful side.

When You're Getting Stressed . . .

You will love your "Little Helper's" desire to do things for you, yet you may be suspicious: "Why are they doing this? What do they want from me? More allowance? Permission to go to the party . . .?" Your child may start to feel that you don't appreciate their help and they wonder if you're rejecting them. You find their constant need for approval and attention irksome—their demands and tendency to be overly emotional makes them feel needy.

Particularly if you're a stricter, counterphobic Six, you may find that your little Two doesn't respect your boundaries—you made it clear that you didn't want to be disturbed. The pressure of their needs makes you feel more anxious: "How can I cope with everything—my work, my child, my volunteer duties?" It all feels too much: "What to do? Where do I spend my time?" A little Two may find your occasional prickliness hard to deal with: "What have I done wrong now?" They can start acting like little Eights, wanting control, and to issue orders to you: "I need you to make my lunch, now!" As they push towards you, offering more help while demanding more of your time, so you retreat, sparking their anger or manipulating you to meet their needs.

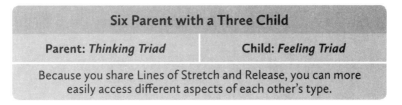

Six Parent with a Three Child	
Parent: *Thinking Triad*	Child: *Feeling Triad*
Because you share Lines of Stretch and Release, you can more easily access different aspects of each other's type.	

What Your Relationship Is About . . .

Your compassion and loyalty blends with your child's optimism and energy. You're both doers—neither of you is scared of hard work if it means getting the desired result. Your child shows you the possibility of your less-explored potential. You demonstrate warmth, and concern for others and the planet. Your child also knows that whether they meet success or failure, you'll be there to support them.

How do you cope when you are full of self-doubt and anxiety and your child is self-confident and seemingly has little fear? In this pair, thinking meets suppressed feelings—but your Lines of Stretch and Release (see page 38) provide enough common ground to make you a good team.

The best time to help your child to open up about their feelings is when you're both involved in an activity—anything from a craft to surfing. Out there on the ocean, for example, distracted by the task, your child may feel more able to talk about what is concerning them.

You may also be part of a church or organization where your child can learn the benefits of helping others—that success may be about holding a great fundraiser rather than being top of the class.

When You're Getting Stressed . . .

While Sixes become more reactive and fiery under pressure, Threes are inclined to become cooler, even icy. Your child has the ambition and confidence you're denying yourself. You mirror your child's hidden feelings of doubt, inferiority, and fear of failure. Under pressure, you may become competitive with each other. You hold back cautiously on your ambitions; they push forward irrespective of the scenario. You doubt your own goals: "Am I doing the right thing?" Your child seems unconcerned. You may even cringe at their boasting: "Doesn't she realize that she's setting herself up for criticism?"

You're both inclined to take on too much and feel stressed as a result. You worry and may run around in circles wanting to get things done while your child may become robotic in their approach. You can both avoid dealing with feelings and, like rats on a treadmill, persist in the pursuit of a goal until you reach burnout.

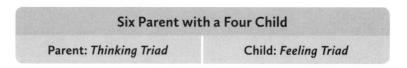

Six Parent with a Four Child

| Parent: *Thinking Triad* | Child: *Feeling Triad* |

What Your Relationship Is About . . .

Because you share so many attributes, these types can be confused. You both fear being abandoned, find parties or groups of people stressful, feel like the underdog, can be reactive and reckless, and mistrust authority figures—you can both experience the world as a harsh place to be. You are also both intuitive, compassionate, and good at listening. Because of these similarities, you may feel that you've found a deep soul connection in your child. Feeling abandoned in some way, when you find acceptance and emotional support in each other, you both feel the other is, "someone who understands me."

As a Six, your pattern of love is an archetypal paternal approach, irrespective of your sex. You want to lead the way—you are the North Star guiding your child, the person your child admires and wants to emulate. You help your child with creative projects, bringing them from dream to reality with your practical, hard-working approach. You meet on a creative level and each can inspire and support the other's endeavors. Your child encourages you to explore your emotions and delve deeper into your inner world.

Together you can be playful, warm, and spontaneous: "Let's stop this homework and go have fun at the park." Your child clearly needs you, which enhances your sense of self. They, in turn, appreciate your steady loyalty.

When You're Getting Stressed . . .

When your child starts becoming inconsistent, critical, melancholic, and overly emotional in their behavior, it's a sign they're moving to the lower side of themselves. Doors may be slammed, angry outbursts can occur, and you may be accused of being boring, conservative, and lacking in any emotional depth. If you choose to retaliate (a sign that you're moving to your lower side), you too can overreact, magnifying a small problem. You can project your feelings onto your child. Sensing their withdrawal, you do the same yourself in a push-pull game you both can play. As your child disappears to play with a friend, you feel abandoned: "I can't even trust my own child to be loyal." They too feel abandoned: "I don't belong in this family!"

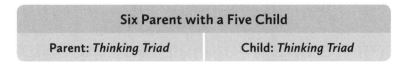

Six Parent with a Five Child	
Parent: *Thinking Triad*	Child: *Thinking Triad*

What Your Relationship Is About . . .

You're an intelligent pair who respect each other's knowledge. You can both view problems analytically. As the adult, you're suited to assume the more active, leadership role. Neither of you is particularly demonstrative, although you bring added warmth to the relationship. The odd hug or kiss will provide the assurance you both need that you're there for each other. Your intuitive knowing, responsibility, and scenario-planning together with your child's calm emotional detachment make the two of you well suited for handling a crisis.

You bring compassion and a more other-focused approach, while your child can be kind and, like you, a good listener. You're very practical but your child often has a less practical approach to life. They enjoy delving into areas that may scare you and push your fear buttons. They're after knowledge but you want a guru (be it a boss in business, a religious leader, a commander, or a politician). You enjoy having someone work with you, whether it's doing the washing or painting the house, whereas your child may avoid such mundane tasks. Fives may appear not to need much nurturing, but in truth they want you to seek them out and offer this support without being invasive.

When You're Getting Stressed . . .

When your little Five withdraws from you (as Fives are inclined to do), you may misinterpret it as a rejection of you, rather than a need to re-energize. As you move towards your child for reassurance that they still love you, they can find the attention overpowering and retreat further: "I need my space!"

Your child may experience your reactive outbursts as immature compared to their contained expression, and you may find it frustrating when they don't react to your outburst. Your ambivalence can create insecurity in your child. "If they don't know, then how can I know?"

You can both be pessimistic. Fives can be secretive, compartmentalizing their lives into what they reveal to whom, but secrecy pushes your trust buttons: "Why isn't he telling me? Is there something sinister going on?"

Your child may see you as too conforming, narrow-minded, and bound by conventions and rules, whereas they are inclined to question these rules and embrace new ways of being. They may say: "Showering removes natural oils from your skin so I'm not going to shower any more." This can create conflict. Whereas you both follow and rebel against authority figures, your child rejects authority and instead puts trust in their knowledge, while wanting to rattle other people's cages. As a result, you may not agree with how they view the things you hold sacred.

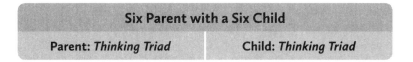

Six Parent with a Six Child

| Parent: *Thinking Triad* | Child: *Thinking Triad* |

What Your Relationship Is About . . .

Both of you are loyal, responsible, hard-working, and dutiful. You're a strong, bonded team when it comes to getting things done around the house, and you share a playful sense of humor. Both of you appreciate the loyalty and safe support you each provide: "Even if the world falls down around me, I know Dad will be there to help pick up the pieces, as I'd do for him." You both value reliability. You'll do whatever is in your power to not be late to pick up your child because you understand their fear—you've been there.

As with all like pairings, the Instinctual Drives (see page 40), can make for big differences in your relationship. Your parenting in particular will be impacted by whether you're a phobic or counterphobic Six. Sexual Sixes are more intimidating and stricter as parents.

Neither of you easily discusses your feelings, yet you express your care for each other in your actions and steadfast loyalty. Mutual trust allows you to test your decisions with and receive confirmation from the other.

As one of the three future-orientated (fear) types (Five, Six, and Seven), planning future sport or leisure outings is good for both parent and child and feeds your need to be strong and physically beautiful. You share an ability to be creative, a belief in helping those in need, a questioning nature, a sense of responsibility, sensitivity, warmth, and compassion for others.

When You're Getting Stressed . . .

As a pair, you might test each other's loyalty: "If I ignore her, will she still be there for me?" You can also unite in your fear: "I don't think Maria and her mom like us." Even if that is not true, this anxiety can quickly escalate, fueled by both of you.

Because you're both inclined to play devil's advocate, you tend to take up opposing positions in an argument. Understanding the other side helps remove doubt and fear, but pushed too far, you can both become reactive and project your insecurities and doubts onto the other. "Yes, but . . ." becomes a common way of dealing with suggestions.

Remember the story of Chicken Little? When an acorn fell on his head, he believed the sky had fallen. Sixes also envisage the worst-case scenario: "Was it the sky? Or could it have been the moon? Whatever it was, things must be pretty bad . . ." You both build on each other's fears: "Who can be trusted? Who really has the answer? What will fall next—the sun?" Because you're afraid, you both become reactive, making accusations and doomsday prophecies. It's fight or take flight; you may take rash action or run around in circles each blaming the other: "Clearly you're the problem!" Pointless and destructive arguments can ensue: "I wonder what's going to be the next thing to go wrong." In this anger dance, you may each be acting out the other's hidden fears and paranoias.

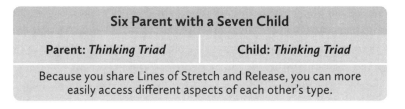

Six Parent with a Seven Child	
Parent: *Thinking Triad*	Child: *Thinking Triad*
Because you share Lines of Stretch and Release, you can more easily access different aspects of each other's type.	

What Your Relationship Is About . . .

If your life was a road trip, your child would be the one with the original idea, who makes the plans and examines options for fun places to go. They're like the accelerator on the car. You would be the one to pack every conceivable first-aid requirement, who reads up on what dangers and risks can be expected and how to avoid them, and who navigates the car. You are the one who applies the brakes. Do this trip together, and you'll both enjoy the journey because you balance each other's strengths and weaknesses.

You are both thinking types and are, as a result, sharp-witted. You share a sense of humor and enjoy good-naturedly teasing each other. While you're inclined to experience your fear directly, your optimistic, spontaneous, busy child keeps active to avoid theirs. While you're cautious, your child throws caution to the wind as a way to enhance excitement. Their upbeat nature helps you to be more optimistic.

You provide a safe space for your child: your loyalty and understanding of practicality and follow-through helps to make their visions real. They help you to leave your duties and enjoy life more: "C'mon, the dishes can wait. Let's go have some fun."

When You're Getting Stressed . . .

You want your child to commit to plans: "Can we agree that you'll visit every Saturday for lunch?" Your child sees this as a direct impingement on their freedom. What if a better option arises?

You scan the horizon to see any problems that may arise, but your child doesn't want their dreams dampened by your doubts and belief in the worst-case scenario: "When I try to talk to my son about problems in the family business, he just gets up and leaves the room. He doesn't want to hear it." To the young Seven, it feels like you're stopping their fun and limiting their freedom: "Do we have to leave the party now?"

When you're a Seven wanting to imagine new and exciting activities and your Six parent squashes your enthusiasm with blunt reality, it can cause anger and frustration. Your child avoids seeing any problems. You'd rather think of all possible problems—it feels safer that way. Their optimism clashes with your overprotective pessimism and the result can be an angry fallout. They say: "You're such a drag. You never want me to do anything but stay at home! You worry about *everything.*"

You retort: "You're so unreliable. All you ever think about is yourself. Me. Me. Me. You never help around the house. And you blow your allowance like I didn't have to work hard to earn it."

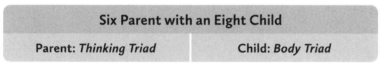

Six Parent with an Eight Child	
Parent: *Thinking Triad*	Child: *Body Triad*

What Your Relationship Is About . . .

You admire your child's ability to face danger and you love them even more when they take up your cause—your child is your little hero or heroine. You are cautious and your child takes risks, yet both of you can be courageous. You act despite your fear while your child acts because it's the way they interact with the world. You love their sense of honor, strength, generosity, charisma, high energy, and directness. They enjoy your reliability, charm, determination, and the feeling that you support them. You share a desire for loyalty, hard work, being responsible, and helping those who have been victimized. You are both doers and enjoy getting tasks done, even if you're inclined to procrastinate at times.

Your child's protective, territorial nature along with your desire for having a safe space creates a home in which you can each expose your vulnerable sides. Your child's decisiveness puts them in the natural role of leader as they get older, while you are there as their faithful advisor.

Your little Eight teaches you to be more assertive and to speak directly, which is something you can find difficult. Your child can minimize your concerns and help you to be your own authority figure. You teach them how to stand back sometimes, to listen, not be so impulsive, to show more understanding and compassion, and to follow their own rules.

Trusting is hard but you can find trust in each other. At times it may feel as if it's the two of you against the world: "Together, we've got this!" While you tend to be more other-focused, your child demonstrates the need to sometimes be more self-focused.

When You're Getting Stressed . . .

Your child may find your constant fears and anxieties annoying: "Why do you always see the worst of everything?" You feel: "Why don't they take my concerns seriously? There's danger in the world, I'm trying to protect them." Your questioning mind may create hostility in your child, who wants autonomy rather than having to answer to anything.

Your child may see you as weak for your inability to decide the way forward or reticence to confront them head on. They may lose respect for you. Frustrated and angry, they rock your secure world, making you more reactive or evasive. Trust is lost and neither feels supported. You become defensive. They act tough: "I don't need you anymore!" They attempt to control. You rebel: "I'm not having a teenager dictate to me." The difference is that your child generally gets over these fights quickly, particularly if they feel they've won. You, on the other hand, mull over the event: "Was I wrong to shout at him?"

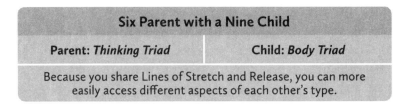

Six Parent with a Nine Child	
Parent: *Thinking Triad*	Child: *Body Triad*
Because you share Lines of Stretch and Release, you can more easily access different aspects of each other's type.	

What Your Relationship Is About . . .

This can be a good bonding relationship, with each giving the other the solid grounding and confidence you're both after. Easy-going, accepting little Nines will go a long way to soothe your anxious, doubting mind.

Inside of you is your child's peace-making, relaxed nature, where you are able to avoid your troublesome thoughts. You mirror each other, which helps bring understanding when you are integrated and the opposite when you're less healthy.

The Six enjoys security, the Nine values stability. You can both be indecisive—you because you fear making the wrong choice (although you don't like others deciding for you), and your child because they don't want to antagonize anyone by making the wrong decision. Both of you tend to "go along to get along," again for different reasons. For you, it's more secure that way (safety in numbers), and for your child it's because then they are less likely to offend.

You both enjoy routines and enjoy dependability over the excitement of the unpredictable, yet it's not all down-the-line values: your child enjoys their autonomy and stepping away from society's norms while you can be a rebel at times. You question others' motives, while your child is unquestioning of others: "Live and let live."

You have a more pessimistic view of the world so your child's optimism is uplifting to you. While trust is generally an issue for you, your child has a naïve ability to trust. Your tendency to be more reactive, even prickly, is balanced by your child's forgiving, easy-going nature. Neither sees yourselves as being exceptional, even when you do achieve greatness.

When You're Getting Stressed . . .

Neither you nor your child is particularly skilled in communicating your feelings or problems. Your child dislikes confrontation, so keeps quiet. You fear that voicing how you feel will destabilize. Both of you hope the other will fathom what's wrong. You can both rage unexpectedly. If your child merges with you, they may become unsure about what they really want—it's your needs they're expressing. Both of you need to learn to focus more on your own needs.

Your child's passivity can become a source of annoyance: "Are they really listening to me? Don't they realize the danger?" Your doubts and fears trouble their cotton-candy world. As you push them to take action, they stubbornly refuse and can become passive-aggressive or numb out. For you, it's infuriating and creates more anxiety: "How can you just sit there? Why are you not taking me seriously?"

Type Seven Parents
and Their Children

Seven Parent with a One Child	
Parent: *Thinking Triad*	Child: *Body Triad*
Because you share Lines of Stretch and Release, you can more easily access different aspects of each other's type.	

What Your Relationship Is About . . .

You're opposites whose strengths can create growth and learning for each other. As a Seven, you love the bigger picture while One loves detail. You're spontaneous; they're measured in their approach. You take risks while they're risk-averse. Chaos can excite you while they like order. You want fun and adventure while they seek perfection. For all your Seven character, inside you is a One seeking order, while inside your One child is a desire for the fun and spontaneity of the Seven.

You bring to your child the understanding that life is more than duty and getting things done correctly. You permit them to be freer and less rigid, while they help with your tendency to become distracted. While you've blown your budget mid-month, your child will have carefully budgeted their allowance. You eat the bumper bag of M&M's in one go, while they carefully calculate their own daily allowance. Both of you can be idealistic and garrulous, although while you're inclined to embellish the truth (it makes for a more interesting story), your child demands 100 percent accuracy.

When You're Getting Stressed . . .

As a Seven, you don't enjoy anything that limits your freedom, which children are inclined to do. When you have a child whose focus is on adhering to the rules, life can be interesting! Opposites can clash.

As you become increasingly scattered and undisciplined, your child can berate you, becoming the adult in the relationship. They may criticize you for being self-centered, overindulgent, and irresponsible: "It's like you've never grown up! You're supposed to be the parent here!" While you try glibly to avoid any issues by telling your child to "Lighten up and start enjoying life for goodness sake," they become judgmental and inflexible.

To them, your desire for pleasure seems wrong and selfish. You run towards what feels more enjoyable, seeking more freedom: "Where did I get such a boring child from?" Neither of you takes criticism well. You confront and rage while they repress and resent. You may deliberately try to shock your child with inappropriate humor or bad behavior. You become an embarrassment to them: "I'd rather you didn't go to the PTA, Dad."

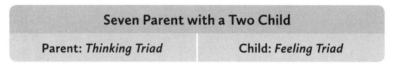

Seven Parent with a Two Child

| Parent: *Thinking Triad* | Child: *Feeling Triad* |

What Your Relationship Is About . . .

Others could be forgiven for thinking you are the same type because you're both social, friendly, energetic, and engaging. You both seek happiness and have a high energy level. You're both generally upbeat, seeing the best in situations and enjoying the good things in life—particularly good food and entertaining. Together, you make any event more lively, fun, and warm.

Whereas you enjoy being the focus of attention, your child is happy to bask in your glory: "I helped Mom to organize this party." You're more self-referencing while your child is more focused on others. You create excitement in your child's life: "Let's have a *Star Wars* party! No, wait—how about going to the woods and having a treasure hunt . . . ? Or we could try out the new burger joint?"

Both of you are generous to a fault, but you help your child learn to receive as well as to give. Social Sevens in particular have a desire to make the world a better place, as does a Two child.

When You're Getting Stressed . . .

If your child feels you drawing away from them, it can trigger a desire to cling on. Having someone demand your attention feels stifling. Their neediness smothers your freedom—yet you have a responsibility to your child. This creates a dilemma, particularly if you're a single parent and don't have the option of handing over responsibility. You can start to feel trapped: cornered by your child.

Your child does what they can to hold on to the intimacy you had: "Dad, can you for once not put yourself first?" Parenting feels unfulfilling, and you feel manipulated. Your child's unmet needs make you feel guilty—a feeling you don't enjoy. Your child is no longer your devoted friend and adoring audience. They can retaliate by making sure you can't have fun, such as saying they feel unwell and want to go home just as the party is starting to liven up. To you they feel like a handbrake—stopping you from getting up and going.

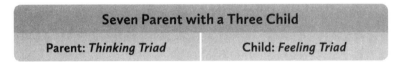

Seven Parent with a Three Child	
Parent: *Thinking Triad*	Child: *Feeling Triad*

What Your Relationship Is About . . .

Woosh . . .! When this energetic, charismatic duo walks into a room, nobody is going miss it—the party has started! Your natural spontaneity encourages your more self-conscious child to ease up and let go. You both have a "can do," youthful approach to life.

You want options. Your child wants goals. These desires keep you both on the move. Being bored is an issue for you, but it's likely that your child will provide the stimulation you enjoy. You both may be so involved with your lives (your latest project, your child's extracurriculars and social activities) that you don't spend a huge amount of time together. Life is on fast forward! You both enjoy the lighter side of your relationship and are inclined to avoid dealing with any negative issues. That's no fun, right? Your child comes with a big bonus in that they seem happy to just get on with things, so you don't need to be a disciplinarian (you can leave that to your partner). Both Sevens and Threes enjoy travel and adventure and aren't averse to risk-taking as you suck the marrow out of life. You enjoy exploring new ideas and pastimes—your child to improve themselves, you to make life interesting. You both have high self-esteem and aren't afraid to state your needs.

When You're Getting Stressed . . .

Both of you enjoy being the center of attention and may miss having an adoring audience, which can become a source of conflict.

While you avoid any sense of failure by imagining that what has gone wrong is only "a small step back from success," your child will negate failure by throwing themselves into another project. Neither approach is healthy. You may also be so focused on the need to be upbeat that you fail to acknowledge or even see when your child is in trouble: "Oh, a few spliffs here and there doesn't make for an addict. She's just a bit stressed out."

You opt for what pleasures you, while your child opts for what looks pleasing. In your mutual desire to impress others, you can both appear superficial. Both of you can mold the truth to suit your needs. You may find that the idea of having a child was exciting, but the reality has put major limitations on your freedom: either you find yourself becoming increasingly frustrated or your partner has to cope with what you can't. The more your child wants attention, the greater the level of volatility. You may say hurtful things without thinking, then escape toward what feels more fun.

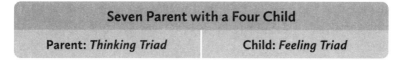

Seven Parent with a Four Child

Parent: *Thinking Triad*	Child: *Feeling Triad*

What Your Relationship Is About . . .

You can both be spontaneous and enjoy stimulation in whatever form you find it—a new store, food, or experience. You share an irreverent sense of humor. For both of you, your dress sense reveals a desire to look cool and different. While you as a Seven seek fulfillment and excitement, your Four child wants to establish a unique identity.

Opposites meet as your optimistic outlook connects with your child's identification with melancholy—at best, this balances your viewpoints. Another difference is that you are extroverted while they are more introverted. You are supremely confident and may find your child's self-doubt and lack of confidence confusing—you help draw out your child to become more engaging. While you are focused primarily on thinking, your child feels deeply. Your child enjoys time alone, but you look for social stimulation. You love a good party, while your child dislikes superficial small talk. Yet you meet in both wanting intensity and experiences. You both enjoy the stimulation of ideas and creativity and will encourage each other in this.

As your child gets older, you may share a passion for the finer things in life—good food, fine wines, fashion, or art. You run through your salary quickly; their allowance also slips easily through their fingers.

When You're Getting Stressed . . .

You're Peter Pan who doesn't want the restriction of adult responsibilities, and they're the lost child. You feel entitled, while your child longs to feel unique and special. Your high level of fiery energy motivates your child away from watery depression, yet it can also mean that you merely avoid dealing with your unhappy child.

Your child may experience you as not showing up emotionally and they could feel abandoned and misunderstood as a result. You don't enjoy confronting painful issues, while your child may relate to feeling what is intensely painful. Your child may experience you as lacking in depth and care when you comment: "Why are you always so down in the dumps? Just get over it and lighten up." Yet the further they sink into their emotional quagmire, the more you fear drowning in emotion yourself and you desire to escape their needs. To up the energy, you may draw other family members into the fray.

Your combined impulsiveness can lead you both into trouble and your mutual resistance to forgiveness can mean that fights last for days. As you become increasingly frustrated with your child, who always seems moody, needy, and self-absorbed, they experience you as confrontational, shallow, and intolerant.

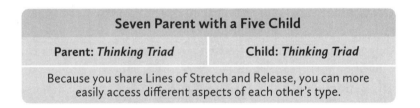

Seven Parent with a Five Child	
Parent: *Thinking Triad*	Child: *Thinking Triad*
Because you share Lines of Stretch and Release, you can more easily access different aspects of each other's type.	

What Your Relationship Is About . . .

Your child loves your wide range of interests and ideas, while you appreciate their questioning mind. You both have a sharp intellect, picking up new concepts fast, yet you may both be less emotionally mature. When you move to your Five aspect, you become less scattered, studying issues in greater depth. Moving to Seven means your Five child develops imagination, spontaneity, and the ability to become more socially adept.

You do have many differences, however. You are the most extroverted of the Enneagram types, while your child is the most introverted. You enjoy being the center of attention, but they do not. They internalize their fear by acquiring knowledge ("The more I know, the safer I'll be") while you externalize and avoid your fear by planning non-stop future activities. Type Seven parents will feel they have failed at parenting if their child doesn't enjoy socializing—preferring to remain alone rather than having a wide circle of friends may be incomprehensible: "They can't be happy all alone, right?" Yet underlying your outgoing Seven nature is a shadow Five who is withdrawn and restrained, and who feels trapped by limited options.

Both of you appreciate independence. You are positive, while your child tends to have a darker view of life. While a good night for you would be having a few events lined up (so if one gets boring you can move to the next), your child would find playing a computer game or watching a documentary or Sci-Fi movie more fun. There are going to have to be compromises here.

You see the world as abundant. Your child experiences life as never having enough resources. As a result, you're generous with what you have, while they're inclined to hold on, minimizing their needs. You encourage them to take risks and enter into the world, while they help you maintain focus and restraint. They don't enjoy sudden unexpected changes in plan, but you'll easily change plans when a more exciting option comes up.

When You're Getting Stressed . . .

Yours can be a tricky combination. If your little Five is planning a quiet night of reading and you arrive home with rent-a-crowd, they'll retreat to the sanctity of their bedroom. You'll be perplexed by their preference for being alone: "Why can't you be more fun? You're young, dammit—you should be enjoying your life." Forcing them to engage isn't a good idea.

They experience you as being intrusive and out of control, and see you as superficial and shallow: "You know nothing about everything." You see them as wasting their lives on irrelevant studies: "Get real. Stop delaying and do something that's going to earn you an income when you're older!"

As you enjoy being the focus of attention, you'll want your child to act as an appreciative audience. They, however, withdraw behind a "Do not disturb" sign, which frustrates you further, causing angry outbursts: "What's your problem?"

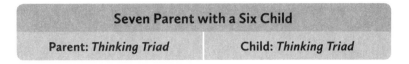

Seven Parent with a Six Child	
Parent: *Thinking Triad*	Child: *Thinking Triad*

What Your Relationship Is About . . .

This can be a great pairing, in which you each bring something to help balance the other. Whereas you escape from your fears through external activities, your Six child scans the horizon for potential dangers and is more anxious. You enjoy the adrenalin rush of risk-taking and adventure, while your child displays caution. Your spontaneity meets their procrastination. While you are confident, your child has issues with self-esteem and self-doubts: "Did I make the right decision to choose Math over Science?"

You both enjoy banter and share a good sense of humor. While you enjoy being the center of attention, your child is happy to be a good, supportive audience. Your child is the more loyal, responsible and hard-working of the two of you, while you bring joy, playfulness, excitement and exuberance to the relationship: "Let's skip class and have a fun day out!"

The exception to this dynamic is if your child is a counterphobic Six, (Sexual Instinctual Drive), as they attempt to go against their fear fixation to prove to themselves that they are not afraid. In that case, your child will be eagerly joining you on that paddling trip down the river rapids or hiking in remote and wild areas.

When You're Getting Stressed . . .

As you assume an optimistic view of life, your child may be frustrated by your seeming inability to acknowledge their fears. Your glass is half full; theirs is half empty. If you try to dissuade them from worrying, it's them who'll believe you're crazy and can't be trusted as a result: "Can't you see this is a real problem? Anything could happen." Your response may be: "Why do you always see the worst-case scenario? You make mountains out of molehills." Be aware that as a fear type, it may be your unconscious, suppressed fears that your child is expressing.

At times you may experience their more conservative, rational outlook as limiting: "Have some fun for once! Learn to be more trusting." To your teenage child, you may seem blind to reality, childish, irresponsible, and unreliable. They want limits; you want freedom from limitations. Their attempts to chastise you won't be well received.

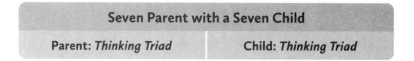

Seven Parent with a Seven Child

Parent: *Thinking Triad*	Child: *Thinking Triad*

What Your Relationship Is About . . .

Hold on to your hats, everybody—this dynamic duo is ready to start the party! If you're in a family with two Sevens, life may be exhausting but never boring. With your extroversion, self-confidence, high energy, drive, positivity, and spontaneous approach to life, neither of you has an "Off" button. You both want everything. (Now.)

Chances are your home will be the cool place to be in your neighborhood. You both love the new and unexplored, and your innovative new ideas will spark other ideas in your child. You're a charismatic team that exudes joy and generosity. You're both happy and you help to make those around you happy too. At an integrated level, you are also both sensitive, appreciative, and able to find joy in the present moment.

You love that your child understands your need for freedom. Together you plan, create, and explore possibilities. You excite each other to live more fulfilled lives. Your child will enjoy not having too many rules and restrictions placed on them.

When You're Getting Stressed . . .

Failures are quickly brushed over: "Problem? What problem?" Both of you want to be the center of attention. Discussions around the dining room table could be a series of attempts to upstage each other.

Little kids are energy-consuming, placing restraints on time and finances. As a result, you may secretly be impatient for your child to grow up fast so you can do fun stuff together. Staying home babysitting when you could be out at a new restaurant with friends doesn't feel like much fun, and parenting can feel like a bad idea as you change yet another nappy. Everyone else seems to be having a good time. You strain at the end of the parenting leash: "I thought this was meant to be fulfilling." Escaping into work, sport, or other activities seems like a good option. Life needs some perking up.

You're both impulsive so may, despite being fear types, engage in activities that involve an adrenalin rush. When you feel like life is becoming too predictable, you may blame the other. You don't engage on a deeper level—but you do engage in rage and becoming increasingly selfish and self-centered. You let each other down: "I know I said I'd come to watch you play, but I got caught up."

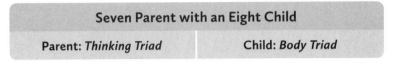

Seven Parent with an Eight Child

| Parent: *Thinking Triad* | Child: *Body Triad* |

What Your Relationship Is About . . .

You both enjoy earthy pleasures and go after what you want with passion and immediacy. Getting your needs met comes easily to both of you. You are both practical, and you engage firmly with the world. Both have a love of life and the energy to match—so adventure and new thrills are appealing to both of you. Together, you're in for an exciting ride!

Neither of you holds back on expressing an opinion. You're both confrontational, and see yourselves as the center of your universes. This can make for big fights when you disagree. Whereas you have a more refined quality, your child tends to be rougher and tougher.

You both make good entrepreneurs. Both of you can be excessive and generous, and may entertain lavishly, irrespective of your financial situation. For you, this may mean getting in caterers or rustling up a gourmet meal. For your child, it can mean blowing their allowance on sweets and sodas for their friends. You like to talk (a lot), entertaining the crowds with tales of your exploits. Your Eight child is quieter and happy to stand on the sidelines while remaining in charge.

Neither of you wants to be controlled by any authorities and both march to the beat of your own drums, being unafraid to push the limits. Neither enjoys limitations or the curtailment of your freedom. While you focus primarily on your own needs, your child wants to protect and care for those close to them, who they see as being weaker than themselves.

When You're Getting Stressed . . .

When disintegrated, you both become self-centered and selfish, but there can only be one sun in your family solar system so conflict is bound to arise. Because you're less straight-talking and direct than your child, you may be accused of beating around the bush, which makes you feel dominated. You attempt to justify yourself through rationalization, but your savvy child sees straight through you. It becomes a clash of your equally strong wills: "You really think you can control me? Yeah, right!" Your resistance invites resistance from your child.

All this energy requires channeling to keep you from turning on each other. It's your child's nature to want to be in charge and they will repeatedly challenge your role as parent. Your child may mock your attempts to remain in control, while you both resort to insults, derision, and ridicule to maintain the upper hand. Things though can go too far and verbal abuse can become physical.

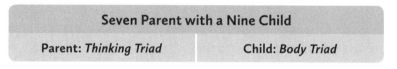

Seven Parent with a Nine Child

| Parent: *Thinking Triad* | Child: *Body Triad* |

What Your Relationship Is About . . .

You are an optimistic, upbeat pair. As a Seven parent, you'll be inspiring your child to explore all manner of extracurriculars, experiences, and activities: "Have you tried the new rock-climbing place across town?" Just as your little Nine has settled into a comfortable routine, you'll be wanting to shake up their world—it's how kids grow and develop, right? As such, you're able to broaden your child's perspective: "If you can dream it, you can do it." Both of you can have broad vision, resulting in a wide spectrum of hobbies and friends.

You allow your child greater freedom than many parents, a trait your autonomous-seeking little Nine will enjoy. You share a sense of humor and may enjoy the banter that comes with telling jokes and seeing the lighter side of things. While you are more energetic and assertive and have greater self-confidence, your child brings a relaxed, listening, steady, gentler, and accepting aspect to your relationship. Be careful that your constant need for activity doesn't exhaust your child.

When You're Getting Stressed . . .

Nines are inclined to ruminate rather than express their feelings directly, and you avoid uncomfortable feelings—so neither of you spend much time focusing inwards. You will quickly gloss over any problems or failures, focusing only on the positives. As a result, conflict is avoided but problems can fester.

Your trait of keeping your options open in case something better comes along meets your child's confusion over what they really want.

Choices can feel overwhelming, so neither of you can reach a decision. Your focus is on what you want to do, while your little Nine will typically merge with you or another family member. If your child has merged with you, neither of you may even be aware that choices are typically focused on your needs, not theirs.

You want to explore everything, while your child enjoys a routine. They can start to feel boring, even limiting, to you, which can be annoying. Where's the fun, stimulating kid you wanted? Yet neither of you are good at discussing problems—you'd rather put a positive spin on things. You both meet in Type One, your Point of Stretch (see page 38) and your child's wing (see page 35), which means you can both become critical. Blame arises. Neither of you owns your responsibility for problems. Your anger fuels your child's ineffectiveness, stubbornness, and indecision. Anxiety arises for both of you, and you may say things you later regret. But your child is so withdrawn, they seem not even to have heard.

19

Type Eight Parents and Their Children

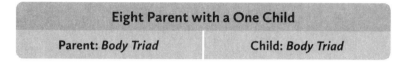

Eight Parent with a One Child	
Parent: *Body Triad*	Child: *Body Triad*

What Your Relationship Is About . . .

At first these two seem very different, yet they share many commonalities. You both believe in justice, fairness, honor, and protecting those you see as being victims. You both rise to the call to make the world a better place—you do so practically, while your child is more idealistic. You are warriors of truth and will make a stand to protect those you love and the community you belong to. It's the reason you were born.

You make the rules but seldom stick to them. Although Ones also make rules, for them it's more about abiding by them and insisting that others do too. You may encourage your One child to break some rules (just not your rules!): "Cut class and come surfing with me!"

Your child focuses on details while you see the bigger picture. Your child sees themselves as being good while you feel badass. Your child is restrictive and upholds the law; in going against society, you feel free and lawless. Little Ones will want to contain their anger, while you have no trouble raging. Both of you have a sense of purpose driving you to work hard, but whereas Eights believe in playing hard, Ones can simply move on to another task.

While Eights are robust and earthy, Ones tend to be more idealistic and airy. Both are strong-willed and both want to be right. Whereas Ones practice self-restraint even when younger, Eights go after life with a lusty passion.

When You're Getting Stressed . . .

A clash of wills happens as a result of you both seeing yourselves as taking the lead. Both want to be in charge—your child in a cooler, more controlled manner that sets an example to others and you with an innate sense of authority: "It's my way or the highway, kiddo!" As your child pushes harder to gain control (because Ones know the right way to do things even when they are young), you push back. Yet they gain your respect for standing up for themselves.

Little Ones can start seeing their brash parent as embarrassing and may even try to keep them away from school or social functions: "You're not meant to behave like that, Mom." They may attempt to criticize—let's just say that won't end well. Ones have repressed their anger. Seeing you launch into an attack, they at last feel entitled to retaliate. As your child reacts, so you act out more. For a One teen in front of friends, this can be mortifying.

You see your child as inflexible and self-righteous: "Won't you just lighten up a bit? You should be out there having fun and enjoying life as I did when I was your age." Sometimes expressing their anger towards each other becomes the way they feel most connected.

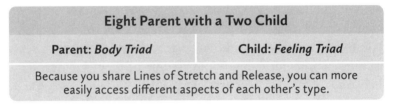

Eight Parent with a Two Child

Parent: *Body Triad*	Child: *Feeling Triad*

Because you share Lines of Stretch and Release, you can more easily access different aspects of each other's type.

What Your Relationship Is About . . .

With this combination, the archetypal "father" (fire) meets the archetypal "mother" (water). On the Enneagram symbol, the Eight moves against the Two and the Two moves towards the Eight. Eights demand attention while Twos give and please, hoping it'll get them attention. This translates as the parent ruling and the child pleasing, which can work really well provided the child is acknowledged. Eights love being the center of their child's world and enjoy attention (as do Twos)—being the focus of their nurturing child's world feels good. In helping the parent, the child receives protection and strong support.

Twos represent the disowned childlike aspect of Eights or their shadow, which has to do with being needy, gentle, and vulnerable. The actual Two child can represent the disowned aspects of the Eight adult. Both can be tender, generous, and warm. Little Twos may try to win over a parent by being "daddy's little princess" or "mommy's little helper."

There's likely to be friendly verbal banter and physical affection between these two, which both enjoy. Powerful Eights can become more loving when they move to their Two aspect, while in moving to their Eight aspect, a Two child can step into their power and claim their own needs. They can express their gentler, often hidden sides with each other. They "get" each other and know that even if they do clash, it'll quickly be over and forgotten. Sometimes their connection can feel threatening to the other parent, depending on their type. In feeling supported by their parent, young Twos can more easily nurture others unconditionally.

When You're Getting Stressed ...

Whereas Eights are straight-talking, Twos are inclined to skirt around their needs and issues. An Eight parent can be frustrated if they feel they are being manipulated—if their firm "no" becomes distorted into some sort of "yes," or if their child blames them for something they feel they didn't do or mean.

Both want to rule and dominate the other, although this is more obvious in the Eight parent. A Two child, particularly a daughter, can become coquettish in order to soften the parent—another form of manipulation.

The child wants to help the parent and the parent wants the child to help themselves, but the loving connection gets broken as the parent toughens up. Trust has been lost. The child who was idealized can become seen as weak and insincere, the parent viewed as uncompromising and controlling. The parent feels smothered and autonomy is lost, which creates resistance.

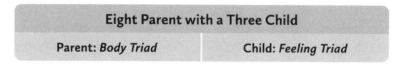

Eight Parent with a Three Child

Parent: *Body Triad*	Child: *Feeling Triad*

What Your Relationship Is About ...

You and your child share many similarities: you both know the meaning of working hard to achieve an end, you're not afraid to confront injustice, you're both generally charismatic in groups, and shine when you're the center of attention. You'll step into the arena of life together, getting what you want from life, and earning each other's respect as you do.

You can't help but notice the confident and accomplished young Three and the Eight parent who exudes an air of "I'm in charge here." Both Threes and Eights are comfortable confronting or going against others. In standing up for themselves, little Threes earn their parent's respect. Where they differ is that Threes want to please and impress others, whereas Eights are more focused on pleasing themselves.

Both parent and child tend to be competitive. Typically, though, your bond means that your competitive spirits are focused on others. You take personal pride in seeing your child achieve and shine their light brightly: "That's my Sarah—she just took the opportunity and ran with it!" It feels good to raise a child who can stand on their own two feet and the young Three is the perfect pupil for you to school toward success.

While you naturally rise to be in charge, your child can easily do so if the situation arises. Both of you tend to brush over any failures and quickly change course in a new direction. You enjoy supporting your child and feel their support in your endeavors, although your child would prefer to claim success as entirely theirs. You are able to see beyond the external success of your child and love them for who they are.

When You're Getting Stressed . . .

When overworked, stressed Threes start to show their inauthenticity by lying about achievements, presenting a false image, or covering up failures. Eight parents may lose trust, which is a big issue for an Eight. Instead of being mutually supportive, you may find yourself starting to compete: "You're no great shakes. I'd made my first million at thirty."

You can become more controlling, checking up on your child: "Is he really where he said he was going? Let me drive past the house to see." Eights increasingly see their child as an extension of themselves, instead of having their own needs and desires: "What I say happens. Understood?" "Shape up or ship out!" The child feels belittled, particularly if the conversation happens in front of friends: "You humiliated me! Nothing I do is ever good enough for you."

"You lied to me!"

"What was I supposed to do when you keep me under lock and chain? I want my own life!"

Neither is inclined to discuss their feelings or to show any vulnerability.

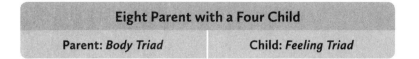

Eight Parent with a Four Child	
Parent: *Body Triad*	Child: *Feeling Triad*

What Your Relationship Is About . . .

To bold, brave Eights whose vulnerable side is seldom seen, young Fours can feel like exotic, fragile creatures. Your child can experience you as an awe-inspiring protector. Naturally elegant and refined, creative Fours can have their brash parent wondering how they bred such sophistication.

Fours are introspective, wanting to withdraw into their own fantasy world. Eights want to take on the world. Neither is prepared to follow accepted social norms, so they form a team: "We'll do this our way. We don't care what others think." You rule by taking action while your child rules emotionally—both of you can learn from the other. Raging Eights meet the child who is deeply connected to their feelings. Eights want action while Fours want depth.

As an Eight, you're intuitive and attuned to the motivations of others, while Fours tend towards being more attuned to themselves. Eights offer little Fours protection while Fours give Eights intensity and the challenge of raising a mysterious child. This relationship seldom runs on an even keel, but that's what parent and child enjoy and admire about each other: "At least my dad's not boring!" This relationship is going to be volatile, particularly during the teenage years, but deeply loving nevertheless. In this dynamic dance of fire and water, you find a child willing to walk into the blaze with you, creating the intensity you enjoy. You both want a reaction from the other. In throwing a hissy fit, your child ignites your anger, but both of you feel more alive as a result.

Eights may be blunt, but their emotions feel large and real to your child: "Here's authenticity. Dad is for real." The Eight parent is like a rock in a Four rainstorm. As the child moves towards you and then backs away, you stand firm. You understand the dance and the dynamics.

When You're Getting Stressed . . .

This duo reveals the opposite sides of the same neurosis, especially when it comes to anger. Eights take their anger outwards. Fours internalize, and their repressed aggression tends towards depression. Eights are the fire while Fours are the water. Eights want to express their will while Fours want to express their individuality. There's a good chance that these needs will be in conflict at times. Neither of you wants to be controlled by the other. If you begin to treat your child as an extension of yourself by objectifying them, they will react strongly. Regular fights can become the way of relating, and it may become common to draw other family members into the fray: "Are you with me or against me?" It can be an exciting and intense way to live. Emotional storms can create a cycle of arguments, anger, acting out, vengeance, and truces before something sparks the process up again.

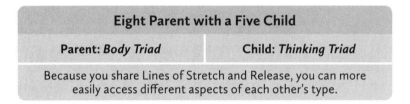

Eight Parent with a Five Child	
Parent: *Body Triad*	Child: *Thinking Triad*
Because you share Lines of Stretch and Release, you can more easily access different aspects of each other's type.	

What Your Relationship Is About . . .

This combination of two very different personalities can complement each other in many ways. Each represents the hidden desires or aspects of the other. You feel naturally protective of your introverted, intelligent child. They admire your confidence, competence, and power in the world.

Both of you can be antisocial, although in different ways. Both have firm boundaries and are independent. Fives are head-centered while Eights are body-centered.

Eights want to engage. Fives need to detach. You may find it hard to understand a child whose interests are academic: "Get outside and play some ball!" Yet you learn from each other's strengths—your child learns to be more in the world and connected to their bodies, while you learn to be more introspective and to think before acting. Young Fives will admire their parent's intensity and straightforwardness, while the parent admires their child's curiosity and questioning mind.

Fives aim to limit their needs and dependence on all things. Eights, on the other hand, lust after all life has to offer. So, it's a case of "less is more" (Five) and "more is more" (Eight). Neither of you wants to be dependent on another person.

When You're Getting Stressed . . .

Both Fives and Eights are self-focused—their own needs take precedence. Fives are the most introverted or withdrawn Enneagram type, and Eights are the most assertive. This means your child may feel insecure and afraid in your powerful presence. (Eights are often unaware of how imposing they can be.)

While Fives like to mull over events and feelings before arriving at a conclusion, Eights are immediate and want answers now. Eights push energy into situations, but this can drain your Five child. The parent needs to learn to hold back, but this can be as frustrating as when the child is put on the spot, becoming uncooperative: "No, I won't!" The Eight shifts away: "I've had him! I don't give a damn anymore!"

When under pressure, young Fives withdraw and become secretive and more introverted while you become more aggressive. Fives like to argue, Eights to fight, so a lot of sparring can occur. As the tempo increases, little Fives may become terrified and feel overwhelmed. You may feel your child is a wimp because they can't confront you directly and are inclined to back down.

Fives will become dismissive; Eights will reject and may become punitive: "I'm not going to let you waste my money studying. Get yourself a job." Fives become cynical: "What, and end up like you, bright spark?"

Eight Parent with a Six Child	
Parent: *Body Triad*	Child: *Thinking Triad*

What Your Relationship Is About . . .

This can be a strong bond, with you providing the strength, security, and safety your child wants and needs—your insecure child loves feeling protected. In return, you enjoy their warmth, playfulness, and the hero status they award you. Both of you have trust issues and enjoy being able to rely on the other for support: "Together we stand." Your child's loyalty helps build your trust. You can become fiercely protective of your child, while they see you as a powerful ally in a hazardous, erratic world.

You both knuckle down and get on with a job, taking responsibility for getting it done. Both of you can fill the role of hero or heroine, over-coming fear to find courage. Your child is more sensitive and can draw out your softer, more vulnerable side. Your child's humor and creativity encourages you to lighten up and enjoy life more.

Sixes sometimes struggle to make decisions and can lack confidence. Having an Eight parent encourages them to become more decisive and assertive. Both of you can take on the role of rebel—Sixes against authority figures and Eights against the world in general.

When You're Getting Stressed...

When stressed, your child becomes more reactive and defensive, while you become tougher and more brazen. Like dogs in a corner, you both attack, and can offend to defend. In this relationship, the parent definitely rules the roost, but Sixes (particularly counterphobic Sixes, who go against fear) can push back hard to show they won't be ruled. You circle each other looking for a weakness. Phobic, fearful Sixes will do what dogs do when under attack—lie down to show they've submitted: "No threat here, see." Like Nines, they can become passive-aggressive and stubborn.

Eights should be careful not to make their child an extension of themselves, accepting that they have their own needs and desires. What you perceive as a weakness, such as their cautiousness, can be a strength.

Sensing weakness, which is something you fear, Eights may belittle a child: "Not much fight in you, is there?" Not being able to fight, and seeing their security under attack, young Sixes may take flight. Trust, that fundamental need for both types, has been lost.

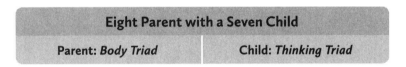

Eight Parent with a Seven Child	
Parent: *Body Triad*	Child: *Thinking Triad*

What Your Relationship Is About...

You're an assertive, energetic, adventurous, independent pair, who lives life to the full. Neither of you enjoys rules, or being controlled or limited in any way. Instant gratification works well for you both: "Let's get a burger with all the trimmings... Now!"

As you're both generous, your child will be organizing events that you happily fund. Your child loves the buzz of social interaction. While they assume center-stage by recounting (exaggerated) tales, your presence is sufficient to let everyone know who's in charge. I've seen Eight parents take kids out to eat after a sports match. They don't just include a friend, but the whole team! Little Sevens will love the juice and energy that Eights bring to their world.

You're both spontaneous, so an idea is followed by action. Eights take pride in seeing their quick-witted, entrepreneurial child live life in the fast lane. You both want to be self-supporting—being tied to a desk and being checked by a boss doesn't work for either of you. You both get a rush from taking risks and seeing it work.

Your child brings excitement, upbeat humor, and fun to you, while you support and encourage their endeavors. Whereas you can be quite silent as you sum up a situation or person, young Sevens seldom stop talking, livening up any social event. You both are self-referencing and both of you have very strong opinions. When it comes to these clashing, neither of you shy away from confrontation; although you're the more aggressive.

When You're Getting Stressed . . .

You share Type Five as your Point of Stretch or Release (see page 39). Here you can both detach from feelings and problems. Neither of you feels comfortable, but whereas your child escapes dealing with painful feelings through activity, you want to deal with adversity head on rather than admit you feel hurt. Both of you can be extremely belligerent.

Problems can arise if either sees the other as limiting their freedom or options: "If it weren't for you!" The trouble increases if you, becoming increasingly stressed, become more controlling, limiting your child's independence. "Think you're the boss of me? Think again," the little Seven shouts. You respond with: "It's my way or the highway. You're just a kid. Try living without the allowance I give you!"

As much as you try to control your child, they will find ways to free themselves. By now, both are totally self-focused and selfish, objectifying the other. You see the other as an extension of yourself. Verbal fights can become physical as you barge your way through each other's lives. You typically have the upper hand. Another parent may have to intervene as the potential for violence becomes the only form of communication.

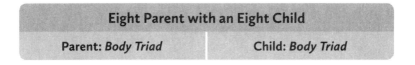

Eight Parent with an Eight Child	
Parent: *Body Triad*	Child: *Body Triad*

What Your Relationship Is About . . .

Two strong-willed, volatile types who aren't afraid of confrontation could spell a rocky relationship. That would be the case when they are under stress (disintegrated), but when more integrated, you make a dynamic parent–child pair.

When you two walk into a room, everyone is going to notice. Your energy and vitality literally fill the space. You have probably spent much of your life frustrated at not having your energy met—but here's a child to do just that. Going up against something solid is stimulating for you, and allows you to drop your guard and show a softer, more vulnerable side. It's fire meets fire: "At last, in Jim I've met my match!"

Together, you've got things under control. Should your child misbehave, they'll have you backing them up. If you decide to go into business together, you can build an empire, each fiercely supportive of the other: "The family can rely on us."

When disagreements arise, they're sorted out directly, and both of you move on quickly. There is mutual respect—like a commander and his courageous lieutenant taking on the world. Both of you are doers who think on your feet. It helps if you both have your own space in the house, as you can be territorial. Your child benefits from feeling that their room is their territory, and no parent is going to invade their space.

When You're Getting Stressed . . .

In a younger child, the parent may laugh off much of the Eight's competitiveness, and take pride in their child's bravado. But as the child gets older it becomes a much more serious breach of trust: "You've betrayed me. No one betrays me and gets away with it."

The young dog and the older one begin to fight for control of the family pack. What was once a fun cycle ride together becomes a fiercely fought competition. Egos come to the fore, and neither of you backs down. Both of you want control of the other.

When under pressure, all the attributes that cemented this relationship become weapons of war. When an Eight father and son started a business together, all went well until it came time for a large payout. The stepmother got involved, and the dispute ended in the high court with the son winning the battle. Determined not to be seen to have lost, the father quickly liquidated the business, handing over the assets to his wife rather than paying what was due. The son lost absolutely everything, and it was an empty and cashless victory for the father, who lost a successful business. There is little chance of reconciliation between them.

The parent will do whatever they can to maintain their leadership role, and the constant fighting becomes exhausting.

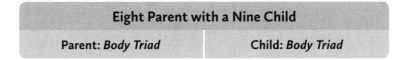

Eight Parent with a Nine Child	
Parent: *Body Triad*	Child: *Body Triad*

What Your Relationship Is About . . .

No matter their sex, Eights assume the role of an archetypal protecting male and Nines the archetypal nurturing female. In this way, both "parent" the other. Essentially, in this duo you have a warrior with a peacemaker—just as they broker peace in the family, you can disrupt it.

You bring excitement and energy to the relationship with your receptive, calm, and laid-back child. To them, you represent the confidence, decisive, and energetic qualities they can feel they lack. Merging with you makes them feel stronger. You enjoy having a calm place to rest before the next storm. With your accepting child, you can drop your guard and expose the softer side of yourself. There's little fear of being challenged.

In some aspects, you represent polar opposites of each other. While both are anger types, you take your anger into the world, while your child steers away from confrontation in fear of disturbing the peace. Although you're both action-centered types and thus fiery, the Nine's more passive approach becomes water to soothe your fire.

Eights assert themselves and need to be in charge. A child gravitates towards the protective presence of the strong leader with great admiration: "My dad's the boss of bosses. He can do anything he wants!" As much as the child looks to the parent for support, so the parent will enjoy being admired.

As an Eight, you're unpretentious. Although your child appears easy-going, when pushed Nines can show the resistance and willpower equal to their parent, particularly if they have a strong Eight-wing (see page 35).

When You're Getting Stressed . . .

Like Fours and Fives, Nines tend to withdraw under pressure while Eights (like Sevens and Threes) tend to confront. Under pressure, the Eight parent gets more reactive, aggressive, and confrontational. Nines resent being controlled and objectified, so will withdraw and become less able to communicate to the point of becoming unresponsive. This drives the Eight to greater anger—it's like fighting an absent opponent.

Eights express their anger. Nines want peace so they largely internalize it, which is frustrating for the Eight, who wants open war. The parent becomes more controlling and frighteningly aggressive. The child resists by being passive-aggressive. Eights communicate their anger directly, while Nines obfuscate. Both point fingers at the other: "If it wasn't for them . . ." The hero has fallen.

20

Type Nine Parents
and Their Children

Nine Parent with a One Child	
Parent: *Body Triad*	Child: *Body Triad*
Because you share Lines of Stretch and Release, you can more easily access different aspects of each other's type.	

What Your Relationship Is About . . .

You make for a complementary pair, particularly if your wing is your child's type and vice versa. You'll share a love of order and the need to do things correctly. You both focus your attention on others—you from a position of nurturing, your child from a sense of higher purpose. With your easy, accepting nature, you help your child to judge themselves less harshly: "You're wonderful just the way you are." Both of you can be idealistic, striving for a better world, although while you daydream about how to create it, your child is working hard to implement it.

When it comes to the question "What should we do today?" you consider all options and can get bogged down by choice. Your child may be afraid that they'll choose the wrong option, so they delay. Nothing gets decided, yet your child will expect you as the parent to make the decision. That's what parents do, right? In all likelihood, though, it will be the child who finally makes the decision, and you'll accept it.

Both child and parent will enjoy daily routines and family interaction. Both are comfortable with things that don't change too much. Your child may be inclined to boss you into what they believe is the correct way to do something: "Mom, you're not cutting the paper straight."

When You're Getting Stressed . . .

Although you are both in the Body (anger) Triad, neither of you enjoys openly engaging in fights or expressing anger, albeit for different reasons—you because you want to maintain peace and your child because it's not the "right" way to behave. Both of you may ruminate over some hurt and then suddenly explode. You'll both then withdraw—the Nine to sulk and the One in indignation or resentment.

You may clash over what each understands to be correct or perfect. You often simply accept your child's criticism rather than call them out on it: "Maybe they're right?" Your child finds criticism hard to accept because it implies that they're not perfect. The parent's inability to confront a problem and seek ways to solve it can make an older One child judge the parent as inept and weak. You may withdraw and act as if everything is fine when it's clearly not.

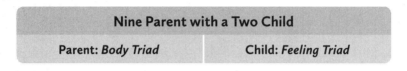

Nine Parent with a Two Child	
Parent: *Body Triad*	Child: *Feeling Triad*

What Your Relationship Is About . . .

Both of you are helpful, good nurturers, and other-focused. You enjoy entertaining (in your case only if it's not too much work) and want friends to feel relaxed and comfortable in your home. Nine parents will welcome their child's friends and will be supportive of their child's desire to engage with others. Your child needs to feel wanted, and you provide the steady love and acceptance they're after. In turn, you enjoy their desire to help you—it makes you feel acknowledged and that your presence matters.

You're both optimistic and want to avoid uncomfortable emotional issues. In assuming the role of Little Helper, your little Two merges with your needs. As a Nine parent, you may find that merging with your child becomes the purpose of your life. Both of you are affectionate and enjoy the sensual things in life. You both enjoy homemaking, baking together to make cookies for friends and family, or making craft items as gifts. Both will enjoy the comfort of a much-loved pet and a warm and loving environment. You're happy to be in each other's company.

When You're Getting Stressed . . .

Typically, you won't want to do too much disciplining as it upsets the peace, while your child won't want to be "bad" and therefore less likely to be loved. From that perspective you won't clash, but when it comes to who holds the power in the relationship, Twos can easily slide into their Eight aspect and start dominating: "Mom just doesn't understand how to do this properly, so I have to help her." As in the Nine–One combination, roles can get reversed, with little Twos calling the shots. Your child may feel that you haven't shown sufficient appreciation for all the "good" they have done and feel hurt and unloved as a result. When Nines numb out, it can feel like a devastating rejection for a young Two: "You don't care!" They want to force a response from you. As they demand attention, you may feel your autonomy is being threatened and will withdraw further.

The road back to togetherness is for the parent to take some time for their own needs and for the young Two to understand that all parents need time alone, and that this doesn't equate to rejection. You can try to find a balance between both of your needs: "After I get back from having my haircut, you and I can make fudge together. That will be fun, right?"

Nine Parent with a Three Child	
Parent: *Body Triad*	Child: *Feeling Triad*
Because you share Lines of Stretch and Release, you can more easily access different aspects of each other's type.	

What Your Relationship Is About . . .

Nine parents provide the safe springboard from which little Threes can leap into stardom, becoming the little hero or heroine of the family. You're both optimistic, and you both enjoy the comforts of life. Both of you appreciate hard work. Little Threes are self-motivating when it comes to school projects, which takes pressure off the parent to impose homework discipline. Your ability to nurture and relax means that your child has an ideal background to support their endeavors. You aren't in competition. You want your child to succeed, even if it involves sacrificing your free time to lift or financially support them.

When you move to your Point of Stretch at Three (see page 38), you are able to communicate your needs, display more self-confidence, and focus on what's really important to you. Your child's Point of Stretch at Nine teaches them collaboration and the ability to let go and enjoy pastimes unrelated to work.

The Nine's acceptance helps a young Three to value themselves, inside and out. Having a parent who accepts them at face value allows them, at least at home, to truly be themselves. This is a huge benefit for a child who often feels they need to focus on having a successful exterior image.

You easily praise your child, which a Three will especially enjoy. You both easily gloss over any of your child's perceived failures: "C'mon, there's another opportunity. You can try that if you want." Threes also enjoy being the center of attention: "Come and watch me in my play, Mom!" Nines will happily indulge them.

When You're Getting Stressed . . .

Although Threes sit in the Feeling Triad, they can struggle to connect with their emotions. Having a parent who gets distracted or who withdraws emotionally can make your child feel unheard, experiencing you as being uncaring. You can experience your child as being too demanding. While the parent becomes too permissive, young Threes may act out and can seem spoilt. You can merge with your child's successes, believing that your role in life is to simply be their devoted supporter, rather than find your own personal fulfillment. You may feel that your child is achieving much of what you were unable to achieve, and so you live vicariously through them.

Threes like to be kept busy, but less healthy and therefore less energetic Nines may find this tiring. While Nines tend to withdraw from conflict, Threes are more confrontational, though not to the same extent as an Eight. So while, in fact, little Threes may not be averse to fault finding, they will often find excuses to leave a playground fight. You will need to be more assertive to maintain the parent–child dynamic.

Threes represent the shadow aspect of Nines—those aspects that are not acknowledged at a less integrated level. Within you is a little Three who wants attention, to show off, and to be recognized. The opposite of the self-abnegating Nine that the world sees is ambition and a desire to succeed no matter what the cost. Depending on their integration, Nines will either be able to acknowledge their inner and actual Three child, or attempt to reject both.

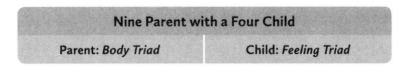

Nine Parent with a Four Child	
Parent: *Body Triad*	Child: *Feeling Triad*

What Your Relationship Is About . . .

Because both the Nine and the Four tend to withdraw, you're both happy to spend time alone or working on projects separately but in the same room. Fours fear being abandoned, but the Nine parent will offer the steady assurance that they are going nowhere. This can be hugely comforting to a little Four. You're a good listener who is in tune with your sensitive child's needs. Likewise, your child may ask "What's the matter, Mom?" when you thought you were hiding your hurt or anger well.

One of the biggest pluses in this pairing is that both of you are very creative. You will happily encourage a love of the arts in your child, understanding their need to explore their creativity. Nines are great storytellers so can make a little Four feel special by creating bedtime stories especially for them. Your child appreciates your presence, where others may overlook it.

Both of you want to be seen and acknowledged, and you appreciate each other's need and desire for connection. Fours battle with acceptance, but Nines offer just that—so, when a teenage Four climbs into your bed to discuss some heartfelt issue, you provide a nonjudgmental space for them to impart their innermost feelings. This pairing often has a deep understanding of the other and can have mutual empathy: "I get that this hurts you."

When You're Getting Stressed . . .

Fours get explosive under pressure, and can become very demanding. They'll be frustrated by their Nine parent who zones out, making them feel unheard—or worse still, ignored. This can cause a young Four to brood or lash out: "You don't love me!"

Your child may feel your chilled vibe is more boring than cool, while their volatility suggests that they live life with intensity. A young Four may envy other children whose parent seems more trendy or exciting: "If only you were more like Kurt's dad . . ."

To a Nine who makes very few demands, your child's "I want it!" can feel precocious and spoilt. Your Four child may have a tendency to pull you towards them only to push you away. It is confusing for such an even-keeled parent to feel worshiped one day and rejected the next, particularly when they can't see what they've done wrong. A Nine's patience and tolerance should see them through any ups and downs in the relationship.

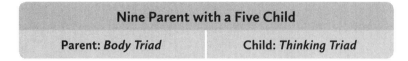

Nine Parent with a Five Child

| Parent: *Body Triad* | Child: *Thinking Triad* |

What Your Relationship Is About . . .

Your optimism balances your child's pessimistic outlook. A little Five is less upbeat and more uptight in comparison with their easy-going Nine parent. For intense little Fives, this place of loving acceptance can be a wonderfully comforting space in which to relax—something the outside world seldom allows. Your warmth and ability to listen will help your child open up and connect with their feelings. Both of you have an off-beat sense of humor that will help you through tough times.

Your being natural and spontaneous encourages your child to come out of their shell—but both of you are inclined to stand outside the party group rather than be the center of attention. Your child may be happy to observe a parent's project if they find it interesting, such as repairing and dismantling a computer. Both of you enjoy time alone and won't place too many demands on the other. You both enjoy the space, particularly as your child gets older and wants to focus on their own projects. You can happily work alongside each other, both appreciating the noninvasive company. This is when your best communication happens—nonverbally, with you both feeling comfortable.

When You're Getting Stressed . . .

As they reach their teens, Fives can adopt some outlandish habits, such as not wanting to wash their hair because it "self-cleans," or housing an imposing collection of spiders or graphic novels. You'll tolerate this and be happy to debate the issue. What does push a Nine parent's buttons is when a child they have merged with withdraws from them. They will feel profoundly hurt—as if they've lost their role in life. This is why it's important that Nines find their own purpose in life and don't make their child their sole focus.

Fives don't enjoy having expectations placed on them, so a parent making "helpful suggestions" seldom works. The Five's belief in their superior intellect can have them criticizing a parent they view as being less smart than they are: "You know nothing!" A little Five may enjoy challenging a Nine parent's belief systems, knowing they're unlikely to retaliate. Yet, because both dislike real conflict, if this becomes extreme the parent will numb out and the child will detach. Nothing happens but an underlying current of animosity, while everything seems okay on the surface.

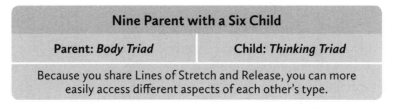

Nine Parent with a Six Child	
Parent: *Body Triad*	Child: *Thinking Triad*
Because you share Lines of Stretch and Release, you can more easily access different aspects of each other's type.	

What Your Relationship Is About . . .

You two "get" each other. Sixes move to Nines to become more playful, less reactive, and more relaxed; Nines move to Six to be able to voice opinions, take a stand, and reduce their fears of being overlooked. This two-way movement helps each to understand the other. Both enjoy routines and stability and the security and comfort of home: "When James was a toddler, he hated traveling. It really upset him to have his routine disrupted." The Nine's calm can be hugely beneficial to this wary child: "At least I'm safe with Mom."

Six kids will happily help around the home, provided you or their siblings are also pulling your weight. They won't enjoy having instructions yelled at them while you relax in front of the TV. Both of you feel that together you make a stronger team than when you are alone. Your child may question your decisions and can enjoy a debate around them. You two also share a somewhat self-diminishing sense of humor and may enjoy private jokes.

When You're Getting Stressed . . .

Trying to coerce little Sixes to do tasks such as homework can have the opposite effect: their resistance to authority arises and a young rebel may emerge. Like stubborn Nines, Sixes can dig in their heels, refusing to co-operate. It's best to work with them: "What will happen if you don't pass this test?" The idea of the consequences typically allows Six children to self-motivate.

Both of you can remain silent about issues that are upsetting you—you both want the other to seek you out to find out what the problem is. Sixes may move from reactive defiance to guilt. Neither of you enjoys confrontation because it threatens your security, yet both can explode with pent-up anger. As a Nine myself, I found that this approach worked best with my Six child: I'd say, "I feel you're angry about something?" and then listen to what he said. This went a long way to broker peace. I did not always agree with him—and I would say that—but getting things off his chest soothed troubled waters.

At its best, this combination supports each other, but when under pressure both may wait for the other to take the initiative. Nines hang back unsure of what to do while Sixes have doubts about what to do. Both procrastinate: "You're not tidying your room, Mom, so why should I tidy mine?" This can be particularly apparent if there has been some disagreement. Who will make the first move back to peace?

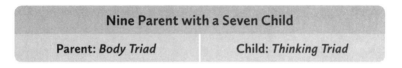

Nine Parent with a Seven Child

| Parent: *Body Triad* | Child: *Thinking Triad* |

What Your Relationship Is About . . .

Both types are upbeat and enjoy socializing and participating in school and other activities. Friends are welcome to come over to play. Your Seven child stimulates you to take action, to do more, and to move out of your cozy comfort zones. From making new friends to trying out new sports or hobbies, your child will lead the way: "Have you ever surfed, Dad? Come surf with me!" In this way, the Seven is good for the Nine, who might otherwise not have been so adventurous. In the role of parent, the Nine's more empathetic and nurturing style works well for the little Seven, better perhaps than if the types were reversed, because you provide a steady platform from which little Sevens can launch themselves into the world.

Whereas Sevens can be demanding and self-referencing, Nines are happy to take a back seat and give up what they want for the sake of pleasing and indulging their children. You happily merge with your fun-loving, confident, energetic, and assertive child, who allows you to feel more seen in the world, even if only as "Callum's dad." You bring warmth and a gentler approach.

Neither of you enjoys dwelling on uncomfortable feelings or going too deeply into issues, and both tend to gloss over any failures or unpleasant situations. You're happy to play the fool and have fun together—at your child's instigation, baking cupcakes could well turn into a decorate-your-face-with-frosting event. Like little Threes, Seven children love to be the center of attention. Nine parents happily allow them to assume this role—and can be relied on for an audience.

When You're Getting Stressed . . .

For you, your child's constant need to be active can feel exhausting and as if your autonomy is being lost in continual demands: "I just want to relax with a book, Sid, why can't you entertain yourself?" The sloth meets the little busy monkey: you enjoy the comfort of a routine, while they want to shake things up with new possibilities. When you get angry, you seldom show it except for an occasional explosion—but afterward you feel bad for destroying the peace.

With the Nine and Seven, the need to withdraw meets the desire to confront. You both avoid pain—you by numbing out or avoiding dealing with an issue (perhaps by throwing yourself into work) and your child by creating new plans and keeping busy. Neither of you wants to really deal with anything negative—sliding smoothly over the surface feels better. Underneath, though, there may be criticism and blame leveled at the other. You may be wary of reigning in your child for fear of confrontation: "You've taken away my freedom!" As a result of avoiding the word "no," Nine parents may indulge rather than discipline.

To get attention, your child can become increasingly impulsive and risk-taking, climbing trees that are too high or riding their bike too fast. If you don't react, they become increasingly frustrated and insecure—because deep down, Sevens are fear types wanting to feel safe.

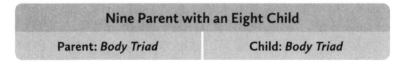

Nine Parent with an Eight Child	
Parent: *Body Triad*	Child: *Body Triad*

What Your Relationship Is About . . .

The Eight child will naturally lead the way in this relationship. They demand that their needs be met. You're generally happy to go along with those demands and support your child. You enjoy merging with their confidence, courage, and energy—traits you find desirable. Your child brings a sense of excitement and an ability to live life to its fullest to your more conservative and steady approach.

There is a story about a large naval ship who comes across what they presume is another vessel in thick fog. They are on a collision course, so the ship repeatedly commands the other vessel to give way. It does not change course—instead the message comes through that they are, in fact, a lighthouse. In this duo, the force of the ship (Eight) meets the immovable lighthouse (Nine). It is energy versus inertia: rage expressed quickly and actively versus rage (mostly) contained or suppressed through passive aggression.

Eights have difficulty relaxing their guard and exploring the softer side of themselves but will find this easier to do with such an unconfrontational, easy-going, and accepting parent. There's little danger of them being attacked or caught off guard. It's the warrior child with the peacemaker parent: the parent teaching the child how to make peace and the child teaching the parent how to be more assertive in the world.

When You're Getting Stressed . . .
Little Eights want the feeling that their parent will stand against them—when they clash and confront, they want to know they'll encounter a solid force. A Nine's inclination to withdraw and be there but not actually there may mean the Eight becomes frustrated: "You're not supporting me." They want to feel that you're right behind them as they go into battle.

It's infuriating when fire meets stagnant water. Eights need straight talk. If you as a parent can't say it like it is, they're going to get frustrated and act out. You're perceived as putting a damper on their fun ideas and plans. They may start to give orders to their "wimpy" parent, who responds by . . . well, not responding. In order to avoid confrontation, you become overly permissive—your child, however, needs to hear you say "no."

They may ignore the rules themselves yet expect you to follow them. You certainly won't enjoy your autonomy being threatened by a bossy, belligerent, badly behaved child. Childlike, you may refuse to be accountable for problems in the relationship: "Problem? What problem?" You bury your head in the sand and avoid dealing with inappropriate behavior: "He's just letting off a bit of steam."

The Eight child can view their parent as being ineffectual—this makes them feel vulnerable, which Eights don't enjoy. Your child may look for a stronger role model, or home may become a battleground of opposing wills, with other family members drawn in to take sides. As they attempt to dominate you, you dig in your heels—suddenly you're not the pushover they expected. Both blame each other for the impasse.

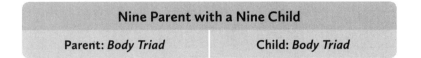

Nine Parent with a Nine Child	
Parent: *Body Triad*	Child: *Body Triad*

What Your Relationship Is About . . .

Both you and your child enjoy a comfortable, peaceful routine. In your relaxed way, you make friends welcome in your home—nothing is too much of a problem. Both of you are tolerant and patient with each other. You'll enjoy a comforting routine: "Wednesday is pizza night, and on Fridays we play a board game and then get a burger and fries at Dave's Diner." A little adventure will go a long way to keep both of you happy—nothing too scary, mind!

After a disagreement, both of you forgive each other easily. You are both creative and will enjoy crafting pastimes and telling each other stories. There's usually a calm and relaxed atmosphere in your home that you both enjoy.

You have many of the characteristics that make for a great parent: patience, acceptance, good listening skills, and the ability to nurture and be affectionate. You have few expectations and are unflappable in a crisis: "My toddler pulled down a heater and chopped off his toe. It was okay, though—I wrapped it in ice, gathered up my older child, and drove to the hospital, where they sewed the toe back on."

When You're Getting Stressed . . .

Your Instinctual Types and wings will create differences between you, but this pair is going to be happy to get along while avoiding any nasty confrontations. Parent and child may merge so that neither really knows their own likes, desires, or opinions: "Where do I begin and where do you end?" Because their needs are so intertwined, neither knows what they want or feels as if they have their own identity—yet not being seen for yourself can cause a huge amount of anger and pain. You may even mimic each other's mannerisms, if not your looks.

Nine parents want everyone in the family to be happy but both of you have the ability to get lost in the mundane. What could rock the blissful Nine boat is a sibling or other parent who changes the peaceful status quo. Both Nines could feel their world is being threatened and may comply to keep the peace, yet subtly try to sabotage the new suggestion.

When it comes to planning what to do and making decisions, you both expect the other to take the lead. There are so many options: "Invite a friend to play, go to the park, watch TV . . ." Both of you hang back, hoping the other will decide. That way, if things don't work out, it won't be your fault.

Both may idealize the other and be resentful when reality strikes. Nothing is said and nothing appears wrong, but anger boils under the surface and both withdraw.

NOTE: For more information on the triads mentioned under each parent/child type, i.e., Thinking, Feeling, and Body types, see page 32.

Afterword

As you no doubt know, the job of being a parent can be the most rewarding undertaking of your life. It can equally be the most daunting and challenging. One moment you're cuddling your cute little bundle of potential genius and the next you're wondering what planet this teen dripping with attitude is from. In our family we chuckle when each grandmother attributes any of their grandchildren's seemingly negative traits as being "from the other side of the family," while each positive talent is clearly the direct result of the genes on their side!

This book is an aid for understanding not only your child better, but also yourself. When I have fallen back into less integrated ways of being a parent, an awareness of my neuroses and the habits I've formed around them has really helped me to shift myself. With insights from the Enneagram, I'm able to stand back and make the conscious choice to change—to work with the higher aspects of my type. This reminds me of an image I once saw on social media. A new dad is holding his baby son. The dad's T-shirt says, "Student" while the baby's says, "Teacher." There's so much truth in that.

I have a gentle, caring friend who is a pediatrician. His wonderful, nurturing wife is a caregiver. A better parenting combination couldn't even be made in a petri dish, yet all five of their children have gone off the rails at times—there have been addictions, unwanted pregnancies, violence . . . "We've stopped beating ourselves up," the wife commented. "Now we just work with what is."

Judging ourselves or other parents is never helpful and constructive. Just as you believe your perfectly behaved child is the result of your perfect parenting skills, they will behave in a way that has you groveling in apologetic humiliation. Parenting is no place for judgment—it's a space to demonstrate acceptance of all types, no matter where they are on their journey toward integration. Be like the father with the T-shirt and stay open to learning.

Relationships are like seesaws. What happens to a person on the one side directly effects the person on the opposite side. (In fact, I wrote a book about this called *What Went Wrong with Mr. Right? Why Relationships Fail and How to Heal Them*.) If we want our children to change, then we need to start with ourselves. I'll share a story here to demonstrate what I mean. A therapist friend of mine was asked to assess a four-year-old boy. The boy was cute and charming, yet when he began to play with her therapy toys, a very different child emerged. As she observed him, the boy started to trash the play area. For 30 minutes, toys of all shapes and sizes, building blocks, and handfuls of sand were flung everywhere. Dolls were beheaded, trains derailed, and bears had their stuffing removed. At the end of the session, pleased with himself, the child grinned at the therapist as she remained calm but concerned.

When the parents arrived to collect him, they were horrified at the demolition job their child had done in the therapy room. Harder still was when my friend told the couple that it wasn't their son she wanted to see again, but them. The couple embarked (a bit unwillingly and defensively) on their therapeutic journey, protesting that it was the child with the problem, not them. In time, as they healed their relationship and themselves, not only did their son's behavior improve, but so did that of their other children.

That's how it happens: as you work with the more integrated aspects of yourself, it starts to show in your child. As you become more open and authentic, you invite them to be the same. Ditto with your partner. Your relationships will never be perfect, perhaps, but what exactly is perfection other than the acceptance of what is, but with greater depth and empathy?

Even the most conscientious and enlightened parents experience parenting problems at times. We may find that one child is a breeze to raise, while another provides a much tougher challenge. Hopefully this book and the Enneagram wisdom it contains will provide some answers, ushering you on a richer, more conscious journey to yourself while gaining deeper, more compassionate insight into your child.

If you have a story to tell because of reading this book, please share it with me by emailing *info@enneagrams9paths.com*.

For more information on the Enneagram, you can visit my website: **https://enneagrams9paths.com**.

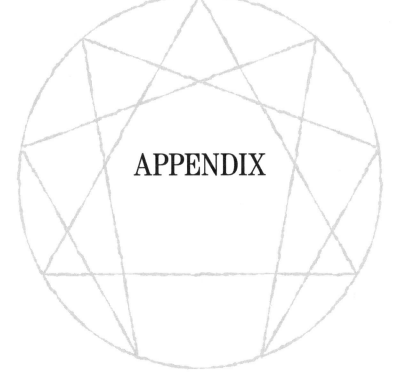

APPENDIX

Quick Type Overview

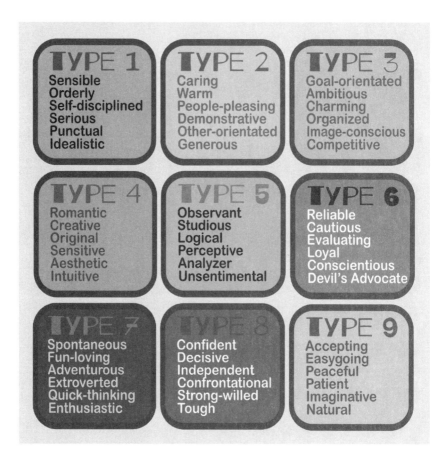

TYPE 1
Sensible
Orderly
Self-disciplined
Serious
Punctual
Idealistic

TYPE 2
Caring
Warm
People-pleasing
Demonstrative
Other-orientated
Generous

TYPE 3
Goal-orientated
Ambitious
Charming
Organized
Image-conscious
Competitive

TYPE 4
Romantic
Creative
Original
Sensitive
Aesthetic
Intuitive

TYPE 5
Observant
Studious
Logical
Perceptive
Analyzer
Unsentimental

TYPE 6
Reliable
Cautious
Evaluating
Loyal
Conscientious
Devil's Advocate

TYPE 7
Spontaneous
Fun-loving
Adventurous
Extroverted
Quick-thinking
Enthusiastic

TYPE 8
Confident
Decisive
Independent
Confrontational
Strong-willed
Tough

TYPE 9
Accepting
Easygoing
Peaceful
Patient
Imaginative
Natural

You find free downloads with more information on Ann Gadd's website:

On the Nine Types: **https://enneagrams9paths.com/free-download/**
On the wings: **https://enneagrams9paths.com/enneagram-wings/**

Lost Messages Your Child Needs to Hear

When we are growing up, there are certain type-related messages which if repeated by a parent, carer, or educator, can help us to develop a healthier sense of self. The late Don Riso and Russ Hudson in their book *The Wisdom of the Enneagram* describe them as "The Lost Messages." Hearing them helps a child to work through their core fear.

Affirming these messages is such a simple thing to do, yet the effect on your child (and even adults) can be powerful and profound. When you speak these sentences to the child, make sure that you make loving eye contact with them and are fully present.

Type One: You are a good human being. You do what's right.

Type Two: You are much loved and wanted for who you are.

Type Three: I love you the way you are. You don't need to be anything else but yourself.

Type Four: You truly belong here in this world and family. I really see the real you.

Type Five: It's not a problem (whatever your needs are). If you need to withdraw that's okay. I still love you.

Type Six: You are safe. You can be sure of yourself and trust both yourself and the world.

Type Seven: I love taking care of you. You will always be loved and taken care of.

Type Eight: It's okay to be vulnerable and show the gentle side of yourself. I will not betray you, and will always be honest and open with you.

Type Nine: You matter. It's important that you're here. The world needs you, and so do we.

What Toys Different Enneagram Type Kids Could Enjoy

When it comes to what toys to buy, some favorites will appeal to most Enneagram type children, such as building blocks, computer games, cars, dolls, and playdough. Certain toys may be enjoyed more by certain types.

When reviewing the lists, also look at wings, and Points of Stretch and Release. The Instinctual Drives will also play a definite role in toy choices. Generally though the following applies to the different types of children:

Type One: Type Ones could be attracted to self-improving toys and books. They would typically enjoy toys that aren't messy such as pencil coloring-in books, spelling flashcards, reading cards, and puzzles. Rules are enjoyed by Ones (and they don't enjoy those who break them), so board games may be of interest. Dollhouses they can keep spick and span are an option. Anything that involves sorting will appeal, as well as toys that teach while having fun, such as a toy cash register, or educational books.

Type Two: Twos enjoy being in friendships, so they'll be attracted to toys that connect them to other kids and provide ways to be liked. Tea sets, jewelry kits (to make a friend pretty), and doctor or nurse sets could work well. Toys that need tending, such as dolls that can drink, toy ponies, paper dolls, doll dress-up kits, and cute toys are a good bet.

Type Three: Three kids look for toys where they can achieve or accomplish things (to gain your praise or their peers' admiration). The latest trendy or branded toy or clothing items and accessories such as watches, bracelets, sunglasses gives them the status they desire: "All the cool kids have them." Apart from the counter-type, Threes generally enjoy being on stage, so microphones, musical instruments, play stages, or puppets would work.

Type Four: Fours want to express themselves and have others see them as unique. They'll be wanting to explore themselves by trying different personas, so dress-up outfits, face painting, and masks that show their uniqueness will be popular. Toys such as mermaids, mystical creatures, fairies, dinosaurs, and unicorns, or books that appeal to their fantasy side keep them occupied, while mosaic kits, glitter glue, painting sets, and musical instruments, allow them to express their creative selves. A toy that can act as an imaginary friend may also appeal.

Type Five: Fives are seeking to enhance their knowledge with intellectually stimulating toys. Not wanting to be depleted by the demands of the world, they're happy to play alone. It's soothing being in a safe space. Books that teach information such as birding, simple mechanics, identifying dinosaurs, different car types, or fun facts work, as well as science fiction. Construction kits also appeal. Anything from Lego monsters, robots, dragons, or "build the solar system" sets. Periscopes, telescopes, and microscopes could interest older children, while nature kits, a bug jar, or ant farms provide hours of entertainment. Collectible toys, be they soldiers, dinosaurs, fantasy characters, or baseball cards are good. Junior science kits, National Geographic kids' toys, robotics, sudoku, and PlayStation are other suggestions.

Type Six: These kids enjoy solving problems, playing with friends, and games that aren't too scary. Paint with water books (you don't have to choose the color), pet-care playsets, rescue dog collectible figures, tea sets, and PlayStation could work. Sixes typically adore pets, so pet toys or an actual pet could be popular. Construction or engineering toys also work well, such as building robots, buildings, or monsters. Farm animals, train sets, baking sets, dollhouses, puzzles, and sudoku are other options. Musical instruments such as a guitar would work, along with books.

Type Seven: Upbeat little Type Sevens get easily bored, so any toy you give them is going to need to provide stimulation for their busy minds. Repetitive won't work. They're after opportunities for fun and pleasure. Activity toys such as Swingball, or ball games, goggles, an inflatable pool, slippery slides, a climbing activity set, bikes, roller-skates, a skateboard, tents, bodyboards, super-hero dress-up outfits, frisbees, scooters, or swords, could prevent boredom. Toys that move, such as remote-controlled toys, provided the controls allow enough variation, could work.

Type Eight: Little Eights are after toys that allow them to deploy their power or meet physical challenges—something that lets them display their leadership and strength. Action or combative toys, such as water rocket blasters, water pistols, or bow and arrow sets, they'll love. Then there's competitive physical games, punch/boxing bags, boxing gloves, baseball bats, and like Sevens, balls, bikes, scooters, or skateboards. If you want to encourage musical talent, then drums, trumpets, and electric guitars are going to appeal more than flutes or violins.

Type Nine: Nine children are attracted to toys where they can be supportive and helpful to others while avoiding games that are likely to cause competitive conflict and tension. They're generally creative so painting sets, dressing-up outfits, sticker sets, clay, musical instruments, or drawing tools are enjoyed. Their desire for nurturing finds expression in cuddly toys, pet care playsets, baking, or tea sets. Nines often enjoy board games—something where they can explore their competitive Three aspect without the fear of causing too much conflict, as a physical sport could do. Individual card games, puzzles, kites, and bubbles, allow them to immerse themselves into a happy, day-dreamy, alone space.

Bibliography

Baden-Powell, Robert. *Scouting for Boys*. "Camp Fire Yarn—No. 4 Scout Law". 1908.

Bays, Brandon. *The Journey*. London: Thorsons, 1999.

Campling, Matthew. *The 12-Type Enneagram*. London: Watkins, 2015.

Chestnut, Beatrice, Ph.D. *The Complete Enneagram*. Berkeley: She Writes Press, 2013.

Ford, Debbie. *The Dark Side of the Light Chasers*. London: Hodder & Stoughton, 2001.

Hanh, Thich Nhat. *The Heart of the Buddha's Teachings*. Berkeley, CA: Broadway Books, 1998.

Hay, Louise. *Heal Your Body*. Cape Town, South Africa: Hay House/Paradigm Press, 1993.

Horney, Karen, M.D. *Neurosis and Human Growth*. New York: WW Norton & Company, 1991.

Horsley, Mary. *The Enneagram for the Spirit*. New York: Barron's Educational Series inc., 2005.

Johnson, Robert A. *Owning Your Own Shadow*. San Francisco, CA: HarperCollins, 1993.

Judith, Anodea. *Eastern Body, Western Mind*. Berkeley, CA: Celestial Arts, 1996.

Kamphuis, Albert. *Egowise Leadership & the Nine Creating Forces of the Innovation Circle*. Self-published. Netherlands: Egowise Leadership Academy, 2011.

Kornfield, Jack. *A Path with a Heart*. New York: Bantam, 1993.

Levine, Dr Amir and Rachel Heller. *Attached*. London: Pan Macmillan. 2011.

Lipton, Bruce H. *The Biology of Belief*. Santa Rosa, CA: Mountain of Love/Elite Books, 2005.

Lytton, Edward Bulwer. *Zanoni: A Rosicrucian Tale*. Whitefish, MT: Kessinger Publishing.

Maitri, Sandra. *The Spiritual Dimension of the Enneagram*. New York: Penguin Putnam Inc., 2001.

_____. *The Enneagram of Passions and Virtues*. New York: Penguin Random House, 2009.

Millman, Dan. *The Life You Were Born to Live*. Novato, CA: HJ Kramer in a joint venture with New World Library, 1993.

Murphy, Joseph. *The Power of Your Subconscious Mind*. New York: The Penguin Group, 2008.

Myss, Caroline. *Anatomy of the Spirit*. London: Bantam, 1998.

———. *Why People Don't Heal and How They Can*. London. Bantam, 1998.

Naranjo, Claudio, M.D. *Character and Neurosis*. Nevada City. Gateways/IDHHB, Inc., 2003.

———. *Ennea-type Structures – Self-Analysis for the Seeker*. Nevada City: Gateways/IDHHB, Inc., 1990.

Palmer, Helen. *The Enneagram in Love & Work*. New York: Harper One, 1995.

———. *The Enneagram: Understanding Yourself and Others in Your Life*. New York: Harper One, 1991.

Pearson, Carol S. *Awakening the Heroes Within*. New York: HarperCollins, 1991.

———. *The Heroes Within*. New York: HarperCollins, 1998.

Riso, Don Richard and Russ Hudson. *The Wisdom of the Enneagram*. New York: Bantam Books, 1999.

———. *Understanding the Enneagram*. Rev. ed. Boston, MA: Houghton Mifflin Company, 2000.

———. *Discovering Your Personality Type*. Boston, MA: Houghton Mifflin Company, 2003.

———. *Personality Types*. Boston, MA: Houghton Mifflin Company, 1996.

Shapiro, Debbie. *Your Body Speaks Your Mind*. London: Piatkus, 1996.

Shealy, Norman C. and Caroline Myss. *The Creation of Health*. Walpole, NH: Stillpoint Publishing, 1998.

Stone, Joshua David. *Soul Psychology*. New York: Ballantine Wellspring, 1999.

Surya Das, Lama. *Awakening to the Sacred*. New York: Broadway Books, 1999.

Thondup, Tukulu. *The Healing Power of the Mind*. Boston, MA: Shambhala Publications, 1996.

Tolle, Eckhart. *The Power of Now*. London: Hodder & Stoughton, 2005.

Wagner, Jerome, Ph.D. *The Enneagram Spectrum of Personality Styles*. Portland: Metamorphous Press, 1996.

Zuercher, Suzanne. *Enneagram Spirituality*. Notre Dame: IN: Ave Maria Press, 1992.

About the Author

Photo by Anthony Gadd

Ann Gadd is an accredited iEQ9-certified Enneagram practitioner, International Enneagram Association Global Conference presenter, holistic therapist, artist, workshop facilitator, author, and journalist. An avid, long-term student of the Enneagram, she offers workshops for beginners as well as advanced students. She is the author of 35 books, including *Sex and the Enneagram*, *The Enneagram of Eating*, the Enneagram Kids series for children, and *Painting by Numbers—The Enneagram and Art*. Ann lives in Cape Town, South Africa.

For more information visit:
https://enneagrams9paths.com
and
www.anngadd.co.za

PERCY PERFECT
The Enneagram Type 1 for Kids
Ann Gadd
978-1-08653-981-3

HAZEL HELPER
The Enneagram Type 2 for Kids
Ann Gadd
978-1-67437-737-7

SALLY STAR
The Enneagram Types for Kids
Ann Gadd
978-1-69533-588-2

ARTHUR ARTSY
The Enneagram Type 4 for Kids
Ann Gadd
978-8-60955-891-6

SEBASTIAN STUDY
The Enneagram Type 5 for Kids
Ann Gadd
978-1-70044-819-4

KATY CAUTIOUS
The Enneagram Type 6 for Kids
Ann Gadd
978-8-62367-334-3

FELIX FUN
The Enneagram Type 7 for Kids
Ann Gadd
978-1-69443-879-9

BEN BOSS
The Enneagram Type 8 for Kids
Ann Gadd
978-8-63713-229-4

POSIE PEACE
The Enneagram Type 9 for Kids
Ann Gadd
978-8-66494-231-6

A Fun Series of Illustrated Children's Books on the Enneagram

Do you want your child to gain a better understanding and appreciation of themselves and others? This Enneagram children's series does just that. Gadd translates the amazing Enneagram into a humorous, easy-to-understand series for children and adults age 3-101 years. Using a simple but insightful approach, Gadd gets to the core issue of each type and their path to emotional health.